REMARKABLE PRAISE FOR
WHERE SHE CAME FROM

"A rich and absorbing book ... In the guise of a family memoir, she brilliantly evokes Jewish life in the Czech lands ... Epstein is unsparing in her examination of the trials of transplantation, and unlike many family biographers, who are in thrall to their characters, she steps out of the frame to observe herself." —*New York Times Book Review*

"Helen Epstein's foremothers become our guides to the ways in which the past can be rescued by attention and empathy. In Epstein's hands, truth becomes not only stranger than fiction but more magnetic." —Gloria Steinem

"Compelling ... a family saga of vivid women ... a story with range and scholarship, a book that accomplishes the demanding task of memoir: to use the poignance of personal narrative to convey less accessible themes." —*Boston Sunday Globe*

"A deeply felt yet refreshingly unsentimental memoir of an assimilating Central European Jewish family and three generations of remarkable women. In chronicling the lives of her own ancestors, Helen Epstein gives us fascinating glimpses of a still unfamiliar world, with its complex history, its hopes, vicissitudes, and its tragic end. A richly informative, moving book." —Eva Hoffman, author of *Lost in Translation*

HELEN EPSTEIN is the author of four previous books, including *Children of the Holocaust*, *Joe Papp: An American Life*, and *Music Talks*, as well as many articles. She is an affiliate of Harvard University's Center for European Studies.

"Rich in detail, this work is told with a strong voice, and the result is a moving account of a family history and the strength of its women." —*Library Journal*

"An appealing and engaging work . . . Blending the qualities of a bestseller mystery novel, a biography, and a docudrama, Helen Epstein immediately draws the reader into her well-researched and eminently readable work." —*Rocky Mountain News*

"In the last half century in our country, one totalitarian regime murdered almost all the Jews and the second declared war on their memory. Now, in the 1990s, Judaism has become a fashion often founded on ignorance or a dangerous idealization. This book is the first I have ever read that gives an authentic picture of Czech Jewry as it was, particularly of its women." —Helen Klimova, Prague Foundation for Tolerance

"[A] powerful evocation . . . elevates the memoir from an attempt at history to an achievement of high art." —*Time Out* (New York)

"Adds a vivid and telling chapter to the reconstruction of Jewish women's history, one life at a time . . . A real-life family saga . . . about Czech history and relations between men and women, Czechs and Jews, rich and poor. It is a compelling account, one that any woman trying to recover her history will value." —*Kirkus Reviews*

"An eloquent memoir . . . a rich personal story." —*Publishers Weekly* (starred review)

Where She Came From

A DAUGHTER'S SEARCH
FOR HER MOTHER'S HISTORY

Helen Epstein

A PLUME BOOK

PLUME
Published by the Penguin Group
Penguin Putnam Inc., 375 Hudson Street, New York, New York 10014, U.S.A.
Penguin Books Ltd, 27 Wrights Lane, London W8 5TZ, England
Penguin Books Australia Ltd, Ringwood, Victoria, Australia
Penguin Books Canada Ltd, 10 Alcorn Avenue, Toronto, Ontario, Canada M4V 3B2
Penguin Books (N.Z.) Ltd, 182–190 Wairau Road, Auckland 10, New Zealand

Penguin Books Ltd, Registered Offices:
Harmondsworth, Middlesex, England

Published by Plume, a member of Penguin Putnam Inc.
This is an authorized reprint of a hardcover edition published by
Little, Brown and Company, Inc.
For information address Little Brown and Company, Inc., a Division of Time Warner
Trade Publishing, 3 Center Plaza, Boston, MA 02108.

First Plume Printing, November, 1998
10 9 8 7 6 5 4 3

Map credit: Erik P. Kraft

 REGISTERED TRADEMARK—MARCA REGISTRADA

The Library of Congress catalogued the hardcover edition as follows:
Epstein, Helen.
Where she came from : a daughter's search for her mother's history /
Helen Epstein.
p.   cm.
ISBN 0-316-24608-5 (hc)
ISBN 0-452-28018-4 (pbk)
1. Epstein, Helen—Family. 2. Epstein family. 3. Jews—Czech Republic—
Prague—Genealogy. 4. Children of Holocaust survivors—New York (State)—
New York—Biography. 5. Jews—New York (State)—New York—Biography.
6. Prague (Czech Republic)—Genealogy. I. Title
DS135.C97E67   1997
974.7′1004924—DC21   97–13845

Printed in the United States of America

BOOKS ARE AVAILABLE AT QUANTITY DISCOUNTS WHEN USED TO PROMOTE PRODUCTS
OR SERVICES. FOR INFORMATION PLEASE WRITE TO PREMIUM MARKETING DIVISION,
PENGUIN PUTNAM INC., 375 HUDSON STREET, NEW YORK, NY 10014.

For Margo

"To be rooted is perhaps the most important
and least recognized need of the human soul . . .
To be able to give, one has to possess;
and we possess no other life, no other living sap,
than the treasures stored up from the past
and digested, assimilated and created afresh by us.
Of all the human soul's needs,
none is more vital than this one of the past."

— SIMONE WEIL —

We think back through our mothers
if we are women.

— VIRGINIA WOOLF —

Where She Came From

Central Europe in 1870

- Riga
- Königsberg

POLAND

Berlin •
GERMANY

- Warsaw

NETHERLANDS

BELGIUM

Dresden •

• Prague   • Cracow

• Paris

FRENCH
EMPIRE

Munich •

HABSBURG

• Vienna

• Budapest

Switzerland

EMPIRE

• Trieste

I T A L Y

RUMANIA

BOSNIA   SERBIA

BULGARIA

MONTENEGRO

GREECE

Czech Republic
1997

Prague ○ • Kolín

BOHEMIA   MORAVIA

Jihlava •
        • Brtnice

MILES

0   100   200   300

1

~

Whenever a telephone rings late at night or at an odd time of day, I still — even now that Frances has been dead for almost a decade — think someone is calling to say that my mother has taken her life. I grew up with stories of women who wanted to die. My mother's grandmother jumped from a window in Vienna at the end of the nineteenth century. My mother's mother repeatedly threatened to commit suicide in Prague. My mother locked herself inside the bathroom in New York, saying she had had enough, that she could not go on.

I had just returned from a trip with my husband and two small children when the telephone rang into the sunny spring afternoon. It was my brother. Frances had not tried to kill herself but was close to death all the same. I had better catch a plane to New York. Fast.

~

During the nights my mother lay dying in a hospital five miles away from her home, I slept in her bed. I had never been in her room alone before and, gazing about at her things, I felt treacherous, as though I were violating a family code. I was, for the first time, looking at her world with my own eyes rather than with hers and reflecting on what I saw.

It was a small, very feminine room. There was grasscloth on the walls and a thick carpet of the same French blue on the floor. Against that blue were layers of objects that the Impressionists liked to paint: pillows, vases, books, a sculpture, two paintings, some plants. There were framed photographs of my mother's clients in the clothes she had designed and a framed floor-to-ceiling mirror with her chalk marker and dolly in front of it. For fifty-four of her sixty-nine years, Frances Epstein had been a dressmaker, making beautiful clothes for women.

My mother was like her room: elegant, multilayered, and much influenced by the French. Her height and weight were average. Her hair, an undyed salt-and-pepper, was well cut. Her face was dominated by large glasses that framed dark eyes and a wide lipsticked mouth. Otherwise, she wore no makeup and only a touch of cologne. Her clothes were perfectly constructed. Her appearance was what she had never given up hoping that mine would be: "well put together." Nothing in the impeccable way she looked divulged her complicated history. You had to look carefully at her face and, of course, at her left arm.

When I first saw her in the hospital intensive care unit, my mother lay eyes closed, a tube in her nose, a tube in her wrist, hooked up to an electrocardiograph machine. There had been no illness, no warning. She had been sitting at her sewing machine when a vessel burst in her brain and flooded it with blood, knocking out her speech and paralyzing her body. My mother's face was gray. Her hair lay limp against the pillow. I placed my hand over hers and she opened her eyes. They had always been eloquent. Now they were opaque. Her mouth moved to form a word but all that came out was a "Huh." I smiled and stroked her hand with growing panic. Frances had survived several concentration camps, typhus, three births, one abortion, one appendectomy, two disk fusions, hospitalizations for back injuries, tuberculosis, and bleeding colitis. I had visited her in the hospital before, but, before, she had always been able to speak. She looked at me. Then she closed her eyes.

That night as I lay in her bed, I thought that my mother knew she was dying. Beneath her outer layer of feminine well-put-togetherness, Frances saw herself as a soldier. She had forged that persona in camp, held on to it in the difficult postwar years that followed, and arrived in America disciplined, authoritarian, and rarely carefree. Her soldier persona froze out emotion and focused on the next task at hand. It did not admit my memories of waiting outside a locked bathroom door or holding her as, exhausted, she wept in our living room. It was a persona that gave her the illusion of control over a life that had been buffeted by forces well beyond her control.

Frances had been in many seemingly fatal situations before. The most dramatic one occurred when she was twenty-three years old and standing in a line of naked women prisoners waiting to be selected for work or death in Auschwitz. She had assessed the situation and determined that she had two strikes against her: First, she had a large scar on the right side of her abdomen from an appendectomy and the Nazi doctor selecting prisoners disliked scars. Second, she was a dressmaker and, as sewing was one of the few women's handicrafts of use in a concentration camp, many hundreds of women claimed to be dressmakers. Before the war, Frances had actually run her own dressmaking *salon,* but her father had been an electrical engineer and, when her turn came, my mother said she was an electrician.

She worked as an electrician for the rest of the war, making it up as she went along, dry-eyed and competent, using her hands. Frances managed not to electrocute herself or anyone else and learned the trade so well that years later, whenever there was trouble with an electrical appliance in our home, she would rarely call a repairman. She would disassemble it, arrange the parts in neat piles, and start splicing wires. Later she would take out her leather manicuring set, then carefully soak and tend her small, well-kept hands.

The second morning, Frances was moved into a neurological ICU, her hands tied to the rails of her bed. Although she seemed unable to move, she had been forcibly restrained. A band of sheeting, stretched tight, cut into the skin of one underarm, held down her chest, cut under the other arm, and was bound to the bed.

"Why?" I asked the nurse.

"She was probably trying to pull her tubes out," she answered pleasantly. "They all do it. They don't know what they're doing."

There was no question in my mind that my mother knew. But how to explain it to a stranger? How to explain that she was as familiar with the varieties of death as anyone in this hospital, that choosing one's death had an unusual and complicated history in our family?

When she was twenty-two, Frances, her first husband, and her parents were deported from Prague to a nearby concentration camp. She herself was ordered to remain there. Her mother and father were ordered to Poland. Although they did not know the implications of deportation, my grandfather was unwilling to cede control of his life to the Nazis. He pulled a small pillbox out of the breast pocket of his jacket. He had enough pills to kill himself and his wife before anyone else could kill them.

Frances then made what she would later regard as the mistake of her life. She admitted to her father that she had found his pillbox a year earlier and, aware of both her parents' propensity toward suicide, had taken it to a pharmacist. When he confirmed that the pills were lethal, my mother asked him to substitute something harmless in their place. The pharmacist replaced the contents of the box with saccharin pills of the same size.

Her father flew into a rage. He told her that she was a brat who had stolen his means of an honorable death. Later that day, her parents were forced to board a train to Poland. That moment of separation from her mother and father had been the most painful of her life. It was then, Frances said, that she had felt the meaning of a broken heart.

I could not find the words to tell the nurse all this, to persuade her to untie my mother's hands, to say I knew that her hospital was not a concentration camp but that we were repeating a family process that had been played out before in another country and another time. I could not tell my husband, who had remained with our children, or my brothers or my mother's one surviving cousin, who joined me every day at the hospital. That night, I lay in my mother's bed feeling that I had failed to protect her just as she had failed to protect her parents.

My father had died fifteen years earlier. He was a very different kind of person from my mother, an athlete and life-loving man, who often said that when he died, he hoped it would be while swimming laps in a well-maintained pool. He had a heart attack while taking a morning walk, and went so fast that he was dead before an ambulance could be called. My mother was fifty-five then. He was seventy-one.

Although she missed him, Frances was one of those widows who blossom when released from long marriage. For a time, she had continued to live and work in the large Manhattan apartment where she had raised three children. But two of us had moved out by then and, without my noisy, space-filling father, the place echoed like a shell. When the youngest of us decided to move out, she sold it and bought a place to suit no one but herself: the first home in which she had ever lived alone.

She chose a small apartment high up over the Hudson River. Every day she ate her breakfast looking out over the George Washington Bridge, the River, and the cliffs of the New Jersey Palisades. Over the first of many cigarettes, she took ten minutes to knock off the *New York Times* crossword puzzle in what was, after Czech, German, and French, her fourth language. Then, after dressing in her meticulous way, she went into her workroom, for my mother could not envision living — at any age — without work.

"*Couturière*," she called herself when she was feeling fine and optimistic, using the French word for designer, which raised her craft to the status of an art. But that fancy word evoked Paris and seemed too grandiose a description for work performed in what should have been the master bedroom of our apartment. "*Švadlena!*" my mother called herself when business was bad and she was forced to do alterations to bring in money, using the Czech word for seamstress. *Švadlena* signified a lower place on the social ladder, and association with what, along with prostitution, was the oldest of women's professions. But whatever word she used to identify what she did, most of her clientele knew that, like a fine glassblower, Frances practiced an art that belonged to another time and continent and — even there — was on its last legs. I always thought that my mother was an artist.

The women in the photographs on the wall of Frances's bedroom were also artists: writers, actresses, singers, or painters. She regarded them as colleagues and they reciprocated her regard. Some had given her gifts of their work: a large etching by one hung on one wall; books by another filled a bookshelf. There were glamorous photos of Jarmila Novotná, the Czech soprano who had been her first client in America; of Vivian Vance, the actress who played Lucy's dizzy neighbor on the *I Love Lucy* television show; and of Hester Lewis, a Hollywood starlet who married a spark plug king, whose party clothes sometimes accounted for half our family's yearly income.

There were other clients whose faces did not appear on her walls. For years, Frances had dressed many ladies-who-lunched, wives and girlfriends of famous men, rich divorcées, along with her more interesting customers. I remembered almost all of them, sitting in their slips on the couch in our living room, where Frances conducted fittings during the day and where, at night, my parents slept. They would lean against bolsters on the black slipcovers that disguised my parent's twin beds, sipping tea and flipping through *L'Officiel* or *Vogue* or *Bazaar* or *La Mode* or a book of fabric samples. From the adjoining workroom you could hear the whirring of the sewing machine, the slashing sound of scissors, and a low murmur of talk. The "girls," as Frances called the mostly European seamstresses, worked there surrounded by boxes of zippers, buttons, threads, piping, ribbons, feathers, snaps, frogs, shields, and weights — the details that, strategically hidden or clearly displayed, lent my mother's dresses or suits their custom-made distinction.

When I could not sleep, I walked around my mother's small, silent space. The workroom here in her last apartment was not the master bedroom but a corner of the living room. There was only one sewing machine, one headless dummy, and one massive iron. But otherwise it looked very much like the workroom I had grown up with. The sleeve of a navy blue wool jacket lay in the grip of the machine needle. There was a half-smoked Dunhill in the ashtray beside it. The *New York Times* crossword puzzle lay — completed — on her cutting table. She had, with her usual refusal to give in to pain, finished it after the medical crisis had begun. The answering machine next to her telephone was blinking. I rewound it and found this conversation:

"The doctor called me," my mother's best friend, Hankah, says in Czech.

"*Ja,*" says my mother, her voice thick.

"The ambulance is on its way. I'll call Helen."

"Helen is . . . in . . ." my mother says in English. She is coughing or vomiting or both. "In . . ."

"Don't talk," says my mother's friend over the sound of my mother's breathing. "I'll figure things out. The ambulance is on its way."

"*Ja,*" says my mother.

"Is the door open so they can get in?"

My mother takes a deep breath. "*Ja.*"

"As soon as I find out where you are, I'll come after you."

I can hear my mother trying to pull herself together. "I can give you — just wait a minute," she says in English. Then, the timbre of her voice intensifies and the language she is speaking disintegrates into bits of speech none of us has ever heard before. "*No blowcha,*" she says. "*Ache the sand. Zate, zate the time. Ze mensch do up on that. Pensch dem sem maygen . . .*"

"Franci, don't talk now," says Hankah.

"*Ja,*" says my mother. Then, her English suddenly resurging, "I'm trying as much as I can. I can . . ."

"Don't try anymore."

"Okay," says my mother.

"I love you and you will be okay."

"Okay," says my mother, with difficulty. I can hear her breathing. I can hear her struggle for control. "Okay. Bye."

I was forty-two when, after five days, my mother died and it felt as though I had been left in the world alone. Although I was myself a mother, although I had a husband, two sons, two brothers, and many friends, with whom my relations were passionate and often complicated, my relation to my mother was the most passionate and complicated of all. So intense was our bond that I was never sure what belonged to whom, where I ended, and she began.

I was the eldest of her three children and the only daughter, a mirror image, people said, of my mother: same dark brown eyes, same wide, toothy smile, same direct and sometimes bossy style. People always said we looked like sisters and, for a long time, I thought that was fine. I wore the clothes my mother made for me, read the books she read, valued what she thought good. I shared my life with her, half-understanding that I was her anchor and that, through me, she lived out alternatives to what had been her own life.

I know that there are mothers who are complete in themselves, who when they need help seek solace in their partners and adult friends. I know that there are daughters who claim their lives for themselves alone, who have no time or sympathy for their mothers. But for a long time, long after adolescence should have ruptured the bond between us, neither my mother nor I were among them. I shared her loves, her disappointments, and her memories. She was the engine behind my energy, my defender when I needed one, my solace. When the break finally came, it was brutal. We came apart in a great explosion that required years to repair.

Our new relation was only a decade old and still not without its strains and conflicting desires, expressed and mute. Since I had become a mother myself, the focus had shifted away from the two of us but left me no less fascinated with Frances. I had always viewed her as a heroine more compelling than any in the Bible, any novel or myth.

I stood, well dressed, dry-eyed, and competent, greeting mourners in the funeral chapel. "It is my wish that my funeral be very simple and my body laid in an unadorned six-board coffin," Frances had stipulated in her will. "There shall be no speeches and the Gustav Mahler *Adagietto* of the Fifth Symphony is to be played. I wish my body to be cremated and I leave the disposal of my ashes to the decision of my children." She wanted no rabbi and no Kaddish, the mourners' prayer recited by Jews since the thirteenth century.

My mother was a Jew who did not practice Judaism. She drew spiritual sustenance not from the Hebrew liturgy, but from the realm of secular European art. Of those arts, music spoke most deeply to Frances and of musicians, Gustav Mahler spoke most directly of all. Mahler had been born in the same country as my mother and her mother and her mother's mother. He once described himself as "three times homeless: a native of Bohemia in Austria, an Austrian among Germans, and a Jew throughout the world. Everywhere an intruder, never welcomed."

In the aftermath of my mother's death, I did not sit *shivah,* the seven days of Jewish mourning. I prepared some meals for my husband and small children, then returned to Frances's apartment, to sift through her workroom supplies, her office papers, her closets and drawers, her kitchen. I wrote letters, made arrangements, discussed endless details with my brothers. I had to concentrate hard on doing things right. In those first weeks after her death, I left the car ignition on, left packages that I had just paid for on counters, lost money, burned food. Every few days, a numbness would steal over my arms or back, my neck would stiffen, and I would call my doctor, certain that a blood vessel had burst in my brain. Whenever one of my sons got sick, whenever my husband and I had a fight, whenever I felt exhausted, I understood for the first time the way my mother gazed at the photograph of her mother that hung over her cutting table.

From the time I was a little girl, I was fascinated by that sepia-toned photograph that hung on the wall like an icon. My grandmother Josephine — Pepi, for short — was not pretty but looked very mysterious with her dark hair, dark eyes, and dark fur collar hiding her neck. She too had been a dressmaker. My mother cut, measured, and sewed under Pepi's unchanging gaze.

They were business partners from the time Frances was fifteen and her parents allowed her to drop out of school to become a dress designer. Pepi's *salon* in Prague was a rare place where the nature of the world was reversed, where women were at the center of things and men were relegated to the margins. It was a place where mother and daughter not only made the family living but served as the hub of a society of interesting women — actresses, opera singers, diplomats' wives, who brought the greater world to them:

Men did not belong in the *salon*, Frances often said. They were a distraction, and besides, they were not supposed to see the tricks she employed to make her customers' waists appear slimmer or breasts higher or shoulders wider than they actually were. My father — who kept the books — might be called in to help wrap a large package or to deliver it to its destination. Occasionally, a customer's husband or boyfriend might be invited to preview an evening dress; or a repairman might come in to fix something. But, as a rule, both workroom and *salon* were off-limits to men. They were premises inhabited by, employing, and catering to women.

I did not, as a small child, understand how unusual such a place was, but I loved being in it. I crawled and learned to walk among the scraps of the workroom floor. I learned not to swallow pins and to keep quiet when my mother was thinking or giving her employees instructions or fitting glamorous women with luxurious fabrics. By being silent and practically invisible, I could eavesdrop on the girls as they stitched seams against a soundtrack of classical music and talked about the work, the customers, and their clothes. Best of all, I could listen to my mother.

It was as she stood at her cutting table, considering cloth, that Frances would sometimes pin her present onto a scrap of her past and tell me a story about my grandmother. Pepi was eight years old when she became an orphan. She was brought up in a small city in Bohemia by her aunt Rosa, who taught her how to sew. Because she was an orphan, she had to learn a trade when she finished school. But she loved to make clothes and when she grew up, she moved to Prague and became so successful that she started her own *salon*.

It was in the workroom that I fell in love with the dead women in my mother's family. At the end of the day, when the "girls" swept up and threw out threads and scraps of cloth, I collected threads and scraps of stories, hoarding them, mulling them over. Each one seemed cut from a different kind of cloth. Each was distinct. There were no seams, only wide gaps in the fabric. My mother would never have made a dress the way she told these stories. There was something wrong in their proportions and some disturbance in her telling that prevented them from making a whole. My mother was a master at joining parts. She would scrutinize the way a sleeve or skirt joined a bodice and if the juncture was not perfect, it would preoccupy her until she found a resolution. If necessary, she would let her mind work overnight, then rip everything apart and fix it in the morning. But she never fixed the way she told her past. The parts never fit. They remained separate and discrete.

Those disjunctures fascinated me. I was never much interested in the construction of clothes but always drawn to the construction of stories, to what was said and what was withheld. Whenever I tried to sew, thimbles fell off my fingers, needles drew blood, and if I tried to use my mother's machine, she was relieved when I got up with my thumbs intact. It was only after my mother died that I noticed that I had begun to enjoy mending holes, replacing buttons, closing up rips in seams. Part of it, I knew, was busywork, the small mindless tasks you choose to do after your world has been shaken and you can't do anything else.

But even then, disoriented as I was, I began to sense that making and repairing clothes was a form of narrative. I sensed that for me, for my mother, and maybe for those other women in my family that I knew so little about, it had to do with warding off suicide.

2

~

After my mother died, several times a week I took to wandering through the university library close to my home. In the stacks I passed scholars and students seeking research to bolster their arguments. I had no thesis to defend, not even a clearly defined question. I browsed through books about death, books about Central Europe, books about women, books about Jews. I was mourning my mother and if you had asked me what I was looking for in that enormous tomb of books, I would have said that I was looking for her.

I rarely passed anyone in the Czech section. Many of the volumes there were old and crumbling, their titles barely legible, like ancient gravestones. Some of the books I looked at had not been checked out in fifty years. Some dated from the time of the Habsburg Empire, some from the First Czech Republic, some from the Communist period. The world my mother came from had been buried by a series of political and military upheavals involving Czechs, Germans, Russians, Nazis, and Communists, each of whom had rewritten its history in their own language. Reading my way through the library stacks in Czech, English, and German, I began to feel like an archaeologist who, instead of collecting shards of broken pottery, was picking up pieces of narrative.

I had in my possession a kind of map to my mother's world. About ten years before she died, I had asked Frances to write down everything she knew of her family and she had produced a twelve-page, single-spaced chronicle of personal history. It read like the libretto of a romantic opera:

"Therese Frucht was born in the city of Iglau in the province of Moravia sometime in the 1850s," wrote my mother,

> *the daughter of a prosperous innkeeper. After an unhappy and hopeless love affair with a young Czech, she was married rather abruptly in an arranged marriage to a penniless young man by the name of Judah Sachsel, who was more a poet than a peddler of worn clothes.*
>
> *They settled in the Jewish section of Vienna, where their four children were born: Heinrich, Rudolf, Emil, and Josephine. After using up Therese's dowry, they had a very hard time making ends meet because Judah was always reading the books he was carrying around in his pockets instead of peddling the old clothes he had draped over his arms. He made up for his inability to make money with absolute love and devotion to his wife and children.*
>
> *Therese loved and played with her children, although Heinrich was always her favorite. Whether this was because he was her first-born or maybe not Judah's son is not absolutely clear, but it did not seem to bother the other three too much. When Heinrich was seventeen, he died of peritonitis, resulting from a ruptured appendix.*
>
> *This event plunged Therese into deep melancholy. She ignored her other three children and disappeared for hours at a time, only to be found by her husband lying on Heinrich's grave. Pride had prevented her for years from contact with her family in Iglau, whom she evidently held responsible for marrying her to*

her husband and their ensuing poverty. Only Heinrich really
mattered. Remonstrations by the rabbi, friends, neighbors, her
husband, and the terrified children had no effect on her and so it
seemed inevitable that Judah found her body one dismal day in
the street. She had thrown herself out of their fourth-floor win-
dow.

When I was a journalism professor, I taught students to verify
the who, what, where, when, and why of a story. How could I
verify this? All the actors in my mother's chronicle were dead.
Not one official family document had survived the Second World
War. The German city of Iglau (population 15,000), then in the
Habsburg Empire, is now the Czech city of Jihlava (population
50,000) in the Czech Republic. There are no Fruchts nor other
Jews left and, apart from the tombstones in the cemetery, no artifacts.

This annihilation of the past is familiar to displaced people of
all kinds. A person whose family has remained in place inherits
possessions — a hat, a cupboard, old diaries, a prayer or recipe
book — that transmit personal history from one generation to
the next. The objects that would normally have been passed
down to me — my grandmother's tea set, my mother's piano —
had been confiscated and crammed into warehouses by the Nazis
along with hundreds of thousands of other pieces of property
belonging to Czech Jews. I was lucky to have a few dozen family
photographs that some of my grandmother's customers had hidden for her during the war and three porcelain figurines. Everything else was gone.

This dearth of a tangible past — people, objects, a physical
context — with which I had grown up and to which I had become accustomed was made suddenly intolerable by my
mother's death. "To be able to give, one has to possess," wrote Simone Weil and, as I went about my daily routines, those words
gave the twelve-page chronicle that had been lying in my desk a
sudden and urgent importance. Long ago, I had read, in the seventeenth and eighteenth centuries when Czech Jews were an observant and important community, some of its members wrote

autobiographical family narratives called *megillot mishpachah,* or family scrolls. Like the Scroll of Esther, read every year during the holiday of Purim, the family *megillot* told a story of Jews overcoming adversity but also provided a multigenerational history. Needless to say, all had been written by men. I liked the idea of taking my mother's twelve-page chronicle and bringing three generations of increasingly secular women to life in an old Jewish literary form.

Before the Second World War, a great library of books including such *megillot* and centuries of community records had documented one thousand years of Jewish life in the Czech lands. Some of these records were hidden by prescient rabbis. But then they themselves had been murdered, taking their knowledge of the hiding places with them into death. Most records documenting Jewish history in Moravia had been destroyed.

If the birth, death, and marriage registers of the Jewish Community of Iglau were gone, I was told, there was little chance of my finding out anything about Therese Frucht. Unlike American women of the nineteenth century, women in the Habsburg Empire were forbidden to join political organizations and are absent from the treaties, books, pamphlets, and newspapers that record public life. She herself was unlikely to show up in the secular business, police, or organizational records of the Habsburg province of Moravia. Feminist scholarship was new to post-Communist Europe: few Czech scholars had examined women's memoirs, diaries, or letters — the kind of materials social historians elsewhere have used to reconstruct the social and cultural life of women.

Within the world of Jewish studies, organized around the writings of learned men, it was all but impossible to find any research on ordinary women like Therese. Until the nineteenth century, Jewish women had minimal education and public presence in their communities. They never had the option of retreating to convents where, like Christian women, they might have created a literature of their own. Their meager literary output was deemed unworthy of the interest of Jewish scholars. Such books as the early seventeenth century *Meneket Rivka,* a handbook for housewives written by a Prague physician's daughter named Rivka, had never been valued by Jewish scholars and had disappeared long before the Nazis burned Jewish books. With the exception of Glückel von Hameln, who wrote her autobiography in the seventeenth century, premodern Jewish literature has preserved almost no women writers.

Czech Jewry itself is problematic, regarded by some scholars as a subset of Germany's Jews. In the sixteenth century, Prague Jews spoke Czech and had built one of the most important centers of Jewish scholarship in the world, and Jewish guilds of printers, crystal cutters, goldsmiths, and musicians displayed an unusual civic pride. But by the end of the nineteenth century, most spoke German and had become so acculturated that their Judaism had become the subject of research. In what would now be called urban renewal, the old Prague ghetto was "sanitized," some of its synagogues torn down and their artifacts collected for exhibit in museums. Czech Jews, like their German cousins, were in the forefront of those in Central Europe who came to worship Goethe and Beethoven instead of God. After the Second World War, within some sectors of the Jewish community, children were taught that their indifference to tradition had brought on the Holocaust.

Although a long tradition of Jewish scholarship had flourished in Czechoslovakia before the war, it all but disappeared afterward. The Nazi policy of extermination was followed by a Communist policy of denunciation that identified Jews with capitalism, imperialism, and the West. Many Czech Jews who had survived the war emigrated. After the antisemitic Stalinist trials of the early 1950s, those who remained in the country vanished from public view. One of my Prague friends who was a child then thought there were no Jews left but herself and her sister. Whenever she heard someone say, "Don't look at me as though I were a Jew!" or "It's as noisy as a Jewish school," she perceived that there were others but was afraid to ask where. My Prague cousin Miki grew up uncircumcised and ignorant of Judaism. His parents, both concentration camp survivors, lived a short walk away from the Old-New Synagogue but his mother never took him inside.

Jewish historiography in Czechoslovakia became a quasi-secret hobby under Communism. Those Jewish archives that had not been destroyed by the Nazis were closely watched by the Ministry of the Interior or, in plainer language, the secret police. It was dangerous to inquire about Jewish records that were contained within state archives. At the university, the little Jewish research that received official sanction focused on Jews of the Renaissance and Middle Ages.

But in November of 1989, half a year after my mother died, the Communism that had driven my parents out of Czechoslovakia finally collapsed. I read the newspaper articles and watched television, wishing that Frances could have seen the Velvet Revolution. Other Czechs who had been living in the West for decades were talking about return. The country was opening up. Hidden archives were being discovered. People who had been accumulating records in secret came out into the open. Prague's once-empty synagogues became a magnet for tourists.

After the Velvet Revolution, I thought, many people would be digging into the past. There was no one alive who could have known the innkeeper's daughter Therese Frucht but somewhere, I thought, there had to be a piece of paper confirming her existence. The political revolution in Europe came at the same time as a worldwide revolution in technology. If that technology was as powerful as everyone claimed, I would find Therese.

I sat down at my computer and composed a letter that I mailed to historians of Jews, historians of women, historians of Czechs, to the genealogical service of the Czechoslovak Embassy, to the Red Cross, the Jewish Community of Vienna, the Jewish Museum in Prague, the Museum of the Diaspora in Tel Aviv, and the Archive of the Jewish People in Jerusalem. I placed advertisements for the Frucht family in the *New York Times Book Review*, the *Bulletin of the Czechoslovak Society of Arts and Sciences*, and the newsletter of the International Society for Czechoslovak Jews. I received a few answers but none retrieved the name.

During that time, I listened to Mahler's *Adagietto*, the music that my mother had requested for her funeral, the music that she viewed as a statement of her essence. Gustav Mahler, like Therese Frucht, had grown up in the Moravian city of Iglau. I read book after book about his life. The most comprehensive was by a French baron who had studied at Yale. I wrote to him too and he referred me to a retired Czech schoolteacher who lived in the town of Humpolec.

Jiří Rychetský was the first of several people I would meet who had long been engaged in their own projects of historical reconstruction. When Jiří was a boy before the war, a fire broke out in the nearby village of Kaliště and he pedaled off on his bicycle to watch the firemen put it out. When he returned home, his mother said that Kaliště was an important place, the birthplace of Mahler, an important composer and a Jew.

After the war, Rychetský became a history teacher in the local high school. Communist doctrine took much of the joy out of teaching history. But Rychetský discovered that the authorities were less concerned about local history and monuments than they were about what was taught in the schools. It was relatively easy for the history teacher to visit local archives in search of documents about Gustav Mahler, his family, and his community. By the 1970s, he had become a Mahler authority, giving private tours through Kaliště and the Czech-Moravian Highlands to musicologists from New York to Tokyo. In Jihlava, he persuaded authorities to place a plaque on the house where Mahler grew up. In Humpolec, he established a tiny museum, the only Mahler museum in the world. He had no support from the government but could call on financial help from abroad as well as on hundreds of his former students working as Party officials, archivists, librarians, and clerks. Years of poring over local archives had familiarized Rychetský with the Jews who had lived in the hill towns on the border between Bohemia and Moravia.

Although most of the Jewish community records had been destroyed, Rychetský told me, the Habsburgs were peerless bureaucrats who had registered much of the same material. It was like looking for a needle in a haystack, but somewhere in the volumes of old registers he continued to consult for Mahleriana, Rychetský believed he would find Therese Frucht. At about the same time, I met an American student en route to Vienna and asked if she could check the Jewish Community records there. She flew off and one summer day, I received a letter.

"Greetings from Vienna," it began.

I've turned up a few things which I hope will be of interest! Therese Sachsel jumped from [what in Europe is] a third-story window in 1890. She died on the fifth of May in the General Hospital at 7:00 A.M. at the age of 46. Her grave is #19, 19, 84 in the Jewish section of the Central Cemetery. It is record #1814 of the 1890 *Deathbook of the Jewish Community of Vienna.*

Heinrich Sachsel died on the 29th of July, 1889, at 2:30 P.M. and was buried on the 31st. At the time he was 16 years old. His place of burial is also 19,19,84. He died of [what looks like] *Bauchfellentzündung* [the script was nearly impossible to make out], which is peritonitis.

The photocopy of that entry in the 1890 *Deathbook of the Jewish Community of Vienna* became my first official document. If it was correct, then Therese was born in 1844 or 1845, when Jews in the Czech lands of Bohemia and Moravia still lived on Jewish Streets closed off after sunset by an iron chain, when a chosen few paid high taxes for the privilege of being "tolerated," and the rest squatted as illegal aliens or wandered, without permanent domiciles, throughout Europe.

No one knows exactly when Jews first arrived in the Czech lands, but they came from Rome in the south and from Byzantium in the southeast. They are mentioned by various Czech chroniclers as inhabiting the city of Prague since the latter part of the tenth century and settling in other Czech towns during the three centuries that followed. They could move about the country freely, own land, and engage in business on an equal basis with Christians until the Catholic Church began, at the end of the twelfth century, to restrict their freedom. Beginning then, Jews in the Czech lands, like Jews in medieval Germany and France, were defined by charters as "serfs of the royal treasury," subjects of the prince or king or emperor who guaranteed them his protection.

"In the name of the Holy and Undivided Trinity," reads a typical charter, promulgated by the Bishop of Speyer at the end of the eleventh century:

Those Jews whom I have gathered I placed outside the neighborhood and residential area of the other burghers. In order that they not be easily disrupted by the insolence of the mob, I have encircled them with a wall. . . . I have accorded them the free right of exchanging gold and silver and of buying and selling everything they use. . . . I have, moreover, given them out of the land of the Church burial ground to be held in perpetuity. . . . Just as the mayor of the city serves among the burghers, so too shall the Jewish leader adjudicate any quarrel which might arise among them or against them. . . . They must discharge the responsibility of watch, guard, and fortification only in their own area. . . . They may legally have nurses and servants from among our people. . . . They may legally sell to Christians slaughtered meats which they consider unfit for themselves according to the sanctity of their law. In short, in order to achieve the height of kindness, I have granted them a legal status more generous than any which the Jewish people have in any city of the German kingdom. . . . In order that the meaning of this matter remains throughout the generations, I have strengthened it by signing it and by the imposition of my seal.

While such charters legitimized Jewish settlement, they did not protect Jews from the enmity of the Catholic Church, which viewed them as rejecting and subverting the true faith and having killed Jesus Christ. Within a decade of the promulgation of this charter, soldiers of the First Crusade murdered the Jews of Speyer, Jews of other settlements along the Rhine, and Jews in one of their two settlements in Prague. After the thirteenth century, when the Catholic rite of transubstantiation of the wafer and wine into the flesh and blood of Christ was made official church doctrine, Jews were accused by Christians of stealing the wafer and poisoning the wine. The Church promulgated a canon requiring Jews to wear a sign marking them as non-Christians and instituted a policy of segregation.

Segregation was followed by expulsion. In 1290, the Jews were

expelled from England; in 1296, from Normandy; in 1306, from
France; in 1349, from those German cities where they had earlier
escaped murder. Everywhere they were subjected to forced conversion and accused not only of desecrating the Host, but poisoning wells, reenacting the Crucifixion on the bodies of
Christian children, murdering them in order to use their blood in
Jewish rituals. After the devastation of plague, Jews were blamed
for transmitting Black Death.

Although Prague itself was the site of a massive pogrom during Easter of 1389, Jews fleeing Western Europe found relative
safety in the Highlands of Bohemia and Moravia, where they established communities under new charters. They were still restricted to a handful of livelihoods disdained or prohibited by the
Church: moneylending, peddling, tanning raw hides, dealing in
secondhand goods. But the Czech lands were less populated, the
charters prohibited forced conversions, and in the thirteenth and
fourteenth centuries, I was delighted to read, bishops complained
that Jews there felt free to employ Christian wet nurses and ignore regulations about their designated attire. No one wants a
martyrology instead of a history and what I was reading indicated that the Jews of the Czech lands had one.

They were not the only people to migrate east. In the thirteenth century, German colonists also streamed into the Czech
lands and established the city of Iglau, after silver was discovered
in the nearby hills. For the next seven centuries, Iglau was a "German-speaking island" in the Czech lands and a bastion of the
Catholic Church.

The Jews and Germans of Iglau lived separate lives. The first
documented evidence of Jewish presence in the city is a thirteenth-
century city law prohibiting sexual intercourse between Christians and Jews, a then customary European edict. Municipal
records attest to the economic impact of the Jewish community
on Iglau for the next nearly two hundred years, until the religious
wars.

The war between the Czech Hussites and the German
Catholics is what makes Jewish history in the Czech lands somewhat different from the history of Jews in other parts of Europe.

A spirit of heresy and humanism took root early in the lands of the Bohemian Crown and found its most powerful mouthpiece in Jan Hus, a preacher in Prague. Hus enjoyed both popular support and the support of the university community. His attacks on the Catholic Church were so powerful and his following so strong that the Council of Constance found it necessary to burn him at the stake as a heretic in 1415.

The Church launched five crusades to defeat the Hussites, and over the next two centuries their descendants, who regarded themselves as "God's warriors against the soldiers of the anti-Christ," fought back. Iglau, like most of the royal cities, remained staunchly Catholic and in 1426 expelled its Jews on the grounds that they were aiding the Hussites. They were not allowed to return for over four hundred years.

Iglau's Jews and perhaps Therese Frucht's ancestors fled to the towns of the Vysočina, or Highlands, that were the stronghold of the Czech Protestants. Rabbinical authorities of the period wrote sympathetically about the *bnei Husim,* or "sons of Hus," also calling them *bnei avazim* (a play on the Czech word *husa,* since *avazim* is the Hebrew word for geese). The Czech Protestants, unlike the later German ones, did not view the Jew as the anti-Christ. They identified with the Israel of the Old Testament. One group, the Taborites, even named their community after the Biblical Mount Tabor and adopted Jewish dietary law.

After 1620, when the Protestants were defeated and the Church tried to extirpate all traces of reform, those Jewish hill town outposts grew. Some of the Czech nobles who had ruled those towns were executed and others, along with thousands of other Protestants, were expelled from the Czech lands. Their estates were confiscated and awarded to foreigners who had fought for the Pope. Czech schools were given over to the Jesuits; Czech culture, driven underground. Some Czech Protestants compared their exile to the Jewish Diaspora. Some — faced with the choice of exile, conversion to Catholicism or conversion to Judaism — took a step unique in history and chose to convert to Judaism.

By the eighteenth century, the Jewish population of the Czech lands had grown and so irritated the Germans that they appealed to the emperor for its limitation. In 1726, the imperial "Family Laws" established a limit of 8,600 Jewish families in Bohemia and 5,400 Jewish families in Moravia. Any Jew wishing to establish a new family had to obtain a family number that was usually passed from father to eldest son. The right to that number became a source of bitter family feuds. Men waited for fathers and brothers to die; youngest sons were forced to remain celibate or marry in weddings that conferred no legitimacy on their children. Thousands of Czech Jews became illegal aliens who lived secretly with their parents and subsisted on charity. Many emigrated to Slovakia, Poland, and Hungary. If Therese Frucht's father was an innkeeper as my mother had written, he and his father had owned such a number and their family had been living in the same town for generations.

The innkeeper was a stock role in the limited occupational repertoire available to Jews in Central Europe before 1848. The distillation and distribution of alcohol were part of a larger system known as *arenda*, whereby a nobleman leased out rights that accrued to his manor. Many of the leaseholders, called *Randars* in the Czech lands, were Jews. In many places the two words were interchangeable.

"At the very end of the village stood a small isolated farmstead," wrote Jakob Kaufmann, a German-Jewish journalist in 1841.

"That's where the Jew lives," my coachman, a sturdy farm boy, said in Bohemian. I'd noticed the shadow of a dark figure in the window, old-fashioned spectacles on his nose, reading in a large gray book. And who else could this be but the village Jew who was perhaps seeking counsel in his Talmud as to how much oil he was to put into his Sabbath lamp the following Friday evening?

It isn't that the Jews have a special relationship with these holy spirits. Nor do they own the taverns which, in most cases, have been built by the lord of the manor and leased to them. One can't therefore hold the Jews accountable for a brandy-plague should one occur in Bohemia.

But a peculiarly pleasant idea is connected with these brandy houses. They are, for the Jews, like a piece of the Promised Land. They are ancestral seats of venerable families who often live for two or three generations in comfortable security.

There were both very rich and very poor *Randars,* according to Kaufmann. "When I think of honest, devout Simon in the village of Obor," he writes,

> my heart swells with pleasure. How enthusiastically he celebrates the Sabbath. . . . Simon not only knows the Bible and the prophets by heart. He has sharpened his wits on the Talmud, he can speak, when he is composed, pure German, and even likes to read German novels. His favorite reading remains Mendelssohn's *Jerusalem* and Lessing's *Nathan the Wise.* He is interested in politics — whenever he reads the Prague newspaper, he spends hours studying world events and neglects his guests. Everything, even England's quarrels with China, or a peasant revolt in France or Spain, seems to him to relate to the Messiah who is taking so long to appear because he is riding on a donkey. . . .

Simon is chronically behind in his rent. He sells whalebone, thread, and tobacco to the peasants in addition to brandy, but he never makes enough money to feed his many children and

> lives on the best of terms with the good Bohemian peasants. Though themselves immensely religious, they are not intolerant of those of other faiths as are most of their priests, or hypocritically tolerant and eloquent about the Enlightenment as are the townspeople . . . but are full of respect for everyone who is religious. They speak of Simon as "Our Jew" in the same way they might say "Our Saint" or "Our hermit."

Simon does not serve brandy on Passover as it is forbidden by ritual law. His farmers visit him nonetheless. Year in, year out, he says his prayers in front of them, turning to the East, putting on his phylacteries, wrapping his prayer shawl around his hat and head. However odd it may look, none of those present will smile. During the eight days of Passover, he often treats them to long religious discussions, explains the origin of the Seder, even translates whole passages from the Hebrew into Czech with such enthusiasm that it seems as though he hopes to convert the old farmers and circumcize them the next day! And the farmers? They sit around, a short wooden pipe between their teeth, their wide-brimmed hats on the side of their heads, elbows on the table, gawking, shaking their heads, and listening carefully. Around them, smiling, stand Simon's children and his wife, Sara, with her high wrinkled forehead. And the farmers, on their way home, shake their heads and murmur into their beards, "He's a pious holy man, our Jew."

It is a charming portrait that Kaufmann paints and one I would like to believe. But in most Central and Eastern European literature, the Jewish innkeeper, like the moneylender and peddler, is almost invariably presented as a parasite living off the guileless Christian. Although the *Randar* may not be rich, he enriches himself at the expense of the peasant, offering him brandy, taking money his family needs for food and clothing, even accepting pledges of unharvested produce in exchange for another shot at oblivion. His proximity to alcohol and apparent immunity to its seduction furthered folk beliefs that ascribed mysterious, demonic powers to Jews. In novels, plays, and stories, his tavern is a place of weddings and other celebrations but also of shady deals, the only venue in which a Gentile, a Jew, a count, and a criminal might meet.

The *Randar* probably heard more confessions than the village priest, and his tavern — the only community gathering place apart from church during the long winters — competed with the

Church for money and souls. The tavern served as restaurant and dance hall, especially on Christian feast days, but also as post office and general store where food, grain, and cloth could be purchased, letters could be written and read. Because the *randar* was literate and multilingual, he became a scribe and translator for the peasants, the repository of village gossip, general information, and, of course, many secrets.

In the Highlands of Bohemia and Moravia making liquor was the job of monks and Jews. Jewish mothers and daughters were pressed into the family business because they were trusted to keep the distilling process secret and refrain from drinking the product. Jewish sons and cousins then distributed it, walking through town with small barrels on their backs, a glass in hand. Brandy — *pálenka* or *kořalka* — was thought to relieve an upset stomach, strengthen the heart, dry up harmful bodily fluids, and even enhance virility.

After 1848, when laws restricting Jewish occupations were abolished and they were free to choose their work, the number of Jewish innkeepers began to decline. One of the few writers interested in keeping their memory alive was Leopold Kompert, a journalist born in a rural Bohemian town in the early part of the nineteenth century, who wrote a novella called *The Children of the Randar.*

"Anyone who enjoys the smell of the woods, the leaves of trees, and the chirping of birds should not enter the ghetto," Kompert begins his story.

> People there have too many troubles and there's no empty space. You need trees and a soul free of anxiety in order to listen to birdsong. The Talmud is too heavy for merry song and sunlight is too strong for the Talmudist's eyes. That's why we are leaving the ghetto for a place where we can find these things — I mean, the house of the *Randar.*

In Kompert's eyes, the *Randar* is the most powerful Jew in his village. Although he attends Jewish religious services, he lives outside the Jewish Street above his tavern, employs Jewish servants, and socializes with Czechs. His wife is the object of the local count's attentions. His children, Moritz and Hannah, grow up playing with their Czech neighbor Honza.

Honza decides to become a priest and Moritz persuades his father to allow him to study medicine. There is no discussion of Hannah's schooling. She will marry the man the *Randar* chooses and keep a Jewish home. Years pass. Her mother dies. Dozens of prospective bridegrooms are presented to Hannah but she rejects them all. She has never outgrown her childhood love for Honza. Then, on the eve of Yom Kippur, the *Randar* and Moritz travel to a nearby town to observe the holiday, since they have no local synagogue, leaving Hannah to mind the inn.

On Yom Kippur, Hannah wakes up alone. She has lost the places her father has marked for her in the prayer book and her Hebrew is insufficient to find the prayers herself. She broods over the fact that another prospective bridegroom is scheduled to visit and decides to run away to Honza and become a Christian. Hannah packs a bundle of clothing and rifles through her father's drawers. When she finds a small sack containing soil from Jerusalem, she spills it out and fills it with money she will need for her getaway.

When her father and brother return, the tavern doors are open and no one is home. They find Hannah with Honza the priest, who tells them that Hannah intends to convert to Christianity of her own free will. Moritz contends that she has no free will: she belongs to her father. Hannah submits and goes home. Moritz becomes a village doctor. The innkeeper dies. Hannah never marries but keeps house for her brother.

Journalists Kompert and Kaufmann provided my first windows into Therese's world. Was my great-grandmother anything like the *Randar*'s daughter? I wondered. Did she read Hebrew? Was she left to mind the tavern alone? Was her Czech lover a childhood playmate like Honza? A musician? A policeman, as in two old Yiddish folksongs about a Jewish innkeeper's daughter who ran away from her father?

On many days, the futility of those questions overcame me and I sat listening to Mahler or for the mail carrier's steps. Sometimes, he handed me bulky offprints from academic journals or envelopes with embossed institutional letterheads. Some days he had nothing and I returned to my books thinking how naive I had been to expect that I could reconstruct what had been shattered. Then one day, he handed me a letter postmarked Prague and bearing an unfamiliar return address.

"Because I myself am engaged in researching the history of the now-extinct Jewish community," it read,

> I know you have written to the director of the Regional Museum in Jihlava, to the National Library, and to the Central Archive in Prague. I put some things together in my mind and that is why I allow myself to disturb you with this letter.
>
> I have at home relatively rich files covering the now-extinct Jewish communities of Bohemia and Moravia. They are mostly documents concerning synagogues, cemeteries and houses, but sometimes you can find in them the names of their owners. . . . Maybe on your next visit you could go to the State Central Archive, or else ask someone who has the time and who knows how to read German Gothic script to do so for you. I don't have the time to do it myself. But if you need me, I will be happy to advise you.

A few months later, I was in Prague.

3
~

What remains of the registers of the Jewish communities of the Czech lands is housed in the State Central Archive in Prague. I had ordered several registers from Iglau and, almost as soon as I opened the first, I looked up for relief. The *matriky*, as they are called, are two-foot-high, hundred-year-old tomes, annotated with goose quill and ink. Sitting to my left and right, squinting, were dozens of Czechs searching for names. It was Prague's first post-Communist spring and they were looking for proof of ownership of property nationalized by the Communist government. They were reclaiming real estate: a factory, a house, a shop. What, I wondered, was I doing there?

That morning, I had left my husband with a book of trolley tickets, a map of Prague, and our three-year-old and five-year-old sons. I felt torn between the demands of family life and the demands of research. My multilingual husband, who had not wanted to be left out of what he perceived as an adventure, became helpless in the face of Czech. My sons found new ways to detain me every morning with broken zippers, blisters, stomachaches, problems that no one but I could resolve right then, on the spot.

This is family, I had thought as I hurtled toward the Prague subway. Family is messy, full of stress, conflicting claims, and the juggling of individual and collective needs — not some pristine paper chase after the dead. Family is not only loving and belonging but wanting, comparing, meddling, resenting, endlessly struggling for dominance and control. What did that have to do with poring over *matriky* in the State Central Archive, my lungs filling with dust?

The registers of the Jewish community of Jihlava I was holding in my hands began in 1867 and, in spidery Gothic script, recorded the growing secularization of Habsburg Jews — the *Samuels* became *Sigmunds;* the *Moseses* became *Maximilians;* the *Izaks* became *Ignatzes.* The women's names changed too, from *Rachel* and *Esther* to *Therese, Josephine,* and *Franziska,* as my great-grandmother, grandmother, and mother were named. My neck began to ache. *Hoffman, Heller, Steiner, Weissenstein* . . . nothing resembling *Frucht.* Then I spotted *Maximilian Furcht,* son of Samuel and Marie, married in 1872.

In the 1880s and 1890s, there were more Furchts: Alois, Elsa, Olga, Adolf, two Josephs, and two more Maximilians. Had my mother or her mother or Therese herself transposed the letters *u* and *r?* I copied down all the names, then hurried to meet the stranger who had written to me about his "rich files of the now-extinct Jewish communities."

Jiří Fiedler turned out to be an elfin man in his early fifties with a pronounced stutter. He worked at a small desk in a children's publishing house and seemed as modest and eccentric as the tiny vase of dandelions on his desk. He was not, he hastened to tell me, of Jewish descent. He had scrutinized his family tree many times searching for a Jewish ancestor to explain his strange hobby and found none. "Some people smoke," he said. "Some people strangle little girls in parks. I bicycle around the country documenting dead Jews."

I smiled politely, as I often do at Czech black humor. Czechs, and particularly Czech Jews, have a love of irony that totally by-passed me. Perhaps, given Fiedler's long and solitary preoccupation with dead Jews, I thought sourly, he was pleased to be talking with a live one. To what, I asked, did he attribute his hobby?

Jiří Fiedler was not much inclined to talk about himself. I made out that he had been born in the old Moravian city of Olomouc, that he was ten when the Nazi occupation of Czechoslovakia ended, and that he saw the German soldiers retreating from the eastern front and concentration camp survivors returning home. They were given temporary housing at his school.

When Fiedler was fifteen, he came across an old Yiddish newspaper. By himself, working slowly and patiently, he deciphered the Hebrew characters as though they were hieroglyphics and taught himself to read Yiddish. He dated his interest in local history to about the same time. Like Jiří Rychetský, he discovered that *místopis,* as local history is called in Czech, was one of the few intellectual pursuits that could be safely enjoyed under Communism. He began to ride his bicycle down back roads near his home, making sketches of buildings and lists of historical landmarks.

After completing his university studies in linguistics, Fiedler took a job as a copyeditor. But on weekends and holidays, he pursued his passion, carrying on his bicycle a sleeping bag, photographic equipment, and provisions. He photographed churches, chapels, fortresses, and castles. At night, while his wife and young children slept, he worked in his darkroom and at his desk, compiling a comprehensive directory of such landmarks in the Czech lands.

By the 1970s, Fiedler had become interested in the synagogues and Jewish cemeteries he glimpsed through the trees. Those cemeteries, he told me, called out to be photographed. The slanting tombstones were so overgrown with vines and bushes that he began to carry gardening tools on his bicycle along with everything else. He tried to enlist the help of his wife and sons.

They were not interested. On the contrary, they resented the time and money he was spending on his strange hobby. So on summer vacations, Fiedler left them to swim and sunbathe while he pedaled down old country roads alone, stopping whenever he saw a telltale crumbling wall. A former schoolmate of his worked at the Jewish Museum and Fiedler repeatedly tried to obtain permission to use its archive. But the Jewish Museum was closely watched by the secret police. He was denied access and continued to amass his maps, his index cards of data on the dead, and his photographs alone.

He could not give it up. He had more information on former Jewish buildings and properties by now than the Jewish Museum: collections of old postcards — neatly arranged by village and town; town plans with Jewish houses marked in red; files of correspondence with dozens of local archivists. By chance, in the late 1970s, he edited a book by a man who enabled him to gain access to the Jewish Museum and even to receive some financial support for his research. By the 1980s, Fiedler had become a consultant to everyone researching Czech Jews. His Judaica collection filled the shelves and cabinets of one whole room of his four-room apartment and included some seventy thousand photographs.

When I told him I had found no Fruchts in the *matriky* but a roster of Furchts, he said that such transposition of letters was common. Who would not prefer *Frucht,* a name that meant "fruit," to *Furcht,* one that meant "fear"? He began to talk to me like a coach to a flagging player. I was lucky, he said. Furcht was an uncommon name in the Czech lands. He could not recall ever having come across it in his travels.

I should rent a car and drive to the Czech-Moravian Highlands, have a look at Jihlava, but not expect to find much there. Jews had been expelled from all the royal cities in the fifteenth century and had returned to Iglau only in 1848. He was all but certain that Therese had been a Czech-speaking country Jew, from one of the hill towns where Jews had been protected by the nobility. Hadn't I said she had a Czech lover? If I started early, I could be back in Prague by sunset. He made a dot for Jihlava on a sheet of paper, drew seven dots around it and told me about those hill towns.

First, *Puklice:* five or six kilometers from Jihlava, with a three-hundred-year-old cemetery. Second, *Brtnice:* seventeen kilometers southeast. Very old community established in the first half of the fifteenth century. Several remarkable tombstones. Synagogue torn down recently to make room for a department store. Third, *Polná*, associated with the ritual murder trial of Leopold Hilsner in 1899. Good museum. I should also try *Větrný Jeníkov, Třešť, Batelov,* and *Úsobí.* There were, of course, no living Jews with whom I would be able to talk in any of these places.

I do not think I would have had the strength to set out on this expedition alone. I did not want my family with me either. Luckily, I had a Czech friend who volunteered to accompany me. Jiří Tichý was half-Jewish, born to a Jewish father and a Christian mother in 1946. During the occupation, his father had been sent to concentration camps and his mother had worked in the Resistance. When Jiří was one year old, in 1947, his father left his family for Israel and never returned.

In the spring of 1968, when travel restrictions for Czechs were temporarily lifted, his mother urged Jiří to fly to Israel. His reunion with his father was difficult and made more so by Jiří's dislike of the country. He was an art student accustomed to hanging out in Czech taverns and arguing about ideas and literature. In Jerusalem, where I first met him, he found few bars, no culture of drinking, a harsh climate, ugly buildings, and a style of life foreign to his own. Although he felt deeply Jewish, he could not connect to the Jewish state. In 1970, *after* the Russian Invasion, Jiří returned home because he could not imagine his life anywhere else but in Prague.

He was twenty-four then, reckless, passionate, and determined to sabotage the Soviet "normalization." First, he took a job in a print shop, where he was thrown out for refusing to produce "some piece of nonsense," then in a theater that the government closed down. Then he worked at the National Gallery and other museums until his activities within the Czech dissident movement were discovered.

He spent most of the 1980s as a menial laborer working in construction for the first four years: "Boots, mud, cold," he told me as we sped down the new freeway toward Jihlava. For the next five, he was a laborer for Prague's Parks Department, "planting tulips, mowing lawns." During that time, he helped distribute underground literature and wrote and published his own volume of essays. Then he was put in prison but the experience was not as bad as he expected. No one beat him up, and he had some extraordinary conversations. Anything was worth being alive to witness the end of Communism, he said. He was now an accredited journalist. He had just revisited Israel as part of the press corps attending Václav Havel. He was as interested as ever in his identity as a Czech Jew and intrigued by my project of tracking down a past which belonged to us both.

Our first stop in Jihlava was the home of Charlotte Janů, a retired hospital administrator in her late sixties. Lotte had been hidden in the countryside with her mother's Christian family during the Second World War after her Jewish father was deported by the Nazis. Since the fall of Communism, she had been in touch with friends in Israel. She saw my project of retrieving Therese as a way of retrieving part of her own life and was our guide in Jihlava. Despite Jiří Fiedler's opinion that we would be wasting our time there, I wanted to see the city in which my mother thought her grandmother had lived.

Old postcards depicted Iglau as picturesque, with one of the largest main squares in Central Europe. In the Czech city of Jihlava, that space is broken by a department store that embodies the ugliness of cheap Stalinist architecture. The layer of industrial soot that seemed to coat every building in Czechoslovakia was especially thick here. The museum was closed. It proved impossible to obtain a city map.

I felt restless and uncomfortable in Jihlava, remembering the ban on intercourse between Christians and Jews; the fifteenth-century expulsion edicts; police reports that listed the names of those few Jews — Kohn, Kopperl, and Weissenstein — who managed to buy their way around the four-hundred-year exclusion; and city ordinances prohibiting the rental of lodgings to Jews. The official guidebook, *Jihlava: City of the Czechoslovak Socialist Republic*, was a bleak example of Communist historiography, which noted in passing that the composer Gustav Mahler spent his youth here.

We walked to the house where the Mahlers lived. The memorial plaque was filthy; the walls stank of urine. The sounds of Mahler's world — horseshoes on the cobblestones, music of the hurdy-gurdy man, brass bands of the imperial military garrison — were long gone. A more pertinent plaque might have memorialized Mahler's description of himself as three times homeless: "a native of Bohemia in Austria, an Austrian among Germans, and a Jew throughout the world."

I was so depressed by the state of the place that I did not notice the sign that read Brtnice Street, the name of one of the seven hill towns on my list.

I told Jiří that I wanted to drive out into the countryside and begin our circle of Puklice, Brtnice, Polná, Větrný Jeníkov, Třešť, Batelov, and Úsobí that Jiří Fiedler had drawn for me. Lotte said she knew someone who had been born in Brtnice. She made a telephone call and came back with the name of an elderly woman. In a few minutes the three of us were driving on a narrow back road through a landscape which had preserved the character and contours of the preindustrial world.

Leopold Kompert's novella *Children of the Randar* might have been set in Brtnice. So might any Grimm fairy tale. The town is surrounded by gentle hills planted with barley and rye, the fields edged by small woods. Smoke rises from cottage chimneys; an occasional wooden cart stands near the road. The scale is child size: small houses, tiny gardens. High above the stream that flows through the village square is an abandoned castle with its park and Renaissance church. The road on which we entered — Brtnice's only thoroughfare — was deserted. We passed the department store that had been built where the synagogue once stood and pulled up in the town square.

Once I turned off the motor of our car, the only sounds were birdsong and the rustle of the wind. I felt a powerful sense of familiarity, as comfortable here as I had been uncomfortable in Jihlava.

Lotte's contact, Mrs. Matlová, was eighty-five years old and, in her muddy, half-open boots and headscarf, surrounded by hens, could have been standing in the eighteenth century as easily as in our own. Lotte explained that I was an American, trying to track down my great-grandmother Therese Furcht, who might have been born here about 150 years ago.

Mrs. Matlová's pale blue eyes looked me over slowly, then she motioned at her pails, her hands. Surely she should clean up a bit and invite us inside. I explained that we were visiting six more towns and did not have much time. Mrs. Matlová continued to look me over and began to talk. It was in 1921, when she was fifteen, she said, that she began working for Mrs. Furcht in the store. Mr. Furcht was born in Brtnice. Mr. Furcht's parents were from Brtnice too, Mrs. Matlová continued — old people who sold old clothes. People used to say *U Šmulíka*, at Shmulik's.

The casualness with which she used the name Furcht took the air out of my lungs. I went numb. I sat down on the bench, scattering the hens, and let my companions ask questions. Was there a town chronicler? Was he likely to be home? His name was Augustine Hons. He was the former mayor, the archivist, and an amateur photographer who had taken pictures of every structure in the town.

I walked to Augustine Hons's house in a kind of stupor, drinking in the air. His street turned out to be a path between woodpiles. A rooster crowed. There were no house numbers or doorbells and we called out, *"Pane Hons!"* a few times before a man who appeared to be about Mrs. Matlová's age came out. With his battered beret and a faded apron over his sweaters, Hons looked like a baker in a Hans Christian Andersen story. He was surprised that anyone from outside Brtnice, let alone America, was looking for him but, if we were interested in seeing his photographs, he would be happy to show us.

We sat down on another wooden bench and Hons came back out with photographs, carefully annotated and arranged in files: the chapel, the castle, the synagogue, the Jewish School. I examined each of them with a sense of growing certainty. My mother had never been in Brtnice; my grandmother had never spoken of it; yet I felt increasingly sure that I was sitting in the place Therese's family came from.

The chapel one hundred feet away, said Mr. Hons, was built by a Florentine architect. In fact, the whole town had something of an Italian flavor because during the Counter-Reformation, the emperor had given it to the Count Rombald of Collalto and San Salvatore. The Collaltos owned Brtnice until the Russians arrived in 1945. They had brought Italian architecture, monks, and musicians to Brtnice. Vivaldi was one of the composers from whom they commissioned work.

The Industrial Revolution, Mr. Hons explained, had bypassed Brtnice. In the eighteenth century, the town was known for its cotton and sheepskin workshops, which had employed a fair number of artisans. But industrialization ended that. Lacking any local industry in which they might find employment, people in Brtnice petitioned to be linked up to the railroad network that was proliferating throughout the Habsburg Empire, but the Collaltos opposed the plan, afraid that they would lose their field-workers to factory jobs elsewhere. No large factory was ever built in Brtnice. Beer from the brewery had to be carted to customers, the Habsburgs moved their administrators to a town more easily accessible, and Brtnice's population — probably about 3,300 at its peak — began to decline.

For the first time I began to have a sense of Therese's world. It was not the poor, dusty, eastern European *shtetl* nor the desperately overcrowded German *Judengasse* but something more moderate and more integrated into Christian life. When Germans wished to characterize a place as sleepy and boring, where nothing ever happened, they used the term *wie in Böhmischen Dörfern*, "like in Bohemian villages."

Brtnice was not a village but a village-like market town. Four separate groups had lived there: the Italian aristocrats in the castle, the German-speaking imperial administrators, the Czech peasants, and the Jews — a community that had grown from a handful of families in the seventeenth century to a peak of sixty families by the time Therese was born, and who owned about one-third of Brtnice's houses. The count and his entourage hunted and entertained. The administrators kept the books. The peasants — for centuries the property of the count — slaved in the fields and forests, looking to their priest and schoolteacher for counsel.

A few Jews leased manorial privileges from the count, renting his inn, his distillery, his privilege of collecting tolls over his bridges. By the eighteenth century, there was a Jewish midwife, a butcher, a tailor, a baker, a bookbinder, and a button-maker. The most successful member of the community had developed a textile enterprise, which farmed out work to neighboring villages, and half of Brtnice's Jews owed him money. But most were traders who left town on Sunday mornings and walked from village to village, starting with empty baskets on their backs, sometimes sheets. They bought up sheepskins, rabbit skins, grain, poppy seeds, flax, old pots and scrap metal, tallow for soap and candles, and, above all, goose feathers. They walked the hills summer and winter, braving dogs and stones thrown by peasant children, and their place in the rural landscape is recorded in the classic village novel of Czech literature, Božena Němcová's *Babička,* or *Grandma.*

"Every day at twilight Tall Moses walked past," she wrote in the mid-nineteenth century.

He was as tall as a pole and had a morose expression and carried a sack over his shoulder. Betsy the maid used to tell the children that he collected disobedient children in this sack and from that moment on, whenever the children saw Tall Moses, they shrank into themselves as though he had drained the blood from them. Grandma had forbidden Betsy to tell them such tales but when Ursula, the other maid, said that Moses was a thief and that everything stuck to his fingers, Grandma didn't contradict her. He had to be a wicked person, this Moses, and he remained a bogeyman to the children even after they no longer believed he carried children in his sack.

Despite their continuing "otherness," Jewish men and women like Moses had regular contact with the peasants, buying and selling, serving as medical, veterinary, and personal advisers. Like medieval troubadours, they also carried news of the world at a time when few newspapers reached the countryside and were so vital to the rural economy that trade fairs were organized so as not to interfere with the Jewish calendar.

The Jewish tavernkeeper, like the peddler, was an integral part of the landscape. His tavern was a gathering place for the community, where weddings and sacred feasts were celebrated one day and men brawled and had to be dragged out by their feet the next. It was for that proximity to and fraternization with the Christian world, and because he did not always close his tavern down on the Sabbath, that the tavernkeeper was looked down upon by pious Jews, even if he was rich and could buy a seat in the front row of the synagogue. His tavern was situated outside the community and — in contradiction to Kaufmann's portrait of the pious Simon — he was often considered an *amhoretz,* an ignorant man unschooled in Talmud and Torah. A *Randar* and his family had to be on friendly terms with the customers who drank his brandy, played cards, confessed in unguarded moments to things they kept from the schoolteacher or priest. How could that kind of environment fail to influence a Jew, not to speak of his children?

Behind the appearance of a solid Jewish community, wrote the literary historian Oskar Donath in the 1920s, social standing was a major issue among the Jews of these hill towns. In synagogue, the front rows were reserved for the rich; the back ones for the poor. A *Randar* would not condescend to friendship with a peddler or a tailor. Business acumen was so keen, as a local saying went, that competitors could "drown one another in a spoonful of water."

Town Jews like those in Brtnice, who enjoyed the benefits of their own synagogue and cemetery, behaved in a paternalistic fashion toward the Jewish families who lived isolated, one or two to a village. During the festival of Sukkot, walkers brought the Jewish villagers the *lulav* and *etrog;* on Purim, they read the *megilla* to the women who could not get to town; all year, they had to remind them of the dates of the Jewish holidays. When village Jews came to Brtnice to observe the Sabbath, town Jews treated them as country bumpkins even as they hosted them in their homes.

To differentiate the Sabbath from other days, Jewish women greeted one another in what they called *žargon* — the *Judendeutsch* that was their regional form of Yiddish — rather than in Czech. There were those who still read Jewish books in Yiddish but "no lack of women who occupied themselves with the German classics," according to Donath. I can imagine that they found the activities of Therese Furcht, the innkeeper's daughter, a rich subject of gossip. On holidays and in their leisure time, according to a museum manuscript from nearby Polná, "the Jews sat on chairs outside their homes, talking shop and picking over their problems with people, including people in their own families."

Nineteenth-century country Jews had enormous families. Jewish patriarchs were regarded by Czech peasants as sexually potent, often fathering twelve or fifteen children with one wife. The Czech Jewish writer Vojtěch Rakous, himself from such a family, claimed his parents were never sure how many children they actually had and wrote a short story titled "About a Person Who Doesn't Know When He Was Born," describing the difficulties of determining his own birthdate in such a family.

With so many offspring to worry about, marriages were a major preoccupation of the women. Purim was the time that matchmakers generally arranged a *beshau,* or "viewing" of prospects from the pool of Jewish families in other parts of Bohemia and Moravia. The size of a girl's dowry was a prime attraction for the groom's family, for the dowry would often be used to establish him in his own business. A groom's Jewish education had long been the prime attraction for the bride's family, although, by the nineteenth century, this criterion was giving way to family reputation and to the groom's ability to earn a good living.

The sayings of the Jews collected in the Polná manuscript include: "No shame in owing people money, a good Jew always owes someone at least five hundred zlatýs"; "Don't lie down with a menstruating woman"; "If you want peace, don't live with your children"; "If you invest in a field, you'll barely have bread and salt for dinner but if you invest in a store, you'll reap a profit and have meat and wine every evening"; and "One person never takes on one hundred but one hundred will gang up on one."

The rural Jews lived in a society that had been re-Catholicized so thoroughly by the Jesuits that, at almost every crossroad, a statue of a saint had been constructed to turn one's thoughts to the Church. They watched the celebrations of Corpus Christi

Day and St. Stephen's and St. Nicholas Day and Three Kings Day and Ascension Day and Christmas Day. They watched the peasants make broomsticks, and throw them into the air, aflame, for the feast of St. John. They were wary at Carnival time when Jews were often dragged, unwilling, into Christian festivities, and warier still around Easter, when the old accusations of Christ-killing and ritual murder came to the fore. Their hours were marked by the pealing of church bells calling worshippers to mass; the seasons by the church processions down Brtnice's main street.

The Christians knew many of the Jewish holidays as well. They knew that the Jewish Sabbath began on Friday evening and did not end until the stars rose on Saturday night. They knew that a Jewish peddler would die of starvation rather than eat food from the kitchens of those peasants with whom he spent the night. They believed that those years when the Jewish Passover coincided with Easter were especially auspicious for planting. And in the fall, when the village Jews arrived in town to observe Rosh Hashanah and Yom Kippur, the peasants would say: "I saw the Jews riding; the snow can't be far behind." When they heard the sounds of the *shofar*, they would joke, "The Jews are blowing to bring in the frost."

In Brtnice, the boundary between the Jewish Street and the Christian ones was all but imperceptible. No expulsion had ever disrupted the continuity of Jewish life there and there had been only one recorded incident of anti-Jewish violence, in 1851. Brtnice's synagogue was not hidden in a courtyard behind a protective wall as in some Central European cities but stood on the main road by which we had first entered the town, with a view of the surrounding hills. Whenever Jews had been persecuted in Vienna or Iglau, they had sought refuge in Brtnice. That was also the case during the Second World War. There were still nine members of the Furcht family living there in 1942, when the Nazis came.

Sitting on Augustine Hons's wooden bench, one hundred yards away from the building where, I later learned, Therese's mother had spent her last years, I grew so excited that I could not move. As if from a distance, I heard Jiří asking for directions to the Jewish cemetery and Mr. Hons telling him that the key was in the courthouse and the courthouse was closed.

Jiří and I set off to the cemetery. The afternoon was golden. Anyone who came here, I told myself, would be drawn to the calm beauty of the town. But another voice inside me was insistent: it said I belonged here.

The cemetery was surrounded by a tall stone wall which we followed until we reached a set of large wooden doors. Across them was an iron bolt, fastened with a padlock. I stopped a few feet away. Jiří and I had been together in the cemetery of Roudnice-nad-Labem, where several generations of my father's family are buried. Tombs had been overturned there, gravestones carried off for use as building supplies, graves dug up by looters in search of treasure or simply teenagers with nothing better to do. I did not wish to see another sight like that one. And what if Mrs. Matlová was wrong? It was one thing to talk about an old employer; another to find a whole, *my* whole, family. I did not wish to discover that my sense of connection was imagined or a longing for something that could not be retrieved.

Jiří felt none of my hesitation. He walked up to the closed padlock, gave it a sharp tug, and the entire bolt fell off the tall wooden door. He opened it, I followed. The grass was high but the graves were untouched. There in the first row, directly facing us, were two tall, marble tombstones which, in bold letters, read FURCHT and FURCHT. I stood rooted in place, a weight lifted from my head, my blood at rest.

4

I returned to Brtnice several times in the 1990s. Mrs. Matlová died
not long after our meeting and Mr. Hons fell ill, but Jiří Rychetský, whose town of Humpolec was not far away, walked with me
along what some Brtnice residents still call the Jewish Street and
the Jewish Bridge. Mahlerites continued to enliven Mr. Rychetský's retirement years. He had helped an astrologer approximate
the exact time of Mahler's birth, and had allowed two young researchers to sleep at his Mahler museum who had subsequently
married. When an archive of Jewish documents hidden since the
Second World War was discovered in Šepekov, in southern Bohemia, Mr. Rychetský traveled there in search of Mahleriana and
found a register of the Jewish community of Brtnice from 1771 to
1835. That book contained the names and pertinent dates of all
Therese's ancestors. Her father, Lazar Furcht, was born in 1811,
the second of eight children. Her mother, Josephine Ullmann,
had been born in 1807, the youngest of twelve. Working in Brtnice's overgrown cemetery with a pair of gardening shears, Mr.

Rychetský had uncovered Josephine's small, half-buried tombstone in addition to nine others that bore the name Furcht.

Over the years, I came to view both Jiří Rychetský and Jiří Fiedler as my companions on the road as well as exponents of a philo-Semitic tradition that began with the Hussites and was embodied in the first president of the Czechoslovak Republic, Thomas G. Masaryk. Not only was I indebted to the two Jiřís for leading me to Brtnice, I felt a spirit of intellectual independence emanate from them that helped me better negotiate the rough, more disillusioning parts of my research.

I had grown up with my mother's nostalgic memories of Czechoslovakia.

My mother often told American friends that she did not know she was a Jew until the rise of Adolf Hitler and that prewar Czechoslovakia was a freer, more progressive country than postwar America. In both my parents' eyes, antisemitism was a German invention, imposed on an enslaved and unwilling Czech nation, an appealing, comforting formulation to me, a child born after the defeat of Nazism.

But as the Jiřís continued to feed me documents and books and ideas, I began to see more than a history that apportioned good and evil along ethnic lines. I read nationalistic and antisemitic tracts written in Czech and liberal texts written in German.

The Furchts, like all Jews in the Czech lands, owed their freedom to the Germanizing emperor Joseph II. Joseph's interest in the Jews was a by-product of his overall vision of empire and pragmatic rather than humane. Aware of the strong, centralized nations of France to his west, Prussia to his north, and Russia to his east, Joseph aimed at unifying his territories, which sprawled from the Dalmatian coast up to Poland and from the border of Switzerland to the Ottoman Empire. He tried to curb the powers of the Church, the local aristocrats, and the national Diets and to impose a unitary administrative and educational system. As a consequence, the structures that had for centuries kept Jews separate and apart were transformed.

The emperor did not suspend the inhuman family laws that allowed only one Jewish son per family to marry and remain in his place of birth. Nor did he allow Jews to live outside the chained-off Jewish Streets. However, his Edict of Toleration offered a program for the "improvement of the Jews," a recipe for using them to his state's advantage. "Since coming to power," he wrote in 1782,

> We have been most particular to ensure that all Our subjects, without distinction of nationality and religion, should share in the public prosperity which We hope to increase by Our care. . . .
>
> Since this, Our gracious intention, cannot be reconciled with the existing laws against the Jewish Nation in Our Hereditary Margravate of Moravia and the so-called Jewish Edicts, We wish to modify them. . . .

To make the Jews of greater service to the state, Joseph gave them permission "to establish their own schools at their own cost with teachers from among their co-religionists." Where that was impossible, Jews were ordered to send their children to the Christian normal, high, and secondary schools

> where arrangements will be made that the Jewish as well as the Christian children may learn everything, but be let out of school at the time of religious instruction, and that they should not be compelled or enticed to any action which goes against their religious practice.

Emperor Joseph II made it possible for Jews to pursue a university education and by 1788, two Jewish physicians graduated from medical school in Prague. He did away with all the requirements that had been used for centuries to differentiate Jews from the rest of the population: the wearing of beards, special colors or clothes, the prohibition on going out before noon on Sundays and holidays, or of visiting places of public entertainment. Henceforth, Jewish dignitaries would even be allowed to wear swords — a special privilege that conferred honor on the bearer. The emperor also expressed his desire for Jews to leave com-

merce and "embrace every type of craft and trade," by apprentic-
ing themselves to Christian masters. He granted the Jews permission to farm and to lease plots of land for twenty years. If they
converted to Christianity, they would be able to acquire property.

But the opportunity for equality that he was offering the
Jews — an opportunity absent from most of Europe — demanded concessions on their part: "The maintenance of mutual
trust demands the abolition of the Hebrew language," the emperor wrote, "as well as of the mixture of Hebrew and German,
the so-called Jewish language. We therefore expressly forbid the
use of this in all public proceedings."

All documents written in Hebrew or using Hebrew letters
would be viewed as null and void. The price of equality was the
adoption of the German language and culture.

"Since We now treat the Jewish nation as almost equal with
other foreigners of related religions," concluded Joseph,

> We instruct them most earnestly to observe most meticu-
> lously all political, civic, and judicial laws of the coun-
> try. . . . We consider it their duty as well as a mark of their
> gratitude that they should not abuse this Our Favor and
> the freedom that has accrued to them, and that they
> should not cause public offense through dissipation and
> excesses, and that they should not falsify the Christian reli-
> gion nor show disdain for it, for a heinous deed of this
> kind would be severely punished, and whoever had com-
> mitted it would be banished from all Our lands.
>
> Given in Our royal city of Brünn, 13th February 1782.

The heart of Joseph's program was linguistic. He understood
that language encodes culture and Germanized the educational
system, in which the language of higher learning had been Latin.
He threw out the Jesuits, who had been charged with education
in the empire since the Counter-Reformation and with the same
aim in mind, he Germanized all record keeping, so that Jews who
had been keeping their personal, community, and business
records in Hebrew characters now had to use Latin ones. Any Jew

who wished to marry had to certify that he had completed a German elementary school. Any man who wished to serve as a rabbi had to obtain a degree at a German university. Anyone who did not have a surname was obliged to adopt a German one.

Lazar Furcht's grandfather, Abraham ben Samuel, and his two brothers were the last men of their family line to identify themselves, in Hebrew, as the sons of their father. In 1788, the three were given the surname Furcht, according to the Josephine naming law. For a price, Jews could choose a pretty name — like Diamant (diamond) or Morgenstern (morningstar), a name based on vocation, such as Zimmerman (carpenter) or Kaufmann (merchant), or on their place of origin, such as Prager (from Prague) and Wiener (Viennese). But poor Jews or those unwilling to bribe the authorities had no choice and were given surnames like Klein (small) or Gross (big) or, in an ironic allusion to the epithet "stinking Jew," Rosenwasser (rosewater). The surname Furcht denoted "anxiety" or "fear."

The naming law, like the rest of the Josephine reforms, met with widespread resistance in the eastern parts of the Habsburg Empire such as Galicia, where Jews lived in larger and more segregated communities. Their Jewish leaders saw Joseph as just another in a long line of tyrants whose assimilationist bargain had to be resisted. Joseph, they believed, was bent not on improving but on destroying the Jews and they refused his project of Germanization.

But in Brtnice, as in most communities of the Czech lands, the majority of Jews viewed the Josephine reforms as progress. The turn of the nineteenth century found them speaking German as well as Czech, reserving *Judendeutsch*, or *žargon,* for the Sabbath and holidays, flocking to public schools, German high schools and universities. They became the first large group of European Jews to receive a secular education. By the 1830s, some had met Joseph's criteria for "usefulness" by establishing factories and bringing the Industrial Revolution to central Europe. They embraced German culture as no other group within the empire.

The pre-Josephine legal framework coexisted with Joseph's "improvements." It is unclear whether Therese Furcht was a legitimate child when she was born. Her father, Lazar, was the second of eight children and his older brother, Jakub, would have inherited the official family number. Although they were not slaves like Negroes in the antebellum United States nor serfs like Czech peasants, Habsburg Jews still could not live, marry, or work without restriction. They were taxed three times more heavily than the rest of the population and they could not leave Brtnice.

The general population did not react enthusiastically to Joseph's plans for the Jews. The crafts guilds did not rush to accept Jews as apprentices and both German merchants and the tiny class of Czech merchants were alarmed by the idea of Jews competing in areas from which they had formerly been excluded. Because Jews entered industry just as mechanization was beginning in Central Europe, they were seen as instrumental in throwing thousands of people out of work. When one Jewish manufacturer in Prague introduced machines into his textile factory and reduced wages, the workers called a strike which turned into an anti-Jewish riot that had to be stopped by the imperial army.

In 1848, the year of European revolution, the peasants were freed from centuries of servitude, unleashing an enormous wave of migration. Jewish residence and family laws were also abolished and, all over the Czech lands, thousands of men began to abandon the Jewish Streets. "Like birds suddenly released from their cages," wrote Erich Kahler, Jews were fleeing "the narrow, stifling and filthy Jewish quarters" of their hometowns for the cities and hundreds of other towns and villages.

Almost everywhere they moved, they found resentment and resistance on the part of both Germans and Czechs. Although Jews took a prominent part in uprisings in Vienna, revolutionary ideals faltered when it came to regarding them as equals. In Prague, the Jewish Quarter was looted by rioters who saw Jews as agents of German industrialization. Czech nationalist pamphlets, songs, and poems depicted Germans and Jews as hated foreigners. "The Jews, vermin of the earth, are indeed scum," read one poem from 1848. "Hunt them without mercy like beasts of the forest. No sooner does a Jew open his eyes than he strips a Christian of his skin. Wherever people find a Jew, they should grab him by the throat. Without hesitation they should hang him right away, hang him, hang him, hang him." The windows of Jewish homes were smashed all over Bohemia and Moravia, a recurrent practice in Central Europe and one which brought the Jewish glazier a steady income. In some places, the National Guard had to be called in or a separate Jewish Guard formed to defend against the Czechs.

Afterward, the Jews were shaken. "The turmoil is over, thank God," one woman wrote to her sister. "When it comes to persecuting Jews, the highly cultured and the lowly uneducated mob join forces. . . . The red thread that has been drawn through the annals of the Jews has not yet broken. . . ." A letter to a Vienna newspaper read: "No matter how furious the struggle between the Germans and the Czechs may become, they will be sure to agree on one point — their antipathy toward the hapless people of Juda." Writer Leopold Kompert, then twenty-six years old, called for an exodus to the United States: "You who do not understand the nature of history, recognize its warning signal! Years ago, when the persecution of the Jews was most violent, a Genoese envisioned the original idea of a new world. . . . It is this America that we now yearn for and that is where you should go!"

Although Moravian Jews were among the hundreds of thousands of people who emigrated to America in 1848, Lazar Furcht remained in Brtnice. Jews had lived there for five hundred years without an expulsion or pogrom and their community now comprised 429 people, or about one-sixth of the town. The Furchts lived over their tavern by the river on the outskirts of town, serving beer and brandy to their customers. They were related to many of the other Jews by blood or marriage. Brtnice's non-Jews knew the family well and they felt safe there.

The Jewish migrations of 1848 led to violence all over the Czech lands. Those Jews who opened stores in small villages where there had never been Jews before met with suspicion and violence. Those hill-town Jews who moved into the city of Iglau for the first time in four hundred years contributed to a rise in rents and to the displacement of local residents. Riots erupted in the city, enveloped the surrounding countryside, and even reached Brtnice in 1851. But Lazar and Josephine Furcht did not leave.

Josephine Furcht was thirty-nine when Therese was born and forty-four when the riots reached Brtnice. In mid-life, she faced a new, promising but uncertain world. Her daughter Therese, unlike herself, would not be obliged to live out her life in Brtnice. She might leave for the city, she might leave the Czech lands, even leave the Jewish community. Those were frightening possibilities for a woman who had grown up at the intersection of two demanding and unequivocal patriarchal traditions.

German culture assigned a woman responsibility in three domains: *Kinder* (children), *Kirche* (church), and *Küche* (kitchen). Jewish culture prescribed three functions: *hallah* (the baking of the Sabbath bread), *hadlakah* (the lighting of Sabbath and holiday lights), and *niddah* (the keeping of family purity).

The Jewish ideal of a woman is described in the Bible's Book of Proverbs and the *eshet chayil* or "woman of valor" prayer recited on the Sabbath by observant Jews.

> What a rare find is a capable wife!
> Her worth is far beyond rubies.
> Her husband puts his confidence in her
>   and lacks no good thing.
> She is good to him, never bad
>   all the days of her life.
> She looks for wool and flax
>   and sets her hand to them with a will.
> She is like a merchant fleet
>   bringing her food from afar.
> She rises while it is still night
>   and supplies provisions for her household,
>   the daily fare of her maids.
> She sets her mind on an estate and acquires it.
> She plants a vineyard by her own labor.
> She girds herself with strength
>   and performs her tasks with vigor.

She sees that her business thrives;
　　her lamp never goes out at night.
She sets her hand to the distaff;
　　her fingers work the spindle . . .
Her mouth is full of wisdom,
　　her tongue with kindly teaching.
She oversees the activities of her household
　　and never eats the bread of idleness . . .
　　　　Extol her for the fruit of her hand
　　and let her works praise her in the gates.

The German ideal follows closely on this model, as is evident in Schiller's classic and much memorized ode to the mother called "The Song of the Bell" in which we follow

the disciplined housewife, the children's mother . . . [who] moves without resting her busy hands, / and increases the profit with her sense of order, / and fills the fragrant drawers with treasures, / and turns the thread on the humming spindle, / and gathers in the clean smooth cupboards the shimmering woolens, the snowy linens, / and manages all of this shining glory well and never rests.

Both the German and the Jewish ideals were highly productive working women who rarely stopped working to rest. Visitor after visitor to central Europe remarked on the obsessiveness of the German *Hausfrau.* "The husband has no wife but a serving maid," wrote Heinrich Heine, "and he still goes on living his intellectually isolated life even in the midst of his family." Although the Habsburg Empire required schooling for girls before Britain and France, girls usually spent only four years in school. Although Jews required their boys to begin their formal Jewish education as early as age three, girls were not sent to school. They were expected to learn informally from their mothers.

"In 1787 I married my wife," wrote Peter Beer, a liberal Jew of the Czech lands.

She is a woman whose mind was not formed, or rather, deformed, by fashionable education, novels and plays, but who was endowed by nature with a direct and healthy common sense and a noble heart, so that she fulfilled all duties as wife, mother and housewife in our forty-seven years of marriage and I believe I can call her, as Solomon did, "A wife among thousands."

Therese Furcht spent four mandatory years in Brtnice's Czech school. Then she stayed at home, helping her mother and father in their tavern. In the summers, Josephine taught her daughter to keep house, to plant and tend a vegetable garden, to keep geese, chickens, and perhaps a goat, to prepare and preserve the food she harvested according to the laws of *kashrut*. During the long winters, she taught her daughter to knit, crochet, and sew. Although there were lending libraries in most Jewish Streets and Therese might have visited Svatopluk, the reading club and library established in Brtnice in 1848, it is unclear what and whether she read.

By the time Therese was growing up, there were Jewish women of leisure in the Czech lands. "Look at the two ladies who are walking through the village, dressed simply and tastefully and wrapped in their green veils," journalist Jakob Kaufmann had written in 1841. . . .

The little peasant children run up from all sides, barefoot and bareheaded, and kiss her hands so humbly that you would think she owns the village along with the young countess. However it is just the village Jewess, Frau Schlikowitz, and her daughter. Their house is the largest and most beautiful in the village and its atmosphere is so aristocratic that the Jews of the neighboring town mockingly call it the Court of Sdur.

Fraulein Schlikowitz — neither the magistrate nor the lawyer nor the priest nor the cantor would dare call her anything else — plays the grand piano, speaks fluent French and Italian, holds forth enthusiastically about

Schiller and Goethe, about Florian and Petrarch. Her face
has the aristocratic shape of a young countess, and her
tender, white elfin hand has never poured a glass of brandy
for a peasant, even though the foundation of this large,
dazzling house . . . is the musty, evil-smelling brandy distillery. She only mixes with the daughters of functionaries
of the nearby town and the village, who consider an invitation to the Court of Sdur as the greatest honor and allow
themselves to be tortured with riddles and charades by the
intellectual, beautiful Jewess. . . .

Even the parish priest visits the Schlikowitz home, although
he scorns the Jewish junk dealer he meets on the doorstep. That
poor, secondhand dealer is fed in the servants' quarters of the
Jewish home, writes Kaufmann, yet it is possible that Frau Schlikowitz might ask him to come up to her drawing room

and spend an hour chatting in honest *žargon,* finally dis-
missing him with a handsome present. For she does not
want to provoke Nemesis: she well remembers a time
when there were no silk curtains at her windows, no luxury coach in the courtyard, no iron box with gold hinges in
her low-ceilinged bedroom. She remembers God with de-
votion for He provided her with all this but she would like
to combine the old orthodoxy with modern Christian
forms. She observes the Sabbath rigorously, she is charita-
ble, and she prays every morning from a Hebrew-German
book of psalms bound in Moroccan leather which lies on
her dressing table.

Mademoiselle Schlikowitz and her mother are new but by far
not unique characters in the drama of Central European Jewry.
Maria Mahler, mother of Gustav, as well as many other women
of the 1830s and 1840s, lived similar lives in the Czech countryside. They read the classics of German literature and played
the piano. They were the spiritual descendants of the Berlin
salonières, the first group of Jewish women to enter Central
European cultural life.

Dorothea Schlegel, Rahel Varnhagen, and Henriette Herz, the product of the tiny, wealthy community of Berlin Jews at the end of the eighteenth century, were educated with the German notion of *Bildung,* the formation of character through careful study and mastery of history and art. They studied German, Latin, French, and Italian — although not Hebrew — and read Rousseau, Voltaire, and Kant. When they were grown, they created for themselves an intellectual life for which Judaism did not allow and brought it into their living rooms.

A friend of Goethe's noted that these Jewesses revealed

more pleasing attention and flattering participation than a national German, and their quick power of comprehension, their penetrating intellect, their peculiar wit render them a more sensitive audience than what regrettably can be found among the often somewhat dull and slow-to-comprehend genuine Germans. Women possess those talents at times in even more amiable form, and thus it happened that Goethe was willing to present his recent poetical productions to them . . . for he could always be assured of a certain response, as I am able to testify from my own observation with regard to Frau von Eibenberg, Frau von Gotthaus, Frau von Eskeles und Fliess, and others.

Although there were never more than two dozen Jewish *salonières* in Berlin, they were a powerful and seductive model. Jewish *salons* were soon established in Vienna and by the mid-nineteenth century, daughters of "good" Central European Jewish families no longer aimed to be productive housewives. They studied languages and literature, aimed to be accomplished pianists, and learned to speak knowledgeably of the arts.

Their education, of course, had no outlet. After Fanny Lewald — a contemporary of Josephine Furcht — completed her schooling in the city of Konigsberg in 1835, she had nothing to do. The autobiography she wrote after becoming the first German-Jewish woman journalist recalls that she "roamed around the house aimlessly" until her father drew up a schedule for her to follow. Every day after breakfast, she practiced the piano for an hour. For the next three hours she did needlework: sewing or knitting. After the midday meal and a siesta, she did another two and a half hours of needlework, then an hour each of piano and penmanship. If she performed well, Fanny was rewarded with "good books" to read in the evening.

There was no place in the Jewish world for girls like Fanny Lewald or the *salonières* who, in the course of abandoning traditional Jewish life for German culture, adopted a view of themselves as damaged human beings. Each repudiated her Judaism. Each converted to Christianity and married out and for decades after, even in the backwaters of Moravia, women like Josephine and Therese Furcht heard about them.

In nineteenth-century Moravia, Jews were positioned midway on the religious spectrum, not as secular as the Berliners but not as observant as *shtetl* Jews either. The Josephine reforms had made it possible for Jews of the Czech lands to rapidly acculturate to Austrian culture; young Jewish men were drawn to secular pursuits and soon there was a scarcity of rabbis in smaller towns like Brtnice. Jewish girls were following the path of Fanny Lewald and their rapid secularization worried the rabbinate.

Fanny Neuda, the wife of one Moravian rabbi, addressed the problem of acculturation in *Stunden der Andacht,* a women's prayer book. To her 107 prayers for a short childbirth or a husband's safe journey, among other concerns, Neuda added a passionate appeal for teaching Jewish women Hebrew. Hebrew, she argued in 1855, would repair a self-regard that was battered by their encounter with the wider world.

"The holy chants of Zion, the wonderful psalms of David, the exalted soulful prayers of Israel remain, for us, a closed book," she wrote, when Therese Furcht was nine years old.

> Why should not our daughters who employ so much time and diligence playing the piano, singing an opera, or learning languages according to what is most in fashion, dedicate one hour a day to the study of that holy language, indeed the venerable mother of languages?
>
> Why not devote a small part of her time to learn that

language which still is the glue that binds together all the branches of Israel that are scattered in all the regions on the face of the earth, in Cincinnati and Bombay, in Tunis and in Warsaw, in Vienna and London, where one can still hear from the Jewish temples that language in which God once spoke from Sinai?

Our daughters must learn to carry the name of Israel with pride and confidence. They must recognize the true inner worth of their people. . . . They must realize that it is a degradation of their own inner selves to feel shame at belonging to a tribe with as distinguished a record in history as any other . . . which, in the midst of thousand-year-long battles against painful enmities, managed to preserve the blessings of joyful family life with noble morality.

Such feelings of shame could be kept out of the lives of Jewish girls and women by restricting their access to literature. But if Therese was anything like her daughter and granddaughter, literature would have become her favorite way of learning about other people's lives and what to expect in her own. She would have become a member of the Czech library, befriended the bookseller in Brtnice, and read everything she could lay her hands on: Goethe, Heine, Schiller, newspapers, pamphlets, the many periodicals that would have made their way to a tavern.

If she did not have the leisure to read, if she worked in her father's tavern, Therese would have listened to the men who talked there, to those who delivered supplies and played music on Sundays when people came in to dance. One of them may have been the young Czech of my mother's twelve-page chronicle, the young Czech with whom Therese fell hopelessly in love. When I walked with Jiří Rychetský along the river to the edge of town where the tavern stood, I imagined that he had the thick brown hair, blue eyes, and the love of music and nature one finds in so many Czechs. I imagined that Therese fell so desperately in love that she took on her lover's world as her own.

Brtnice was a hotbed of Czech nationalism during her adolescence and, like Hannah in Leopold Kompert's novella, Therese would have turned her back on Judaism and adopted her lover's cause. She would have been indignant at the way the Austrians treated Czechs, as colonizers always treat the colonized — as lesser people, buffoons who spoke an unintelligible language. Czech peasants had long been required to kneel before Habsburg officials and kiss their hands before transacting business. By the time Therese was growing up, it was enough for the peasant to behave in a self-deprecating fashion and to address an official as "my gracious lord." German-speaking officials, however, were still entitled to administer corporal punishment (a slap on the face or a caning) to anyone they found insufficiently respectful. "It was taken as a matter of course at home that Slavs performed none but the inferior types of work," writes one of Therese's contemporaries,

> while leadership always rested in German hands. And should any among the Czechs attain some degree of prosperity, he would immediately seek, in his contacts with the settlers and townspeople, to deny his parentage. . . . Educated men or landowners who openly admitted to their Czech descent were rare exceptions — and in the country parts they were looked upon by German official quarters with suspicion.

The Jews of Brtnice belonged neither to the colonizers nor the colonized but bounced between the two. They were trilingual, speaking Czech with their neighbors, German with the authorities, and a remnant of *žargon* at home. But by the time Therese was a young woman, some Jews had begun to see themselves as Czech. "My home, like yours, is the Vltava land," wrote Siegfried Kapper, a Jewish poet to a Czech friend. "Like you, I extoll its wondrous good. Like you, I curse its murderer's hand."

Who would not wish to belong to the people among whom she lived in a place as lovely as Brtnice? There were a limited number of Jewish boys Therese's age. It is a staple of life and literature — the attraction of the forbidden, the violation of the code, the secret, its discovery, the unequivocal opposition of the families.

The Furchts would have been, at best, suspicious of their only daughter's lover. Freedom was a new development in their lives, one they could not yet trust. Only in 1867 could a Christian and a Jew have a civil marriage without one of them undergoing conversion. The Furchts were privy to the casual antisemitism of their patrons and Lazar Furcht may have followed the national debate over the possibility of Jews ever becoming Czechs.

Reviewing Siegfried Kapper's poem, the Czech writer Karel Havlíček Borovský asked:

How can Israelites belong to the Czech nation when they are by origin Semitic? It would be easier to consider Germans, Frenchmen, Spaniards, Englishmen and so on to be a part of our nation than Jews, since these nations all have more in common with us than Jews do. Thus it cannot be said that Jewish inhabitants of Bohemia and Moravia are Czechs practicing the Mosaic religion. We must consider them to be a special Semitic nation that happens to live among us and sometimes understands our language or can speak it. . . .

Clearly, all Jews — regardless of the country or part of the world they inhabit — perceive themselves to be one nation, to be brothers, and not merely to be fellow believers. And the bond that binds them to another is much stronger than the one that binds them to the country they inhabit. There is surely no need to prove that one cannot have two homelands, two nationalities, or serve two masters. Therefore, anyone who wishes to be a Czech must cease to be a Jew. . . .

We would exhort the Jews, if they wish to abandon their natural language and literature, to join the Germans and their literature, since German has, over the years, become a second mother tongue to the Jews.

Therese's Czech lover might have believed what is expressed in so much of nineteenth-century literature: not only that Jews were Germanizers but that they were parasites who grew rich at the expense of the peasants, poisoning them with alcohol, seducing them into buying things they did not need. In the only Grimm fairy tale about a Jew, *The Jew in the Thornbush*, as in many nineteenth-century Czech novels, Jews are portrayed as willing to do anything for money. Where would thieves dispose of their stolen goods if there were no Jewish junk dealers? As for the (dark) beauty of Jewish women, "So great was his fear of dishonor, so deeply still rooted were the prejudices against those unhappy children of Abraham," wrote an Austrian poet, "that in this terrible moment they even overwhelmed his tender feelings for the beautiful daughter of Israel."

In my mother's twelve-page chronicle, it is Lazar and Josephine Furcht who put an end to the affair and arranged for their daughter to be married to a Jewish peddler. But the documentary evidence shows otherwise. Jihlava's business and police registers show that, instead of being married off like centuries of women before her, Therese left Brtnice in 1868, unmarried, to live and work in the city of Iglau.

Lazar disappears. It may be that he died during the Prussian war or during the cholera epidemic that followed. Town records may provide another answer: the lease on the count's tavern was discontinued when the authorities decided to transform it into a starch factory and Lazar was suddenly out of work. "When the lease expires," Jakob Kaufmann wrote, "the days of fear and lamentation begin, as if Jerusalem were to be destroyed for the second time." In such cases, the tavernkeeper lost not only his livelihood but his home and was turned out into a world in which he had no place.

There is no record of Lazar Furcht's death and no tombstone for him in the cemetery. What various registers do indicate is that when Therese moved to Iglau, her mother, Josephine, moved into Count Collalto's poorhouse near the bench in Augustine Hons's yard where we sat the first day I came to Brtnice. Therese, accompanied by her cousin Franziska, is recorded in an Iglau register, working as a seamstress for a Jewish woman named Zelenková.

"I will be a dressmaker; I will be a plain-work woman; I will be a servant, a nurse-girl, if I can be no better," Jane Eyre declares after fleeing Mr. Rochester's house. As a Jew entering a city where Jews had been banned for four hundred years, Therese Furcht could not have worked as servant or nursemaid in a Christian household and the Jewish community was still small. Postal service, railway, and clerical jobs were restricted to men. Teaching school was still restricted to Christians. Sewing was the only work available to a poor young Jewish woman who wished to remain respectable.

The city of Iglau had a population of 25,000 then, including 1,179 Jews. Midway between Prague and Vienna, it was a main station on the new railway, a garrison of the imperial army and the site of a booming textile industry. By 1868, it had become a magnet for Jews leaving their ancestral towns and villages.

The new Jewish community in Iglau was very different from the Jewish community Therese left behind in the hills. Affiliation was voluntary, not mandatory, and rather than a modest *shul*, the Jews of Iglau had built an imposing, neo-Moorish structure for their synagogue. They maintained a strict separation of women and men and conducted services — apart from the sermon — in the traditional Hebrew. But they were already becoming "top hat" or "four day" Jews, Jews who attended synagogue only on the Day of Atonement, the two days of the Jewish New Year, and — unlike their similarly liberal cousins in Germany — on August 18, the birthday of the emperor Franz Joseph.

Therese Furcht entered this community as part of a new group: unmarried Jewish women living apart from their family of origin who worked for wages. The number of such women was then growing all over nineteenth-century Europe, and would reach into the millions. According to municipal records, she lived at 79 Grosse Pfarrgasse, a dark and narrow street that ran between a large church and the town square. She and her cousin Franziska and eight other young women worked, slept, and took their meals in the home of their employer.

Mrs. Zelenková catered to the tastes of the growing group of wealthy women in Iglau who no longer sewed for themselves but had their clothes sewn for them. Successful men spent more and more of their time away from home, moving into a world that was being made ever wider by the railroad. The wives' confinement within the home and enforced idleness were symbolic of their success.

Iglau's wealthy women — and a growing number were Jews — became excellent cooks and fanatical housekeepers. They retreated into novels, developed romantic fantasies, physical ailments and/or psychosomatic ones, and invested their hopes and energies in the lives of their children. Decades later, in the narratives of Viennese psychoanalysts, the vestigial feature of their Judaism is an obsession with keeping things clean.

These women added a fourth *k*, for *Kleider* (clothes), to their trio of domestic occupations. Buying clothes was a distraction, one of a very few chances to exercise choice, and one of the few activities which put a woman in active touch with a larger world. They subscribed to fashion magazines published in Vienna or Berlin. They spent hours with their dressmakers choosing fashionable styles which connected them to the glamorous international realm of fashion.

The Jewish dressmaker becomes a stock Jewish figure just as the Jewish innkeeper disappears from Central Europe. Sewing, of course, was a necessary woman's skill that had, for centuries, provided women with a way to earn money at home. By the nineteenth century, it was providing a way for women — especially women from middle-class families who had somehow lost their means of support — to leave it.

Jihlava's municipal records do not show how long Therese worked as a seamstress for Mrs. Zelenková. They shed no light on the Czech lover mentioned in my mother's twelve-page chronicle. But they do indicate that around the corner from 79 Grosse Pfarrgasse lived a man named Joachim Sachsel, who was married, worked for the railway, and had a younger unmarried brother in the Bohemian city of Kolín. Newly discovered records of the Jewish community of Brtnice show that on April 4, 1872, Therese was married to that brother, Judah Sachsel, by Rabbi Pollack of Třebíč.

The documents show that Judah was thirty-one and Therese

twenty-six when she married, old for Jewish girls of the time. Her dowry was provided by Brtnice's Jewish community since Lazar Furcht had disappeared and Josephine Furcht was living in Count Collalto's poorhouse. Instead of moving to the bride's place of birth, as was the custom, the Sachsels moved to the groom's in the Bohemian city of Kolín.

5

I arrived in Kolín more than one hundred years after Therese and Judah Sachsel. It is a city due east of Prague, noted for its fine Gothic cathedral, the baroque buildings of its central square, and its location on the Elbe River. I parked, walked into the square, and began to draw elderly pedestrians into conversation. One grandfatherly man told me that during the days of the First Republic he had bought books at Sachsel's bookstore. Those were the days when farmers spread their wares out over the cobblestones every Sunday and the whole town turned out to stroll through the covered arcades around them. The arcades were gone now and so were the Jews. Had I been to the Jewish Street? The houses had fallen into terrible disrepair. He dropped his eyes and took his leave.

It was in Kolín that I became aware of a subtle change in the way people behaved when I said I was a Jew. With varying degrees of discretion, they examined my face for "Jewish" (dark, myopic) eyes, a "Jewish" (large) mouth, a "Jewish" (hooked) nose.

Some found a way to express their appreciation of "Jewish anecdotes" as we talked, jokes and ironic vignettes that I felt a subtle pressure to supply. One man, examining my straight nose, said he found my pronunciation of Czech nasal. But none of this prepared me for the evening when my family and I were having dinner in a Prague restaurant and my sons' antics drew the attention of a wedding party.

I encountered the young bride in the washroom. We were standing side by side in front of a mirror washing our hands. I congratulated her on her marriage and she, in turn, asked how old the boys were and what were their names. When I replied "Daniel" and "Samuel," she clapped her hands together and exclaimed, "You're Protestants, like me!"

"Actually, no," I replied. "We're Jews."

The bride's hands flew to her cheeks. Her eyes lit up. *"No, jéje!"* she exclaimed. "You're my *first* Jews!"

Standing at that Prague washroom sink, I felt confused. I grew up in New York City, where being Jewish was about as remarkable as being a farmer in Kansas. Here, I was a representative of what Jiří Fiedler had called the "now-extinct community of Jews." How to respond? The bride looked so pretty in her white dress. Her excitement was genuine. She was probably no older than twenty-two, born in the early 1970s. She had obviously read about Jews; they interested her and here was a whole family of them! I started to laugh and invited her and her equally young husband to our table to talk.

Unlike older Czechs who had lived alongside Jews all their lives and had witnessed their deportation, they did not search our faces. Nor did their questions have the knowing, historically informed character of older Czechs. Soon they moved to matters more pressing to them than Jews: how could they best learn English? what did Americans learn at business school? what should the groom expect of his new managerial job at IKEA? We drank and told stories about American corporate culture. They invited us to stay with them next time we were in Prague. I left the restaurant thinking that we had given them the impression that Jews were a giddy bunch.

In Kolín, I felt anything but giddy. The director of the regional museum, with whom I had been corresponding, led me through his collections — geological exhibits and early archaeological evidence of Kolín — to a large glass case that displayed a Torah curtain. I stood there, reading the neatly lettered plaque explaining what the object was; that a curtain hung over the cabinet which, in every synagogue, contained the Pentateuch. I recalled standing in a Boston museum, looking through another glass case and reading about the ritual objects of a Native American tribe. I had felt ashamed, as though I were trespassing. Now I began to feel the meaning of the word "extinct." For centuries, the Jewish community of Kolín had been second only to Prague's in size and significance. Along with Roudnice, Mladá Boleslav, and Náchod, it was one of the four oldest Jewish communities in the Czech lands.

The old man in the square had said that the Jewish Street had fallen into disrepair. Many houses looked abandoned and I could feel my body cutting off emotion the way it did when as a child I listened to my mother talk about the war. Therese had moved into this street, into Judengasse 8, in 1872. The drab gray buildings had all been renumbered since then but it did not matter — they were all the same warrens of rooms with no view. The picturesque hills and forests of Brtnice were a memory. Kolín's Jews lived in a closed-in and overbuilt prototype of the Central European ghetto. It was, and still is called the *židovna*, a word akin to "Niggertown," usually rendered in English as Jewry.

The Sachsels, as Therese Furcht had no doubt been told, could trace their roots in Kolín back to 1618. Although Judah Sachsel was a mere peddler and his father an old-clothes dealer, Mr. Rychetský told me they belonged to one of the largest and best-documented Jewish families in the Czech lands, which had given the Jewish community of Kolín several of its mayors. They were a branch of the Saudek family, whose name derived from the Czech transliteration of the Hebrew *Zaddik* — the sage or righteous man. Some of the Saudeks had assimilated into their Czech surroundings without a trace. The Sachsels were the religious branch who, in compliance with Joseph II's 1787 naming law, had taken on the German surname Sachs, an acronym for the Hebrew *zera kadosh,* or "seed of the Holy."

When Therese arrived in Kolín in 1872, almost a century after the Josephine reforms and one generation after the opening of the ghetto, the Jewish community was still tightly knit. Its members knew that, normally, the daughter of a prosperous tavern-keeper would not have been married to a poor peddler. There had clearly been some irregularity if not a scandal. The bride's dowry had been provided by the community in Brtnice. Her father had disappeared. It is probable that the Jews of Kolín would have looked down on any bride from an obscure hill town in the Moravian countryside but the fact that she had been raised above a tavern made her particularly suspect.

Its chroniclers portray Kolín's Jewish community as liberal but rather prim. "It shall be remarked that Kolín Jews have never sold spirits," wrote one. Those honored by appointment to the Burial Society — the highest honor for a male member of the community — were discouraged from even visiting taverns and forbidden to play cards on Mondays, Thursdays, fast days, holidays, and *Rosh Chodesh,* the first of the Jewish month. The community prided itself on its hospitality to travelers. In contrast to Brtnice's Jews, who spoke Czech in their daily lives, had a modest synagogue, no local rabbi, and honored the Sabbath by chatting in *žargon,* Kolín's Jews spoke mostly German, had a magnificent baroque synagogue, a network of some two dozen Jewish welfare organizations, and a health insurance system established in 1811.

Town records mention Jews as early as 1376 and provide a running commentary on conflicts between Jewish merchants and their Christian competitors. The Jews were accused of all the customary acts in the anti-Jewish lexicon and when Europe was being attacked by the Ottoman Empire during the sixteenth century, they were charged with conspiring with the Turks and setting the fire which, in 1541, devastated parts of Prague. For this alleged conspiracy, they had been expelled and settled in Galicia.

Eight years later, they returned in greater numbers than when they had left, bringing back with them Yiddish, Polish customs, and such women's names as Golda and Pufl. They still felt secure enough to lodge repeated complaints with the Town Council and records show that quarrels continued to center around business competition. The meat of Jewish butchers, for example, was considered better than the meat of Christian butchers; Christian butchers petitioned the Town Council for more restrictions on Jewish suppliers and the council eventually prohibited Jews from keeping any animals except workhorses. Because this necessitated buying rather than producing their own milk and cheese, many Jews secretly kept goats in the small plots of yard behind their houses. But the grass was much greener on top of the town ramparts which abutted those yards, the goats had no trouble jumping up to graze on them, and the joke of the district soon became that goats were defending the town of Kolín. As a result, in 1603, Kolín's Jews were expressly forbidden to keep goats.

There were almost no yards left by the time Therese arrived in Kolín. Because of the ever-growing number of residents, each *židovna* — also the term for any building owned by a Jew — had numerous additions to its yard and roof and each addition had been subdivided again and again. As many as one hundred people lived in each of these dilapidated buildings. The birthrate was high and although the family laws criminalized all Jews who had no family number, few left Kolín willingly. The Town Council was repeatedly pressured to limit the number of Jewish families. It was asked to prevent Jewish bakers and grain traders from selling to Christians or from setting up stalls in the town square, where, the Christians complained, they made too much noise, or from using the town cistern. Jews were polluting it with dirty kegs, they claimed, and, finally, a separate well was dug in the Jewish Street. But the Jewish population continued to grow.

Although both Christian and Jewish authorities tried to draw a line between their communities, the records attest to their failure. Individual Christians borrowed money from Jews as did the municipality itself. Jews who could afford it rented houses from Christians. Sex acknowledged no barrier either: in 1624, a Jewish widow was fined because her adolescent son had allegedly seduced a succession of Christian laundresses. After the Josephine reforms were introduced, Jewish children began attending school with Christians. On Saturdays, Christian children reportedly wrote on blackboards for Jewish classmates not permitted to write on the Sabbath. By 1848, when Kolín's National Guard was mobilized, Jews and Christians served side by side.

A nostalgic memoir of Kolín in the 1880s, written fifty years later, tells the story of an irate citizen who went to the mayor's office to protest Jewish observance of their harvest holiday, Sukkot. Jews had built wooden booths in the Judengasse, he complained, making it difficult to walk by day and presenting a major safety hazard at night. The "wise mayor," as he is called, pretended outrage. He assured the plaintiff that the police commissioner would instruct the Jewish community to take down the booths within eight days (when he knew the holiday was over) or face a stiff penalty.

In 1990, as I walked through the *židovna*, the only sign of construction was a pile of sand outside one of the low doorways. The door was open and as I peered into the darkness behind it, a young man in jeans emerged. His name was Milan Šálek and when I identified myself as the great-granddaughter of a woman who had once lived on the Street, he stuck his spade in the sand. Milan had once had a Jewish girlfriend, he said, and I felt he was examining my face.

The girlfriend had emigrated, Milan said, and now that Communism was over, he and a partner were engaged in what, in the United States, was called "sweat equity." The house, like other houses on the Jewish Street, had been abandoned for years. They had raised the capital to buy it from the municipality and construct a pension and wine bar, betting on eventual tourism to Kolín. For years, the bureaucrats had been planning to gentrify the Street and turn the old synagogue into a concert hall, but, of course, nothing had been done. The cellar of the house was six centuries old.

Milan invited me into the cave-like, damp space. My head grazed the ceiling and, by extending both my arms, I could almost touch the walls. Inexplicably, just as I had felt sitting on Augustine Hons's bench in Brtnice, I felt a wave of familiarity. This might have been where members of Judah's family, if not Therese herself, lived. Jiří Fiedler later confirmed that the building had been owned in the mid-nineteenth century by an Ephraim Sachsel. In the overcrowded ghetto, people had probably lived in this humid cellar. This was where Milan intended to store his wine.

He had done some research into the Jewish community. Like the young bride in the Prague restaurant, he was intrigued by Jews and thought that other young Czechs were too. He planned to give his bar and pension a Jewish name for the sake of authenticity. Also, to be slightly racy, a little provocative. He thought maybe U Rabína, At the Rabbi's.

Czechs do not hesitate to call a tavern U Ježíška (At Baby Jesus's) but I was brought up short by the idea of a wine bar called At the Rabbi's. Political correctness was clearly not important in Kolín. Creating a new life for the Street was. I wanted to root for Milan. He was smart, warm, attractive, and a postrevolutionary hero besides. Under Communism, people had lost the habit of work. He was working day and night with his own hands to rebuild this wreck of a building and turn it into something living. But I found myself pursuing what, for me, was an unfamiliar line of thought: Milan would serve pork along with beer "at the Rabbi's"; money would change hands there on the Sabbath.

So what? I asked myself. I am not an observant Jew. I sometimes eat pork and often use money on the Sabbath. Some Jews back in Lazar Furcht's time were keeping their pubs open on the Sabbath and many Czech Jews of my grandparents' generation saw nothing wrong with eating pork. I had no claim on the dilapidated old house. Yet that cellar spoke to me and when I told this to Milan, he merely shrugged and said, "It's in your blood."

His words startled me but seemed apt at the same time. For Milan, I thought, "blood" was a neutral term, associated with people, place, and history, not with extermination. But I had neither the vocabulary nor the inclination to find out whether that was so. Milan suggested that we take a look at Kolín's synagogue, built in the seventeenth century, just across the street. It had been considered one of the most beautiful in the Czech lands.

Unlike Brtnice's synagogue, Kolín's is hidden from the street behind a house that used to be the Jewish School. Milan opened a door, said, "Take a deep breath!" and led me through a stinking passageway into a courtyard filled with trash. The dog that was chained there began barking and an empty can came sailing out the window.

"Gypsies." Milan indicated an open window of the building through which the passageway had been constructed. The outer wall of the synagogue, some of its leaded windows broken, was facing us. The interior was more or less intact, Milan told me, but the municipality kept the building locked. Next time, if I could let him know when I was coming, he would get the key.

The Gypsies would eventually be evicted, he said when we returned to the house that would be At the Rabbi's. There were four hundred thousand Gypsies in the country, who spoke their own language, lived in the worst parts of town, would not assimilate, he said. *There were two kinds of Gypsies,* was what several Czechs had told me. The educated Gypsy was a successful musician, actor, even teacher. This Gypsy spoke Czech and was sometimes indistinguishable from a Czech. But the second, far more typical Gypsy, was the thief or prostitute, or Gypsy who did nothing at all, who lived in filth, ten or twelve children in one room, preferring superstition and tradition to modern life. The educated Gypsy might be a good neighbor. But then his relatives came to visit, decided to move in, and soon the building was gone. It was a familiar line. I had heard it back home in the United States, applied to many groups, and I did not tell Milan I thought that it might have been used in Kolín by his grandparents about mine.

When Therese Sachsel arrived on the Jewish Street in 1872, Kolín had "two kinds" of Jews. The first kind were as well educated as members of the Czech middle class. They spoke Czech as well as German, sent their sons to German *gymnasia* and universities, and lived an increasingly secular life beyond the confines of the former ghetto. Some had stopped living by the Jewish calendar, had stopped observing Jewish law, and did not look much different from the Czech population. The second kind — to which Judah and Therese Sachsel belonged — continued living on the Judengasse, a stone's throw from the synagogue, observed the Sabbath and Jewish holidays, and spoke not only Czech and German but their own *žargon*.

Sunday was the first day of the working week, when carpenters hauled their work to the square for display, and peddlers like Judah Sachsel set off for the countryside, just like in Brtnice, each on his own circuit, or *medineh*. On Monday, the Christian week began, storekeepers opened their shops, and children went to school. On Friday, the peddlers returned, mingling in the Street with housewives preparing for the Sabbath.

Just before sundown, those women brought their *šoulet*, the Czech name for the traditional Sabbath casserole of *cholent*, in a special clay pot with an identifying mark on the handle to Spiru's *šoulethaus* for baking. But despite those marks, a rich family's *šoulet* pot occasionally was confused with the pot of one that was poor, a reminder that all Jews were equal before God. Every Friday evening before the first star appeared, the *shames* walked through the Street with a small wooden mallet, knocking on doors and calling, "*Schabes licht zind zu!*" ("Light the Sabbath candles!"). For twenty-four hours, the Jewish Street was quiet. Shops and storefronts were closed except for those few whose owners risked community censure by smuggling in a quick customer or two. Then, on Saturday night, the *shames* made his rounds again, calling "*Schabes is aus!*" ("The Sabbath is over!").

Therese, who had grown up on the outskirts of the far more casual rural Jewish community of Brtnice, had to adapt not only to a new marriage and a new place but a new way of life. An only child, she now had to contend with Judah's older sister, forty-year-old Rosa Sachsel. My mother's twelve pages describe Rosa as "an avid student of the Talmud." Even if what my mother recorded as "Talmud" was actually Bible or women's prayers, an innkeeper's daughter as a sister-in-law must have been a bitter pill for Rosa to swallow.

I imagine that Therese knew more Czech folk songs than Hebrew prayers, and that she resented taking orders from Rosa in the secondhand clothing shop that was the Sachsel family business. Suddenly, she was expected to attend *shul* and was censured if she did not regularly visit the *mikveh*, the women's ritual bath. On January 12, 1873 — barely nine months after her wedding — Therese gave birth to her first child, Heinrich. Family speculation about whether Judah was, in fact, Heinrich's true father echoed one hundred years later in my mother's twelve pages. Soon there were two more sons. Rudolf Sachsel was born in 1874; Leopold Sachsel in 1875.

Three sons in three years. No space. No money. No mother. A peddler husband. A bossy sister-in-law. I see Therese at thirty alone at home, living in a town she hated, exhausted by the care and feeding of three babies. She could not or, as my mother believed, would not return to Brtnice, where her mother, Josephine, was living, perhaps working, in Count Collalto's poorhouse. Her only hope was Vienna.

For most of Therese's lifetime, since 1848, ambitious people in the Czech lands — Jews and Christians alike — had been leaving towns and villages for Vienna. Many Jews had settled there and had prospered. The Sachsel family would too.

There is a gap in the documents here: When and why did they leave? Who facilitated their journey? Did they have relatives who helped them settle in the city? Records show that there were both Furchts and Sachsels living in Vienna between 1875 and 1879, when Therese, Judah, and their young family arrived. But there is no other data.

Suddenly I found it difficult to continue my work. I had loved doing research in Czech. It had been the language of my childhood, the code I shared with my parents, the language of lullabies and fairy tales and trust. Although I made many grammatical errors when I spoke, I felt more myself in Czech than in any of the other languages I had learned. I was fearlessly fluent, like a child using fingerpaint.

German, on the other hand, has always stuck in my throat. My body never let the language inside me although I grew up hearing it spoken by my mother, her employees, her clients and friends. I mispronounced and mauled words so badly that they became unrecognizable and one of the easiest ways for me to make my mother laugh when I was a teenager singing choral music was to garble a section of Mozart in German. I had always assumed that such deliberate clumsiness was a form of revenge and show of solidarity with my mother but I have come to feel it as an inheritance from Therese Furcht. In the mid-1870s, she moved to Vienna with high expectations; in 1890 she ended her life there.

Long before I knew anything about Therese or Vienna, when I traveled through it as a student, the city had felt to me like a giant mausoleum. Now, after reading volume after volume of Austrian Jewish history, I knew how deadly it had been for Jews. Generations upon generations of Jews had been murdered and humiliated in Vienna, some thrown into boats without oars and left to the mercy of the Danube River. Its politicians had discovered the usefulness of antisemitism early on; Adolf Hitler had studied it there and the Viennese became his most ardent followers.

Coming from Kolín in the mid-1870s, I told myself, Therese was unburdened by this knowledge. It was then Kolín's Czechs who were in the throes of an exclusionary, often antisemitic national revival. As part of their fight to reclaim their nation, Czech leaders wanted to dislodge the Jews from their middleman niche in rural commerce and replace them with Czechs. They boycotted Jewish businesses and portrayed Jews as agents of German colonization. It was the German Liberal Party that was regarded by Jews as the bastion of progressive thought. Jews saw Emperor Franz Joseph, descendant of Joseph II, as the champion of Jewish civil rights. They named their children for him, and thronged to synagogues to celebrate his birthday every August.

Vienna, the Habsburgs' capital, promised immigrants of all faiths and nationalities a place where, as Schiller wrote near the end of the eighteenth century, "every day is Sunday, every day the spit turns on the hearth." Thousands of Germans, Czechs, Italians, Hungarians, Bulgarians, Ukrainians, Slovaks, Galicians, Rumanians, and Turkish immigrants were drawn to it. But for the Jews who migrated there in the mid-nineteenth century, the city represented far more.

The first large group of Jews from the Czech lands came to

Vienna during the 1860s. Leaving cities like Kolín or small towns like Brtnice, most — like the families of Sigmund Freud, Stefan Zweig, and Moritz Benedikt — rushed to cut loose from their provincial ghetto past and embrace the boundless Viennese future, educating their children to believe that Vienna was theirs. "Here all the streams of European culture converged," Stefan Zweig would write.

> At court, among the nobility, and among the people, the German was related in blood to the Slavic, the Hungarian, the Spanish, the Italian, the French, the Flemish; and it was the particular genius of this city of music that dissolved all the contrasts harmoniously into a new and unique thing, the Austrian, the Viennese. Hospitable and endowed with a particular talent for receptivity, the city drew the most diverse forces to it, loosened, propitiated and pacified them. It was sweet to live here, in this atmosphere of spiritual conciliation, and subconsciously every citizen became supernational, cosmopolitan, a citizen of the world. . . .
>
> Adapting themselves to the milieu of the people or country where they live is not only an external protective measure for Jews, but a deep internal desire. Their longing for a homeland, for rest, for security, for friendliness, urges them to attach themselves passionately to the culture of the world around them. And never was an attachment more effective — except in Spain in the fifteenth century — or happier or more fruitful than in Austria. . . . Everywhere, as scholars, as virtuosi, as painters, as theatrical directors and architects, as journalists, they maintained unchallenged high positions in the intellectual life of Vienna. . . . They felt that their being Austrian was a mission to the world; and — for honesty's sake it must be repeated — much, if not all that Europe and America admire today as an expression of a new, rejuvenated Austrian culture, in literature, the theater, in the arts and crafts, was created by the Viennese Jews who, in turn, by this mani-

festation achieved the highest performance of their millenial spiritual activity.

Zweig's family was prototypical in its progress up what Leo Spitzer has called "the emancipatory avenue that had initially been opened by Joseph II's Edict of Tolerance." At the beginning of the nineteenth century, Zweig's great-grandfather had abandoned peddling for shopkeeping. By midcentury, his grandfather owned a textile mill. By the end of it, his father was a millionaire.

Zweig's father was, in his son's view, circumspect about his wealth and status. He avoided dining at the Hotel Sacher because "it would have been distressing or unbecoming to him to sit at a table next to a Prince Schwarzenberg or a Lobkowitz." Other so-called stock exchange Jews, however, felt no such compunctions. They built their new homes in the palatial style of the Schwarzenbergs, Lobkowitzes, and Collaltos. They let their money, their retinues of servants, and elegant two-horse carriages talk. Their wives established secular and sumptuous households imitative of Viennese aristocrats. They cultivated the arts.

Their sons flocked to the universities where, by 1880, one-third of all students were Jews. A university degree, for Christians, had traditionally been the ticket to a teaching or civil service career in Austria-Hungary but these positions were restricted to Catholics, not open to Jews unless they converted. As a result, most Jewish lawyers and doctors were self-employed, as were the great number of Jewish writers. Scholars have pointed out that, in an age when the press was the only mass medium, many of Vienna's newspapers were owned by Jews and well over half its writers — even some working for antisemitic publications — were Jewish.

Individual Jews such as Arthur Schnitzler, Theodor Herzl, and Sigmund Freud became emblems of Vienna. An entire class of Jews — clerks, office managers, and salesmen — comprised the then new phenomenon of white-collar, salaried business employees. Together, the stock exchange Jews, the professional men and artists, and the salaried employees were a new, secular Jewish society, replacing the provincial and traditional one.

In the traditional Jewish community of Kolín, *yichus,* or social status, accrued to those who hewed to tradition: Judah and his pious sister, Rosa, cleaned and mended old clothes with no sense of shame. They were part of an old family and the gap between rich and poor on the Jewish Street had never been very wide. In Vienna, *yichus* attached to the Jew who shed his past. The gap between rich and poor had grown enormous, splitting off parts of the Jewish community from one another. Judah Sachsel was a throwback, an anomaly in upwardly mobile Jewish Vienna. The Jewish trade in used clothing had always been viewed by Christians as a conduit for stolen items or a breeding ground for disease. Now Jews too saw Judah as no better than a junk dealer, a recycler of the old in a city that prized the new.

In Vienna, Therese was an embarrassment or completely invisible to her cousins from the Czech lands, another poverty-stricken mother in a rented flat with a toilet in the hall and no running water. I see Therese crushed by Vienna, by the imperial scale of the buildings, the endless maze of streets, the hundreds and thousands of strangers. I see her walking slowly in the street, pregnant again, her six- and five-year-old sons running wild over the cobblestones. Her third son, Leopold, had died in Kolín but another, named Emil, was born in 1879.

In 1882, she gave birth to a daughter, whom she named Josephine after her mother, who had died, impoverished, the previous year. The Sachsels — six of them — lived in the outlying Hernals section of the city, a working-class neighborhood which a relative whose family also emigrated from Moravia would later describe, not concealing her dismay, with the cry, "But no one we knew lived there!"

There is almost no record of Vienna's Jewish poor of that time. Jewish writers were heavily invested in their new story and their schedule of cultural events and balls. Whether they reveled in their new status or satirized it as writers like Arthur Schnitzler or Karl Kraus would do, they saw it as the only reality. Antisemitic writers, busy setting up the new "stock exchange" and professional Jews as targets for their increasingly virulent campaigns, also found it convenient to ignore the Jewish poor. Sigmund Freud, who lived as a poor Viennese Jew for part of his childhood later dismissed it with the remark, "Those were hard times and not worth remembering."

Emil Sachsel would later hand down to his son only two things down about this period: "Heinrich took care of us," and, "It was always cold." It was the same in every major European city of the time: Freezing winters. Stifling summers. Noise. Bed-bugs. Worry about the rent. The "Viennese disease" — tuberculosis — was rampant. Therese had already lost one son. With no antibiotics, no money for a doctor, every cold sharpened the state of watchfulness that is the lot of any mother of four children. She had no close family in Vienna.

Hernals was a workers' neighborhood, dangerous for Jews, particularly around Easter, when rowdy crowds filed down a re-construction of the Via Dolorosa that ran from St. Stephen's Cathedral in the center of the city to the site of a former Lutheran church. Therese was unlikely to have found it comfort-able. There is no confidant or friend, no coffeehouse or other place of solace named in my mother's twelve pages apart from the Prater, Vienna's great expanse of park, where Therese often walked and tried to catch a glimpse of the empress Elisabeth.

Many women of the empire loved and identified with Elisa-beth, their beautiful and unhappy young empress, but Jewish women composed a special prayer for her. They empathized with Elisabeth's position as an outsider in Vienna and, particularly, with her difficulties in marriage. Elisabeth had been sixteen when she married Franz Joseph, who was kind to his young wife but slept on an iron bed, rose at four every morning, and dutifully put the rituals of his court and his bureaucracy before his personal life. Faced with a rigid imperial protocol, Elisabeth retreated into an obsession with her body: her skin, which she scrubbed with moldy lemons, her waist-length hair, which she dressed in innu-merable ways, and a succession of much discussed diets.

Less than a decade after her marriage, Elisabeth began disap-pearing from Vienna, abandoning her husband and children and wandering through Europe. Her behavior was condemned at court, where she was regarded as an incompetent empress who had inherited the strain of insanity that ran in her Bavarian family. But thousands of women like Therese Furcht saw themselves in her and lived out their own fantasies of escape in her wanderings. Like them, Elisabeth had more children than she could care for. Like them, Elisabeth suffered from a series of ailments — headaches, backaches, and depressions — that kept her bedridden and unable to perform the duties expected of her.

Her eldest son, the crown prince Rudolf — after whom countless Jewish sons, including Therese's second, were named — was her favorite. Like the empress, he was an outsider in court, unhappy with and frustrated by his ceremonial role. Like the empress, he was a great favorite of Habsburg Jews. In January of 1889, he shot himself and his lover in the Vienna Woods.

The empress Elisabeth was fifty-one at the time of her son's suicide. She stood vigil over Rudolf's corpse and then his grave and was reported to have gone mad. For much of February, Vienna was swathed in black and people camped out for days along the route of the funeral cortege. The royal suicide also prompted a wave of imitations. One man hanged himself in spectacular fashion by tying one end of a rope around a window handle, the other around his neck, and then jumping out the window. A trapeze artist performing without a net dove to his death before an audience. Every week, corpses washed up on the banks of the Danube. The daily *Neue Freie Presse* instituted *Lebensmüde,* a column that recorded the names and strategies of suicides under the title "tired of life."

In July, without warning, Therese's beloved eldest son, Heinrich, fell ill and died. He was sixteen years old. His appendix had burst and the family was unable to get medical assistance. Heinrich had been the mainstay of the family, Therese's confidant, her safety net. Now, like the trapeze artist, she had none. All winter, she spent whole days at the Central Cemetery, where she lay on the earth over Heinrich's grave. Spring only increased her sense of loss.

Therese was one of Vienna's anonymous poor. Had she died a natural death, I would never have found her name in a newspaper. But because she was a Jewish suicide in a city where much of what was written and read was written and read by Jews, I found her in the *Neue Freie Presse.* In the column *Lebensmüde* that first week of May, 1890, is a report that Therese Sachsel, the wife of an old-clothes dealer, fell out of a window and into the courtyard of her building "in a fit of insanity." She was not yet fifty years old. Her only daughter, my grandmother Pepi, was eight.

6

~

It *was Judah's sister, Rosa* — then nearly sixty — who rescued the family. According to Kolín's municipal records, Rosalia Sachsel was, at twenty-eight, an unmarried woman of average height, brown eyes and hair, employed as a cook. At thirty-seven, she married for the first time and, at forty-one, she gave birth to a son who died as an infant. Her husband also died, leaving her to run Sachsel's Used Clothing, a shop on Golden Lane, alone. Rosa lived behind the shop in that narrow, partially covered alleyway that turns off the Jewish Street a block away from "At the Rabbi's" and runs down toward Kolín's square. Dark, with old gables, ir-regular windows, and eternally damp courtyards, it contained, according to a twentieth-century memoirist, everything in the world but gold.

In May of 1890, Rosa scraped together the money for a train ticket to Vienna and arrived at her brother's flat to find a dismal family scene. Judah was ill and desperate. There was no one else to feed or comfort the children or manage the household. Therese had not only broken with her family in Kolín, but had not forged any new connections in Vienna. Her children knew no relatives.

Therese had forever marred the family history: in Jewish tradition, a Jew who takes her own life cannot be buried alongside other Jews. It was only because witnesses swore she was "unsound of mind" that Therese could be buried in Vienna's Jewish Cemetery. But disgrace did not alter Rosa's sense of duty. Aunt Rosa, as the children were instructed to call the elderly stranger, packed up their belongings, bought railway tickets back to Kolín, and installed everyone in her two small rooms.

Judah Sachsel never recovered from his wife's suicide. He died nine months later of intestinal illness. When Rudolf, the eldest boy, turned fourteen, Rosa persuaded relatives who owned a gift shop in Vienna to take him in as a boarder and apprentice. That left only Emil and Pepi.

At twelve, Emil Sachsel was a tall boy with a strong, sunny personality. He learned Czech quickly, made friends, and was soon defying his pious aunt by rowing on the Elbe on Sabbaths and on Yom Kippur. At nine, Pepi was a small, fragile child deeply marked by the deaths of her eldest brother, her mother, and her father. She spoke very little in any language. She did not make friends. Like her father, she read and developed severe digestive troubles.

Aunt Rosa fought for Pepi's health. *"She spent every kreuzer she could spare to buy goose liver for her,"* wrote my mother, *"while she herself lived on potatoes and cottage cheese."* She kept close watch over her niece, worrying that — like her mother — she might be drawn into the Christian world. Emil soon found Aunt Rosa's restrictions intolerable. When he turned thirteen, he ran away, lied about his age, and joined the imperial navy. At ten, Pepi was left alone with Aunt Rosa in Kolín.

In her twelve pages, my mother describes Pepi as a shy, phobic child who refused to use the outhouse in the yard because she was afraid of rats, who had nightmares, and who listened more than she spoke. Aunt Rosa often told her that she was poor, an orphan, and a Jew. To compensate for this triple disadvantage, Pepi had to be compliant and as competent and capable as she could be. Toward that end, Aunt Rosa kept Pepi at home when she was not at school. She taught her to sew and while Pepi repaired old clothes, her aunt repaired the hole in her niece's education: prayers, Bible, and the Hebrew language.

It would have been in keeping with Aunt Rosa's persona as a Jewish matriarch to have sent Pepi to the German-language Jewish school. Jews sent their children to such schools in order to guarantee their observance of the Jewish calendar and control their social contacts. Like middle-class Czechs, they also regarded German as the ticket to a wider world.

But Rosa did not send her niece to Kolín's Jewish school. Kolín was a hotbed of the Czech revival and the German-Jewish school a major source of controversy in the community. Although Rosa herself spoke German with Pepi, she may have sympathized with Czech nationalism. Or perhaps she thought she was doing a better job teaching her niece Judaism than any teacher. Whatever her reason, it was a crucial decision, one that was to affect the direction of Pepi's life. Six days a week, Pepi attended the Czech public school. At a time when two-thirds of Bohemian Jews declared German to be their language of daily use, Pepi was speaking Czech and being introduced to her third culture.

In Vienna, Pepi had memorized German myths and Habsburg exploits in Central Europe and Spain. In Kolín, children learned Habsburg history but also Czech history revived by the nationalists. Pepi learned to love the founding myths of the Czech nation and the three daughters of Krok: the priestess Teta, the physician Kazi, and the princess Libuše, who had built her castle in Kolín. Libuše, as Rosa probably told her, had even entered the Hebrew literature through *Zemach David,* the work of the Renaissance astronomer and chronicler David Gans, who wrote that

> a girl ruled over the land Bohemia . . . famous for her art of necromancy. She could also foretell from the features of the face and the lines of the palm and she told the future to many people. She was chosen by the Slavs to become their mistress and princess, to rule over them and govern them reasonably, wisely and deliberately.

While Princess Libuše was alive, according to the medieval chroniclers, she employed a personal militia whose leader was the clever and powerful Vlasta. Vlasta refused to obey Libuše's husband, Přemysl, built Děvín, a castle for young women overlooking Prague, and launched a war against Přemysl. Men were prohibited from carrying weapons within Vlasta's domain, forced to work the land, and obliged to marry the women who chose them or face execution. After eight years, Přemysl's men defeated Vlasta's women. The women of Děvín died in battle after massacring all their male prisoners.

These tales are only a small part of Czech mythology. But in the context of the patriarchal and misogynist Austro-Hungarian monarchy, they are a light in the dark. So are the stories that assimilationist Jewish writers had added to the legends of Libuše. In them, Libuše was said to have prophesied the arrival of an industrious and peaceful people (the Jews) who would come to Bohemia in search of asylum. They would bring good fortune to Bohemia, she said, and could remain in the country until the river Vltava flowed uphill to Prague Castle. In yet another myth, the Jews helped Libuše's descendant Prince Hostivít drive the Germans out of his territory.

These legends seem more wishful than authentic, not only because a woman is at their center but because they are among the few I have ever heard in which Jews appear as a positive and integral part of another nation's history. They are the most poignant literature of the Czech-Jewish movement of the nineteenth century, evidence of a deep and mostly unmet yearning to belong.

In the early 1890s in Kolín's public school, Pepi learned that the Czechs had, for centuries, been colonized. Like the Jews, they had been deprived of their rights, their nationhood, and their language. Although she rarely forgot that she was a Jew at school — a cross hung on the wall just as it had in Vienna — Pepi became aware that Jews were not the only people who suffered oppression. She hurried to learn Czech and to lose the Viennese accent that marked her not only as a foreigner but as an enemy. She did not, at first, forge any close ties at school but by the time she was a teenager, she had found the relationship most essential to adolescence: a best friend.

Gisela Saudek was born into Kolín's upper middle class and, had she and my grandmother not been distant cousins, their friendship might never have grown. The two girls, my mother wrote, were passionate readers who *"read whatever they could lay their hands on in the large Saudek library."* That library contained translations of all the major European writers, including the French novelists who created Nana and Marguerite Gautier, "La Dame aux Camélias." These "kept women," their lovers, their clothes, and the conduct of their lives became the subject of long discussions between the girls. When Aunt Rosa discovered a book by Zola under Pepi's mattress one day, *"pandemonium broke out with loud wailing that Pepi would be corrupted and that she would become fair game for every seducer who would leave her with an illegitimate child."*

A girl's reading, in both Christian and Jewish traditions, determined her morals. "The educated man can and must . . . know and read everything," according to the *Ceremonial Gift for German Maidens,* a widely read Christian analogue of Fanny Neuda's Jewish women's prayerbook, but "it is only fitting for educated women to know that which can afford true poetic delight." Prolonging a girl's childishness was viewed as a way of preserving her chastity and spiritual purity. Contemporary literature, particularly the realistic novel, sullied that purity, raised unrealistic expectations, and reduced a girl's value as a marital partner. Generations of fathers took measures to prevent their daughters from reading and Aunt Rosa was unusual only in that she had stepped into that paternal role herself.

Although she lectured Pepi, Rosa did not complain to the Saudeks. Gisi's father was a formidable figure, one of Kolín's most successful Jewish businessmen. Gisi's mother was prominent in Jewish philanthropy. Rosa was a poor, distant cousin, grateful for Gisi's friendship with her niece. One hundred years later, Kolín's archivists and museum workers still speak of the family with deference. Gisi's older brothers included a writer, a physician, and an internationally famous graphologist. Gisi herself became a Czech-German translator, a cultural journalist, and probably the most famous woman ever to have lived in Kolín. She was sixty when she was gassed in Auschwitz. The Regional Museum owned her portrait and a carton of her papers.

I sat for an afternoon in the small museum office, sifting through that cardboard carton, skimming her one published book of interviews with the prominent Czech poet Otakar Březina, her articles and reviews, unpublished manuscripts, despairing letters to publishers, brief letters of rejection. There was a pen-and-ink drawing of Gisi, a cartoonist's vision of a weird, bespectacled female intellectual. Although the carton contained not a single photograph, it held a far more informative portrait: the first draft of a novel, titled *Diary of a Jewish Girl 1897–1910.*

Certainly, I thought, Gisi's best friend, an orphan whose mother had jumped out a window, would appear in it. I held my breath and raced through the manuscript, looking for Pepi. Nothing. Maybe Gisi had meant more to Pepi than my grandmother had meant to her. Maybe class difference had played a role. I could not find her. But as I read the only autobiographical account in Czech about a Jewish woman's life before the twentieth century, I felt as though I were holding a time capsule in my hands, a letter from Pepi's world to mine.

"September 22, 1896." The real Gisi was then thirteen. Her heroine is transferred from the Jewish to the public school.

I like to go to school. It's more diverse than it was in the Jewish School. Only the cross in the classroom makes me feel anxious. . . .

I was so happy that I wouldn't be going to the Jewish School anymore, that I would never again have to cross the street on Sunday with my schoolbooks. As soon as the boys saw them, they realized we were Jews and let loose: *Jews, you killed Lord Jesus!* or *You crucified Lord Jesus!* That hasn't stopped. They remember me and still yell it. How could Jews know how to kill someone? And a sacred person like Lord Jesus?

November 15, 1897: My teacher, Miss Voděnková, treats me badly — as she does all of us Jewish girls. . . . She tells me to pick up a piece of paper from the floor. And then she pretends to catch herself: "Excuse me, I always forget that you don't do anything on Saturday. . . ." I would like to write on Saturdays but the other Jewish girls would view me as a traitor. It's stupid that we always have to differentiate ourselves from other people.

June 3, 1897: Everything around us is Czech but we are not only Jews, we also want to be German! . . . I try to think in Czech but it never works; suddenly I realize that if I thought out loud, it would be in German!

When a Polish Jew, dressed in a caftan, arrives at the doorstep of her home begging, she writes, "I wouldn't have let him in but Mama would have been angry. Why does he come here all the way from Galicia? To turn our street into an eyesore? They make a business out of begging." On August 18, when services are held in synagogue in honor of Franz Joseph's birthday, she worries what the Czech guests think of Jews honoring the emperor, "who looks upon the Czech lands and the Czech nation as his legal property, with which he can do as he wishes." She is ashamed that the synagogue is not "quiet as a church" but "noisy as a Jewish *shul*" and that her rabbi speaks German.

With its close focus on what was then called "the Jewish Question," Gisi's diary is as remarkable for what it contains as for what it leaves out. She does not recall the riots that broke out in Kolín four years earlier, after a Christian girl's body was found on a bank of the Elbe. The medical examiner revived the medieval superstition of ritual murder, told the press that the German-language Jewish school was responsible for the death, and triggered an outburst of violence against the Jews of Kolín. Street mobs broke windows on the Jewish Street and beat up individual Jews. The police ordered Jewish businesses to close and Jewish children like Pepi and Gisi to remain inside. Two companies of infantry were posted in the city.

Although educated Christians, clerics, and several Popes had condemned accusing Jews of ritual murder, Christian rabble-rousers and politicians had kept the superstition alive. In trial after trial across Central and Eastern Europe, Jews had to explain that they were explicitly forbidden by Jewish law to eat or drink human blood. Just before Pepi had been born, another Christian girl had disappeared before Passover in the Hungarian village of Tisza-Eszlár, fifteen Jews had been arrested, and a professor of theology in Prague had written *Five Letters on Talmudism and the Blood Ritual of the Jews* "proving" that Jews practiced ritual murder.

Gisi's omission of the events of 1893 from her diary attests to the overwhelming sense of shame Jews felt then and during the internationally famous Hilsner Trial — which she also ignores. In April of 1899, the body of a nineteen-year-old dressmaker was found in Polná, near Brtnice. "Under the body," read the indictment, "there was an insignificant pool of blood, no bigger than a hand. . . . The body of Anežka Hrůzová had been completely bled and the traces of blood found under the body did not correspond to the amount of blood one would expect to find near the body after a murder of this kind." A vagrant Jew named Leopold Hilsner was indicted. Across the Czech lands, the windows of Jewish homes were shattered by street mobs.

The Hilsner Trial divided the Czechs as the Dreyfus Affair split the French. It was seen as a test of medieval superstition against modern education, of the humanist Czech Protestant tradition against "Roman" clericalism, of knee-jerk nationalism against justice. The Jews had their Zola in Thomas G. Masaryk, later the president of Czechoslovakia. He beseeched his fellow Czechs and Christians to search for truth, "because the belief in ritual murder casts disgrace on the Czech people." After Hilsner was found guilty and sentenced to death, Masaryk, then a philosophy professor in Prague, defied public opinion and appealed for a retrial. The second trial also resulted in a guilty verdict but Hilsner's death sentence was commuted to life imprisonment by Emperor Franz Joseph.

The Hilsner Affair was an enormous shock to Czech Jews. In the streets, children mimed the motion of a knife slitting their throats and sang, "Shoes and stockings, buttonhook/Every Jew's a born crook!" and "Don't buy from Jews, coffee, sugar, sturgeon/For Jews it was who killed our lovely Virgin!" Jewish writers would later publish stories that detailed the making of matzoh in hopes of clarifying Jewish traditions but the superstition of ritual murder hung on.

Gisi does not even mention Hilsner in her diary. But she is obsessed with the questions Jews discussed in the wake of the affair. How is a Jew different from a Christian? Should Jews remain Jewish? Could she transform herself into an ordinary person by conversion? Are Jews a race? Is Houston Stewart Chamberlain, who believes that the coming century will be dominated by a struggle between German and Jewish forces, right? Should what he terms "mongrel" Jews rid themselves of their negative characteristics and become more like the "blond dolichocephalic Nordic type" German? On the other hand, should she believe Dr. Theodor Herzl's analysis of the situation of the Jewish people?

"I love our garden," she writes.

> I love its smell after the rain, its butterflies and beetles. But I always think that other people experience nature differently than I do, that they have a "love of nature" or a "feel" for it. People say that Jews don't have that feel. Last night, Papa said that Miss Voděnková had stopped him on his way to his factory and had said, "Don't be in such a hurry to get to work. Look how beautifully spring is unfolding this year!"
>
> Miss Voděnková didn't say that out of the blue. But what *is* the correct feel for nature? What's included in it? Is it only the fields and how they look or what we plant in them or what grows there by itself without having anything to do with us? . . . I have to pay attention to how my Catholic classmates talk about nature and everything in it, whether they do it differently from the way I do.

Gisi notes that her mother is better dressed than most Czech women and is never seen carrying a goose under her arm. She compares the grandeur of Kolín's cathedral to the austerity of its synagogue. And she describes the conflicts in the once observant but now assimilationist Saudek household, where one brother has lost all interest in Judaism and another is trying out Herzl's Zionist ideas.

When he raises those ideas with his father, Mr. Saudek replies,

> You think we need to show them ourselves where they should expel us to? To admit that we don't belong here? I'm at home here just like anyone else. Our family has lived here for three hundred years. I know that we Jews should renew our national life. But I can't. I can't and I don't want to go back.

Pepi's aunt Rosa, of course, lived the life that Mr. Saudek did not wish to go back to. She was a devout practicing Jew who attended synagogue regularly, was engaged with the families who lived on the Jewish Street, and found intellectual interest in Judaism. She was also a poor woman who worked hard, expected her niece to perform daily chores, and employed no servants. When Gisi finished school at fourteen, her father insisted that his daughter remain at home until she married. "The man who wants a wife smarter than himself hasn't been born yet!" he replies when she begs to attend Mínerva, the new *gymnasium* for girls in Prague.

Pepi did not even think of continuing in school. Aunt Rosa expected her to earn her living and contribute to the family income. A few professions had opened up to women since Therese Furcht's time, such as teaching, nursing, or clerking with the postal service. But teaching was reserved for Catholics and Pepi's only real option as a respectable, working-class Jewish girl was to become a seamstress.

Aunt Rosa would not allow her niece to live with strangers as Therese had done. In her opinion, a female was always in danger of being seduced and provincial Jewish girls like Pepi risked falling into "white slavery" at the hands of Polish Jews who kidnapped them for use as prostitutes in Turkey and South America.

She secured an apprenticeship for her niece in the workrooms of Zwieback's, the famous department store in Vienna, and lodging with the relatives to whom she had sent Rudolf Sachsel six years earlier.

In 1897, at the age of fifteen, Pepi took the train to the city that her mother had come to one generation earlier. During those last years of the nineteenth century, the imperial court still drove the economy and set the tone for a strict hierarchical society that ranged from the nobility to the military and civil administration to the artisans and small shopkeepers, factory workers, and servants. Every group had its etiquette, its dress code, and its annual masked ball. In such an environment, style was more important than substance and fashion a religion.

Appearance was an obsession in Vienna. Architect Adolf Loos described it as a city of artificial facades, like the ones Potemkin had built in Russia to disguise the poverty of the population. Others pointed to the elaborate obsequiousness of the populace and the military pomp of the army that diverted attention from its obsolescence to its well-pressed uniforms. Impeccably fashionable dress was demanded of both men and women but women regarded clothes as essential to their power. They dressed not only for dinner, but for receptions, teas, riding, theater, opera, or balls where a fateful encounter might change their destinies. Dress designer Inez Exton recalled,

> If a day passed when no man, adolescent or overgrown, followed a lady in an utterly obvious fashion, she felt something had to be wrong with her. She needed a new hat or a new dress? It was the age of unliberated pulchritude, the age of the femme fatale. Our femininity was a dangerous weapon and we used it.

Pepi Sachsel entered the world of Vienna's fashion industry as an apprentice at Palais Zwieback, located in the center of the city on the Kärtnerstrasse, with branches in Graz, Budapest, and Karlsbad. In the *salons,* furnished with Persian carpets and deep easy chairs, clients lay back as clothes were modeled for them and dropped phrases in French while fingering silks, velvets, and brocades. Salesladies were called *vendeuses* here, Pepi noted. Dresses were called *robes* and fur coats *fourrures*.

Most of the time, Pepi worked in the stark, ugly, and poorly ventilated *ateliers,* where seamstresses and apprentices labored ten or twelve hours a day, six days a week, well out of view of the tearoom, restaurant, and American bar. Every day but Sunday, Pepi got up at dawn in a corner of her relatives' flat, dressed, and made her way to the Kärtnerstrasse, where she entered the Palais by a side door. On ordinary days, she hauled hot, twenty-pound irons from their burners to women who stood ironing, then hauled them back to be reheated. On better ones, she was sent on errands. On the best ones, Pepi assisted at a fitting, standing mute with a supply of chalk, pins, and padding, taking in the culture of the *salon.*

She learned that Zwieback's, despite its splendor, was not the very best salon in Vienna. Most aristocrats had their clothes made by the *couturiers* Spitzer or Grünebaum. Although some members of the nobility patronized Zwieback's, it was the Jewish upper middle class — the wives and daughters of bankers, civil servants, and industrialists — who composed its clientele. For them, Zwieback's label was a status symbol, one that they did not hesitate to display.

Like me, Pepi loathed Vienna. *"It was not what she had expected,"* wrote my mother.

> But she kept her eyes open, and took in everything she saw. A little technique, a little watching at the cutting table, but most of all the shapes and styles of the dresses she saw on the wealthy clientele. At night she read until she fell asleep from sheer exhaustion.

On arrival, Pepi had discovered that Rosa's relatives had committed her elder brother, Rudolf, to an insane asylum several months earlier. He had been suffering from melancholia; there had been no alternative, they said. Horrified, Pepi wrote Aunt Rosa to come to Vienna and get him out. When the old matriarch once again came to the rescue, she found Rudolf Sachsel at the asylum depressed but sane, and nursing a broken arm and leg whose cause he would not explain. The doctors argued against his release, convinced he would commit suicide like his mother. But Aunt Rosa prevailed. She packed up Rudolf, now twenty-three, and took him back to Kolín, but left her fifteen-year-old niece in Vienna.

An adolescent girl was prey in turn-of-the-century Vienna, whether she was a *höhere Tochter,* "daughter of the upper middle class," or a *süsses Mädel,* "sweet young thing." Gisi Saudek, who occasionally visited her relatives in Vienna, belonged to the first group. She was given her own room, taken to ride horses, to attend theaters and museums, and to walk through the imperial capital.

A working girl like Pepi was regarded as a "sweet thing." She was a familiar figure in every nineteenth-century European city, immortalized as Mimi in Puccini's *La Bohème,* living with the fear of eviction, starvation, or illness, vulnerable to predatory men who tried to win her sexual favors without the shame or potential legal problems that attached to prostitution.

Both the *höhere Tochter* and the *süsse Mädel* are well represented in turn-of-the-century Viennese literature, the plays, novels, psychiatric case studies, and personal diaries of the time. Gisi herself describes a visit with her Viennese relatives in this way:

My stupid uncle, the vulgar idiot! He came into my room this morning. I looked up at him and he came closer and closer. He had a very strange light in his eyes and then, suddenly, he put his hand under the lapel of my bathrobe. It was so awful that I tell myself that it couldn't have happened. I washed the place twenty times but it didn't help. I can still feel it. I can't wipe it out.

I can't stay here. What should I do? How will I explain that I want to leave? I can't tell the truth, not even to my parents. If I told them, it would stay with me forever. . . . I long to go home and swim in the river, to wash off the dis-

honor of that awful paw which touched me. I pushed him
away so that he almost fell down on the floor. He laughed
stupidly. He was embarrassed. Then he disappeared. My
father worries when I go out with boys. He's always afraid
I'll compromise myself. So he sent me to these old relatives. . . .

The predators are striking as much for their reductionist
view of women as for the fact that they include the cream of the
Jewish elite. The elegant playwright Arthur Schnitzler kept a
diary of his sexual encounters ("Gisela M. is boring. She makes
mistakes in her dress, which disgusted me. I was brutal with her
and bothered no more about her. Jeanette bores me too. . . .")
and the number of orgasms he had during each one. The venerable Zionist leader Theodor Herzl wrote a poem that begins,
"Snakegirls, girl snakes are a dangerous brood" and described a
public official who "cancels out whatever minimal contribution
he may have made as a physician to the general welfare of
mankind by being the owner of three debt-free but ugly daughters whom he permits to roam around freely without regard to
people's aesthetic sensibilities." Otto Rank, one of the more progressive of psychoanalysts, wrote, "The woman is born to acting.
In recognition of this fact, Shakespeare permits only men to play
in his theater since he wanted to make an art out of acting. With
women it is nature."

Pepi would not have escaped Vienna's ubiquitous brutality toward young, single women nor its rabid antisemitism. One million people lived in Vienna in 1897 and the Jews, less than 10
percent of the population, stood out more than ever before. Gustav Mahler, Arthur Schnitzler, Karl Kraus, and Theodor Herzl
dominated the city's cultural life. The city's most prominent
newspaper, the *Neue Freie Presse,* was owned, and largely staffed
by Jews. The "stock exchange" Jews were still highly visible as
were their wives. And as black-coated refugees from Russian
pogroms streamed to Vienna, this picture was filled out with
thousands of *Ostjuden,* who begged or peddled in the streets.

All these Jews gave right-wing Viennese politicians an easy

way to focus the discontent of their constituents. For Catholic Vienna, Jews were both ancient and modern enemies. Jewish capitalists like railway magnate Baron de Hirsch, Jewish socialists like Viktor Adler, Jewish thinkers like Sigmund Freud, Jewish beggars like the *Ostjuden* all became targets of politicians looking to capture the vote of the "little man."

Every day, Pepi worked among the daughters, wives, and girlfriends of this "little man," experiencing how deeply antisemitism was rooted in Vienna. Karl Lueger was campaigning for mayor of Vienna on an explicitly antisemitic platform, promising that "Christian antisemitism forces Jewish economic supremacy to retreat . . . and sees to it that Christian people remain masters in their own home." A Viennese member of Parliament proposed a law offering bounties for the shooting of Jews.

Jewish responses to antisemitism varied. Many Jews adopted the corrosive self-hatred of journalist Karl Kraus, a brilliant satirist who formally left the Jewish community in 1899, or Otto Weininger, who wrote a philosophical justification of antisemitism and converted before committing suicide. Others found comfort in distinguishing classes of Jews: Viennese of Moravian parentage looked down on the Jews from Hungary, who looked down on the Poles and Galicians, who looked down on the refugees from Russia. "We were always being told that these were "fine" people, that others were "not fine," wrote Stefan Zweig.

> This constant categorization . . . seemed to be most ridiculous and snobbish, because for all Jewish families it was merely a matter of fifty or a hundred years earlier or later that they had come from the same ghetto. . . .
>
> A "good" family therefore means more than the purely social aspect which it assigns to itself with this classification; it means a Jewry that has freed itself of all defects and limitations and pettiness which the ghetto has forced upon it, by means of adaptation to a different culture and even possibly a universal culture.

Some Jews were proud militants like Joseph Bloch, a Galician-born rabbi and politician. He served in the Austrian Parliament, published *Dr. Bloch's Austrian Weekly,* a journal of Jewish and Austrian interest, and challenged any libel against the Jews he encountered. Many men in the free professions, like Sigmund Freud, found it helpful to join the fraternal Jewish association B'nai B'rith. Some became adherents of Theodor Herzl's Zionism. But when his *Jewish State* was first published, it created more anti-Zionists than Zionists in Vienna. The Chief Rabbi called Zionism a step backward into the ghetto. Herzl's editor, Moritz Benedikt, refused to let the word "Zionism" appear in his newspaper until he published Herzl's obituary.

Had Pepi been raised in Vienna, she might have become the prototypical, self-hating Viennese Jew. But with Aunt Rosa, she had developed a strong Czech and Jewish identity. *"After six months at Zwieback's,"* wrote my mother, *"it became clear that she would be better off making dresses for the ladies of Kolín than to watch others dressing the ladies of Vienna."* Pepi wrote that she wished to return home and Aunt Rosa welcomed her back.

In Kolín, she began to sew for the wealthier members of the Jewish community, including Gisi Saudek, and was soon bringing enough money into the household that her aunt could turn to religious study full-time. For the next eight years, Pepi developed a dressmaking business. During the day, she sewed coats and dresses. In the evenings, often with Gisi, she strolled under the covered arcades of Kolín's town square in what was called the *corso,* girls linked arm-in-arm walking one way, boys the other.

Those years might have been happy ones for Pepi, my mother had written,

> had Aunt Rosa relaxed her eternal vigilance over her niece's honor and virginity. There was, of course, a particular young man to whom Pepi became attracted — a fact that could not stay secret for a long time in a small town. The affair never got beyond some secretly passed letters and poems but touched off a storm with Aunt Rosa because he was a Christian.

Aunt Rosa warned her niece that she would come to the same end as Therese, that she would be seduced and abandoned, and driven to death by despair. She was still a poor, female, Jewish orphan with no dowry. The young man's family was equally horrified. He was sent away to study in Berlin, away from the Jewish girl in Golden Lane.

Pepi was eighteen in the year 1900; Aunt Rosa was sixty-nine and wanted to see her niece married. An appropriate suitor had been in the picture for some time, following Pepi around Kolín since grade school. Oskar Weigert, the son of a local Jewish family, was to take over his father's fabric store after he completed his apprenticeship in Prague and Aunt Rosa thought her niece fortunate in drawing his interest.

But Pepi had no interest in him and little interest in marriage. French novels had done their damage: from them, Pepi had concluded that the best part of love was premarital. After marrying, a woman's options were grim. She became a housewife like ordinary women. Or she defied convention, like Anna Karenina or Madame Bovary, and died. Or, like Nora in *A Doll's House,* she left her marriage and children and lived outside of society in a world that, as yet, had not been described in literature.

It was that uncharted world to which Pepi and Gisi were drawn at the turn of the century in provincial Kolín. "Don't get caught," a friend tells the heroine in Gisi's diary. "Our world is elsewhere. . . . Even the Czech world is too narrow. You should go to Paris, move in journalistic circles, learn something, and come back a finished person."

As it turned out, the girl who would eventually go to Paris was not Gisi but Pepi. By her twenty-second birthday, in April of 1904, Aunt Rosa's pressure to marry Oskar Weigert became intolerable. Gisi had long argued that Pepi had enough talent to find her place in the big city, that she should pack her things and set out for Prague. A few decades earlier, Florence Nightingale had written that orphanhood was a woman's prerequisite to an interesting life, that a woman's mother, father, siblings — often her entire family — needed to be dead so that she might be spared the obligations of a dutiful relation. Aunt Rosa seems to have excused Pepi from that familial obligation. And Pepi seems to have been independent and healthy enough to leave her aunt behind.

Rudolf Sachsel, now twenty-seven and living in Prague, agreed to be her chaperone. In 1904, extracting promises and issuing warnings, Aunt Rosa let Pepi go.

7

~

Until I began writing about her, Pepi was, for me, the photograph that hung over my mother's cutting table: the dark-haired woman with the fur collar, Pepi as my mother saw her. But now that she was becoming real for me, I examined all the photographs that survived the war, the ones my mother did not frame. In every one, Pepi looks as though being photographed is a trial. I wonder what she'd look like if she smiled or if she knew that photographs would become the only conduit between herself and her granddaughter, that I would spend hours studying them for clues to who she was.

In one of the first, taken in Kolín in 1902, Pepi is still a country bumpkin. Her collar and hat are trimmed with white lace; her dress hangs, shapeless, from her shoulders. In a later one, taken in Prague, she is standing beside a friend, wearing a close-fitting lace blouse and skirt and one of those absurdly huge hats that were then the rage. It is about a decade into the new century; Pepi is already citified, in her mid-twenties, and embarked on adult life.

In March of 1904, when my grandmother moved to Prague, it was still a provincial city, taking its political and social cues from Vienna. It was also an ethnically divided city. Ninety-five percent of the population was Czech; only five percent was German. The Czechs were riding the crest of a nationalist wave that was entering its final, triumphant decade. The shores of the tiny German-speaking island were eroding on all sides but the Germans still refused to regard the Czechs as anything other than a minor and culturally deficient nation.

"German Prague! What a collection of solid citizens!" wrote reporter Egon Erwin Kisch.

> Nothing but owners of lignite mines, directors of mining companies, executives in the Škoda armament works, hop-dealers who commuted between Saaz and North America, sugar and textile and paper manufacturers, and, of course, bankers, and then all the professors, officers, and higher state officials who were accepted in this well-heeled clique.

There was no German proletariat. The twenty-five thousand Germans who constituted but 5 percent of Prague's population possessed two gorgeous theaters, a vast concert hall, two universities, five colleges and high schools, four advanced technical institutes, two newspapers issued in both morning and evening editions, large meeting halls, and an animated social life.

> The average German avoided any contact with the city's half-million Czechs other than that strictly demanded by business. He never lit his cigar with a match from the Czech School Fund, while a Czech never used a match from the little box with the imprint of the German School Association. No German would let himself be seen in the Czech Citizens' Club, while no Czech was ever caught in the German Casino. Even the instrumental concerts were confined to a single-language group, the swimming pools were unilinguistic, and so were the parks, the playgrounds,

most restaurants, coffeehouses, and stores. . . . If the
Comédie Française or the Moscow Art Theater or some
world-famous singer gave a guest performance in the
Czech National Theater, the German press of Prague ignored it utterly, and it never even occurred to those critics
who blithely juggled the names of Coquelin, Stanislavsky,
or Chaliapin day after day in their articles that they might
step across the street and see these figures in person. . . .
Emperor Franz Joseph came to Prague once to visit the
Czech Jubilee Exhibit. Our paper gave column after column to the receptions, the decorations, the ovations, to
every turn of the spokes of the imperial caleche — and
then suddenly our description broke off with the sentence:
"The Emperor then stepped into the fair grounds." That's
about all our German readers ever learned of the existence of a Czech fair.

The last occasion on which Germans and Czechs could be recalled to have sponsored a joint cultural event, Kisch wrote, had
been a celebration to mark the hundredth anniversary of the poet
Friedrich Schiller's birth, in 1859.

Pepi, like many Jews of her generation, was able to live and
work in both worlds. She felt at ease strolling down the wide
promenade of Ferdinand Street where, every Sunday, the Czechs
would walk their children, and on the Graben, the German
promenade, where German students would show their fraternity
colors. The Graben was home to Prague's fanciest shops, including Moric Schiller, a salon and fabrics shop that displayed the title
"by appointment to the Court." It was at Schiller's that Pepi had
stopped before a shiny plate-glass window like a provincial heroine new to Paris in one of Zola's novels. *"She marched into the dress
salon,"* wrote my mother, *"and asked to see the boss."*

Mr. Schiller had been amused by the spunk of the young
woman who had walked in from the street. He asked Pepi what
made her different from thousands of other girls with no skill to
sell but sewing. Pepi replied that she had apprenticed at
Zwieback's in Vienna, that she had run her own dressmaking

business in Kolín, that she loved clothes and enjoyed helping women look beautiful.

"*To her own and Rudolf's surprise,*" my mother wrote,

> she was taken on as a worker in the atelier with beginner's wages, of which she religiously sent half to Aunt Rosa. Within a year, her knack for fit and sense of color had come to the attention of Mr. Schiller, who asked more and more for her to be on hand at fittings until the clients themselves began to ask for her.

People who knew her say that although Pepi was not pretty, she had grace and a quiet charm. During that first year at Schiller's, she must have impressed Moric Schiller as a Jewish girl from a "good" family that had somehow gotten left behind. Mr. Schiller, like most men in Prague's clothing industry, was Jewish and familiar with the *draussige*, or "folks out there," as city Jews called their rural cousins. Just a generation earlier, most of those girls had gone out to apprentice after they turned fourteen. Only recently had most Jewish girls from "good families" been expected to appear helpless in the face of work and not disgrace their families with earned income.

By 1905, Pepi Sachsel had been working for eight years and had the skills of a good seamstress. Thanks to her Kolín schooling, she spoke an excellent Czech. Vienna had secured her German. Aunt Rosa had familiarized her with some Yiddish. She was equally popular with the Czechs, Germans, and Jews who composed Schiller's clientele, avid about fashion, tactful, practical, and calm. Her employer noted Pepi's interest in details of the business and that, unlike the other girls, she seemed to have no interest in marriage. Two years after he hired her, when she was twenty-four, Mr. Schiller promoted Pepi to buyer and *directrice* of his *salon*. By 1906, now addressed at work as Miss Pepi, she was accompanying him on buying trips to Vienna and Paris and receiving flowers at Christmas from appreciative women among her clientele.

Pepi's entry into the fashion world could not have been more perfectly timed. As more and more clothing became machine made, clothing made by hand was transformed from a staple of everyday life to a luxury item. Prague had joined the ranks of major cities like Paris and Vienna with the opening, in 1903, of a department store featuring a reading room and spacious buffet, and there were more than a hundred shops where women could buy ready-made clothes. Women of means, however, preferred to have their clothes made to order at a *salon* or *maison*. "Elegant dress serves the purpose of elegance not only in that it is expensive, but because it is the insignia of leisure," wrote Thorstein Veblen. "The dress of women goes even further than that of men in the way of demonstrating the wearer's abstinence from productive employment."

As handmade clothing became a sign of higher social status, *haute couture*, literally "high sewing," was gaining recognition as a creative art. In 1900, during the Paris Exposition Universelle, one million people for the first time viewed an official exhibit of *haute couture*. More than a dozen *maisons* were represented and two of the most prominent — Callot Soeurs and Paquin — were run by women.

Since her adolescent reading of French novels, Pepi had dreamed about Paris, its theaters, shops, museums, and cafés. Now, on business trips with Mr. Schiller, she walked through the places she had read about — Rue de Rivoli, Place de l'Opéra, Les Tuileries — absorbing color, style, language, and culture. She studied the etiquette of the *maisons*, learning their conventions, the workings of publicity, marketing, design, production, and delivery.

Pepi's introduction to *haute couture* came at a time of major change. Only a decade earlier, women were still weighed down with eight pounds of clothing. Boned corsets pushed up their breasts and flattened their bellies into a line called *sans-ventre* (no stomach), pushed out their behinds, and constricted their waists, defying an international reform movement that had been challenging these practices for half a century. Starting in America with what Europeans called the *Bloomer-Kostüm*, the reform clothing movement had gained support from feminists, physicians, and sportswomen. English designers of the Arts and Crafts movement, German designers of the *Jugendstil,* and Viennese members of the *Wiener Werkstätte* all created clothes that did not require corsets and Gustav Klimt led the growing number of painters who painted models dressed in the new style.

Soon after Pepi began traveling to Paris, designers there capitulated to dress reform and the rigid, controlled clothes of the past decades gave way to loosely draped, flowing ones that were light, whimsical, and airy. Orientalism pervaded the *maisons,* determining shape, cut, and line. Models went barefoot, wore harem pants, kimono-style sleeves, and turbans. Around them wafted the heavy scent of incense and patchouli oil.

Although Prague lagged several years behind Paris in accepting the new styles, Pepi returned home from her trips laden with fabrics and models that she thought would sell in Prague. Although the *maisons* took great pains to safeguard their originals, they were unable to prevent their invited audiences from memorizing as many details of the clothes as they could, then making sketches. Women like Pepi hurried home and adapted what they had seen to the needs of their clientele. The speed of it all, the glamour, and the thrill of secrecy could not have been farther removed from the used-clothing shop in Golden Lane in which Pepi had learned to sew. There, the primary criterion for a dress was utility; here, it was beauty and up-to-the-minute style.

In Prague, Pepi became a source for women eager to know what women were wearing in Paris. She became accustomed to travel, to hotels and restaurants, to negotiating foreign cities in a language she did not yet speak. She was moving into the twentieth century faster than her older brother, Rudolf, who was still a quasi peddler, selling a variety of gift items from his apartment.

Just as in Vienna, the Jewish peddler and tavernkeeper were becoming folklore in Prague. No longer residents of Kolín's watchful Jewish Street, Pepi and Rudolf Sachsel lived in urban anonymity, two of some twenty-five thousand Jews scattered about Prague, about fourteen thousand of them Czech-speakers and eleven thousand German. I do not know if Pepi lit Sabbath candles on Friday nights as she had done with Aunt Rosa, kept a kosher home, or attended synagogue. But I suspect she did not. Her travels surely coincided with some Jewish holidays. Saturdays were prime business days in Prague and most Jews, like most Protestants and Catholics, had left religious orthodoxy behind when they left the countryside. There was no rabbinical seminary in Bohemia or Moravia where a prospective religious leader might study, and few native rabbis.

"While I was still a child," wrote playwright František Langer, who was born into a family of Czech-speaking Jews,

> I used to watch father every morning bind his phylacteries round his stout arm, but later this ceased to be a regular habit and eventually became a rare one.... For many years we kept to kosher food, but this was mainly due to Julia, a devout Christian, who during her youth had worked for our aunt, a strict Jewess, and who saw to it that we observed not only the proper regulations regarding food but also other precepts of the Jewish religion.

The secularization of the Langer family was so complete that its youngest son, Jiří, suddenly decided to travel to Galicia in order to study with the Chassidim of Belz — men he considered "authentic" Jews. When he returned wearing a black, broad velvet hat, a frayed black caftan, and *peyes,* the Langers were horrified.

"For the last three generations, when the Jews had been allowed to live outside the confines of the ghetto, those in our part of the world had not looked in any way different in their outward appearance from other citizens," his older brother later wrote.

> The attitude of our family to Jiří seemed to us at the time to resemble the situation in Kafka's novel *The Metamorphosis,* in which an entire family finds its way of life completely upset when the son of the house is suddenly changed into an enormous cockroach, and consequently has to be hidden from the rest of the world, while the family strives in vain to find some place for him in their affections.

Most twentieth-century Prague Jews associated orthodoxy with a way of life that had ended in 1848. The Langer family, like

Pepi Sachsel and her brother, looked and behaved like the Czechs of their neighborhood. "Would not Jiří's appearance now make us all seem guilty of pretense and hypocrisy?" asked Langer.

> My brother's get-up scared my father and his strata of society in yet another way. It disturbed his feeling of security and permanence; maybe it aroused in him memories of stories, long since forgotten, about the misery and congestion of the ghetto, of a life without freedom and rights, of an existence full of humiliation and injustice. This was no mere concern about conventions or business interests. It was a spectre from the past that had come among us; somebody risen from the dead had come to warn us.

There were still a few old Prague Jewish families, Langer noted, who practiced Judaism without attracting attention to themselves by their clothing, a kind of religious aristocracy "uncompromising in their orthodoxy." But Prague's twenty-four synagogues stood half empty for all but four days each year. Many Czech Jews were entering mixed marriages.

German-speaking Jews were, if anything, even more removed from tradition. They sent their children to German schools, where they were taught by Catholic clergymen and retained, as Franz Kafka would later write, "an insignificant scrap of Judaism." In his bitter letter to his father, Kafka wrote that, so far as he could see, Judaism was

> a mere nothing, a joke — not even a joke. Four days a year you went to the synagogue where you were, to say the least, closer to the indifferent than to those who took it seriously, patiently went through the prayers as a formality, sometimes amazed me by being able to show me in the prayer book the passage that was being said at the moment, and for the rest, so long as I was present in the synagogue (and this was the main thing) I was allowed to hang about wherever I liked. And so I yawned and dozed through the many hours (I don't think I was ever again so

bored, except later at dancing lessons) and did my best to enjoy the few little bits of variety there were, as for instance when the Ark of the Covenant opened, which always reminded me of the shooting galleries where a cupboard door would open in the same way whenever one hit a bull's eye; except that there something interesting always came out and here it was always the same old dolls without heads. . . .

At home it was, if possible, even poorer, being confined to the first Seder, which more and more developed into a farce, with fits of hysterical laughter. . . . The whole thing is, of course, no isolated phenomenon. It was much the same with a large section of this transitional generation of Jews, which had migrated from the still comparatively devout countryside to the cities.

The first generation of Prague Jews, like Kafka's father, were too busy building businesses to educate themselves. But their sons studied Goethe, Schiller, Beethoven, and Wagner. Like their cousins in Vienna and Berlin, they measured social standing not by the traditional yardsticks of piety or Jewish scholarship but their knowledge of Latin, Greek, and German classics. They also adopted the German bourgeois view of women.

Once valued as clever partners and even financial supports of their husbands, Jewish women were now totally excluded from business life, expected to cultivate the domestic arts and remain ignorant of any form of sexuality. Meanwhile, as the late Ernst Pawel — biographer of both Herzl and Kafka — wrote incisively, the humiliation of working-class girls by middle-class males of all ages was taken for a law of nature, and Jewish men, quick to acculturate, adopted it along with other secular habits. Jewish women were tacitly prohibited as premarital sexual partners. It was Czech women — servants, governesses, shopgirls — who were seen as permissible and necessary partners in sexual initiation and practice before marriage.

Few of that extraordinary generation of Prague Jewish writers examined the evolution of these male and female roles, which

seemed to them fixed in stone. Of all of them, I feel closest to
Egon Erwin Kisch, an unpretentious and observant reporter who
seemed unburdened by the recently acquired cultural baggage of
his contemporaries. But even to him, "patriarchy" meant potbel-
lied editors who cut his stories rather than a system that locked
women out of public life. In his vivid sketches of Prague's under-
world, women appear only as prostitutes or "sources" who tip
him off to his man. When he wrote about women, they were
usually freaks: a pair of Siamese twins joined at the hip, a Czech
"ladies orchestra" deported from Portugal. He is typical of his
generation when he writes disdainfully in his memoirs:

> She was conscious of the fact that she bored me and did
> her level best to arouse my interest, but the revelation that
> she was an employee at the Post Office of Poděbrady did
> not go far toward impressing me. So she moved up heavier
> artillery. She asserted that she understood a little German.
> Courteously I pretended both surprise and disbelief.

"Girls, weren't they those white and stupid creatures, to
whom one brings flowers in the dance hall?" wrote Max Brod,
friend to artists and an early cultural Zionist. "I like to associate
with women . . . and I always notice admirable traits in them.
Once their light, airy dresses, another time a charming remark,
quiet goodness."

Gifted Jewish women, like the writer Hermine Hanel, fled the
city, complaining of its misogyny. Hanel described in her memoirs how her aunts

> played the piano, the violin, and the guitar, they sang,
> spoke English, French and Italian, they cooked and sewed,
> they painted on silk and on china, they read and wrote let-
> ters, they flirted, danced, exercised and skated, they chat-
> tered and laughed. They knew everything and yet nothing
> thoroughly and prepared for their future profession as
> housewives. . . . The young aunts often fell in love, were
> enthusiastic about actors and singers. Foolish virgins,
> warm-blooded, uncalculating.

A handful of Jewish women in Prague created their own intellectual world by following the *salonières* model. Berta Fanta, a pharmacist's wife, became hostess to poets, scientists, and philosophers and opened her home to Albert Einstein and Rudolf Steiner. She gave costume balls and parties with guests creating *tableaux vivants,* "living pictures" that presented figures like Hero and Leander, Hansel and Gretel, Goethe, Cyrano de Bergerac. Fanta did not convert to Christianity but, like earlier *salonières,* began to distance herself from anything she viewed as Jewish and provincial. "My father-in-law visited me yesterday after fifteen years," she wrote in a diary entry of 1901.

> It was as if a representative of a strange world sat next to me. . . . The fact that there could be three books lying on a table unused at the same time and costing so much was the most striking to him. . . . Then came all the naive questions, why Else was going to university . . . what we were doing in Podbaba since we were not running a dairy farm. As a tree sinks in a thick forest, he will one day die without leaving a vacuum. . . .

Ida Freund, Fanta's sister and also a *salonière,* arranged exclusive dances at which only a strict one-third of the guest list were Jewish. According to her niece, even this one-third had to be approved by a Christian friend.

How did Pepi retain a sense of self in this world that was in so many ways a smaller version of Vienna? The only explanation is that she spent most of her time in Schiller's *salon.* Performing the centuries-old women's work of making clothes in a room that had little of the intellectual content of Berta Fanta's *salon,* but none of its subtle contempt for women, protected her. In Prague of 1910, just as in New York of 1950, men were excluded from the fashion *salon.* The owner, like Mr. Schiller, might be a man, the goal of the fashion enterprise might be to snare a husband or a lover, but the process itself centered around and provided work for women. It helped that Pepi excelled at what she did and that Mr. Schiller noticed and rewarded her. It helped that she enjoyed the company and support of her older brother. And it helped that she had been raised as a poor orphan, accustomed to viewing work as a way of life.

But she must have found the weight of Prague's small, judgmental community oppressive and Aunt Rosa's worries about her future a trial. Respectable unmarried women of Pepi's age did not even go out at night alone in Prague, Rosa complained, and here was her niece taking the night train to Paris with her employer. *"The fact that Mr. Schiller was a happily married father of three children made no difference to her at all,"* my mother wrote. *"What would people think?"* Pepi was almost twenty-five years old. It was necessary for her to earn a living. But in Jewish tradition, an unmarried life was all but not worth living and Pepi was trying the patience of a suitor who wanted to marry her despite her handicaps of orphanhood and poverty.

Oskar Weigert would one day inherit his father's drapery business in Kolín, Rosa argued. He was a known quantity. He was willing to marry Pepi and allow her to continue in her work at Schiller's at a time when not only Jewish tradition but Austrian law required women to stop working when they married. What more could she want? An orphan with no dowry could not afford to be so choosy.

I study Pepi's face in the photographs and think she must have been very stubborn, far stronger than the fragile woman that my mother remembered. This was the child orphaned at age eight, the spunky young woman who rejected Vienna and set off for Prague. But she was also a woman of her time and place, a woman deeply wounded by loss and indebted to the one relation who had saved her from an orphanage. Aunt Rosa argued that Pepi could not live alone and that she could not rely forever on her brother Rudolf.

Rudolf Sachsel, now thirty-three, had been courting a young seamstress he had met when waiting for his sister to finish work. Olga had been working at Schiller's when Pepi arrived and had watched resentfully as she was promoted up from the workroom into management. *"She thought Pepi a penniless upstart,"* according to my mother's chronicle, and she made clear to Rudolf that she would not share their new household with her prospective sister-in-law. Since Rudolf planned to open a shop with Olga's dowry, her wish carried weight.

Years later, Pepi told my mother that she never wanted to marry. She was sure that she would never fall in love again the way she had as an adolescent, with the young man who passed poems to her in the arcades of Kolín's central square and was sent away by his parents to study in Berlin. But she could not continue living with Rudolf. Her brother Emil was living in Vienna. She could not live alone. There seemed no point in opposing Aunt Rosa's wishes and those of a man who said he only wanted to make her happy.

Thirty years earlier, her mother had been forced to marry a stranger, leave her home, and move to a place where she knew no one. Oskar Weigert was no stranger and there was no question of leaving Prague. But, fundamentally, a woman's options had not changed since Therese Furcht's marriage in 1873. It was a rare woman, even one with a private income, who refused to marry. On June 16, 1907, in the Vinohrady Synagogue in Prague, Pepi Sachsel became Josefa Weigert.

8

~

When her new husband did not initiate sexual relations, my mother wrote, Pepi was surprised but relieved. She did not love Oskar Weigert and had not looked forward to the sexual component of marriage. She did not enjoy taking charge of her new household, and was frightened by the peculiarities of the man she now shared her home with who was so different from her brother Rudolf. Oskar Weigert walked oddly, would occasionally drag a foot or fall down and suffer short blackouts after which he did not know where he was. When one day he had to be taken to a hospital and Pepi was told he had progressive syphilitic paralysis, she confided in no one.

Syphilis was as widespread in Prague as everywhere else in Europe. Contemporary novels and plays are full of references to syphilis and its victims. The Wassermann test had recently been developed to identify the disease and the popular press was filled with advertisements of doctors who treated it. But there was no cure. Speaking of *Lustseuche,* or the "lust epidemic," was unacceptable in polite society, particularly among women, and British journalist Vera Brittain wrote that she found out what syphilis was only when she worked as a nurse during the First World War and came face-to-face with its victims. When Danish writer Isak Dinesen learned she had contracted it from her husband, she kept the nature of her illness a secret from her family.

Pepi kept the nature of Oskar's illness secret too. Silently, even as she conducted fittings and supervised her seamstresses, she worried whether her sharing of sheets, dishes, silverware, and bathroom with her husband would infect her as well. It was common knowledge that women — not only prostitutes but wives of infected men — died tortured and mysterious deaths from the disease. Pepi developed headaches, backaches, and constant fatigue. She found it difficult to concentrate on her work and began to behave in inconsistent, erratic ways. When she fainted on the sidewalk after leaving the store one evening, *"Mr. Schiller determined to get to the root of the change and obvious hysteria in his* directrice," my mother wrote. *"He elicited the whole sorry story of her life and sent her off immediately to a* Nervensanatorium *in the mountains of Austria."*

In 1908, word of Freud's "talking cure" had reached sophisticated circles in Prague. It is tantalizing to imagine Pepi Weigert, age twenty-six, as an early analysand and infuriating not to know with whom. The prospect, however slim, of finding Pepi's case history sent me to the library of the Boston Psychoanalytic Institute and I steeped myself in the Minutes of the Vienna Psychoanalytic Society, the memoirs of its members, and their studies. Masturbation rather than syphilis seemed to be their overriding concern. Working women were rare among the patient population. According to Freud, Wilhelm Stekel wrote, there were six types of typical female anxiety neurosis: virginal anxiety, or the anxiety of the adolescent; anxiety of the newly wed; anxiety of the woman whose husband is a premature ejaculator; anxiety of the woman whose husband practices *coitus interruptus;* the anxiety of widows and voluntary abstinents; and anxiety of the woman approaching orgasm. He and most of the other analysts I read paint an extraordinary picture of the tortures of marital life during the first decade of the twentieth century but I could not find Pepi or her concerns in it.

During the first decade of the century, there were hundreds of *Nervensanatoria* in Central Europe, treating "nervous illness" with rest, seclusion, an array of diets, hot-and-cold water therapy, massage, electric shock, hypnosis, exposure to light, as well as talk. It is fortunate that Pepi found a sympathetic and reassuring doctor who heard her history and calmed her fears. She told him her losses: eldest brother, mother, and father before she was nine; her two remaining brothers a year later. She told him of her work and marriage and the discovery of her husband's disease. Her doctor was able to persuade Pepi that anxiety was an appropriate response to her situation, that she would recover her equilibrium and find a way to lead a normal life.

But while Pepi was taking her talking cure, Mr. Schiller was talking with Aunt Rosa and Pepi's two older brothers about divorce. Divorce was rare in Prague. No Sachsel had ever been involved in one. But Aunt Rosa, incensed that her family doctor had known about Weigert's illness and not alerted her, declared that, under Jewish law, a marriage that had not been consummated could be annulled.

"When Pepi returned to Prague," my mother wrote,

> *she found herself installed at the apartment of a cultivated widow whose home had become too large for her after her husband's death and the marriages of her children. A friend of Mr. Schiller's, she was delighted to have Pepi as her companion and paying guest as she had to augment her widow's pension. . . .*
>
> *The sanatorium had done Pepi a world of good. Although psychoanalysis was still in its infancy, the progressive doctors had been able to make it clear to her that hers was just a case of hysteria and overidentification and assuage her guilt feelings over the impending divorce. The only residue of her marriage was an agoraphobia which appeared on her return to Prague.*

In 1910, a civil court granted Pepi a divorce. At twenty-eight, she was once again a single woman.

During what had become years of haunting the library stacks, I had told the Czech librarian, Zuzana Nagy, parts of my grandmother's story and, like the three Jiřís, she had become something of a companion. Zuzana was born in Prague to survivor parents; I did not have to explain to her why I had no family papers. When I mentioned to her that I would love to know where in Prague Pepi might have lived when she returned, Zuzana frowned. Then she set off into the stacks and pulled out an elegantly bound volume titled *Adresář Královského města Prahy, 1910.*

The Prague telephone directory had a marbleized cover and thick white pages that were neither broken nor brown. I opened the book, looked under *W*, and gasped when I found *Josefa Weigertová, švadlena,* dressmaker. I stroked the cover, repeating my grandmother's address and telephone number of sixty years and a world earlier as if they were poetry:

Josefa Weigertová, švadlena.

568-I Ovocný trh 17.

It was the first time I had ever seen her name in print. For a few minutes, I tried to think of a way of stealing the *Adresář*. Then I photocopied the page.

The life that lay behind those two lines of print, a dressmaker's life, is rarely described in literature and most certainly not in the literature of Prague. The Jewish dressmaker was invisible to men of ideas, regarded neither as artist nor businesswoman but as one of a class of females that provided free sex in exchange for small gifts, romance, and attention. A "little seamstress," such as the one with whom Franz Kafka was involved, was less expensive to maintain than a courtesan and more respectable than a whore. The notion that such a woman could take pride in her work or be an interesting subject to write about was absurd. There were still only a handful of women in the professions. Until after the First World War, all institutions of higher learning except the university school of medicine and the humanities would remain closed to women in Prague.

The *salon,* where many women created thriving professional lives, was ignored by historians. This was the era of Socialists and Communists, mass production and "authentic" factory workers.

Within this framework, Moric Schiller was just another *bourgeois* exploiting the seamstresses in his workroom and the society women they served. The *salon* spawned no new ideas, engaged no issues, and belonged to that category of human activity that carries on irrespective of war or political upheaval.

But from the point of view of Pepi's generation of women, the *salon* was a place where they could congregate the way their mothers had done in synagogue or church and the way their husbands did in their clubs and coffeehouses. Clothing was evolving into a means of expression. And for the women like Pepi who made the clothes, the *salon* was a rare institution that allowed a woman to acquire expertise and authority at a time when few women had authority over anything. It was, along with the convent, the brothel, the birthing room, and the all-girls school, a feminine realm, where women could speak.

Women had always viewed their dressmaker as ally, confidante, and intimate adviser. Vera Brittain, writing of the years before the First World War, described the acquisition of an adult wardrobe as a girl's ritual of maturation. Even comparatively liberated English girls, she wrote, graduated from school

> with only two ambitions — to return at the first possible moment to impress her school-fellows with the glory of a grown-up *toilette,* and to get engaged before everybody else. . . . Although I was then more deeply concerned about universities than engagements, I shared the general hankering after an adult wardrobe which would be at least partly self-chosen.

Princess Pauline Metternich had described the dressmaker's intimate role in this ritual, noting that her dressmaker, Frederick Worth, "had a rare insight into women — an unerring instinct where they were concerned."

Dressmakers, as the nineteenth-century French novelists showed so well, were implicated in their clients' lives. Because so many of them were dependent on their husband's or lover's monetary allocations and because many husbands came to the *salon* at the final fitting to inspect the product themselves, dressmakers were often asked to become accomplices, to fiddle with the bookkeeping, to overcharge or undercharge, to credit their accounts toward future purchases.

Pepi enjoyed the confidences exchanged, the sorrows shared, the conversations about marriage, affairs, troubled and troublesome children. She loved the actresses, opera singers, *demimondaines,* and dowagers who opened up windows for her onto other realms of life. There were the boring customers, of course, those who did not wash, and those who fussed and complained. But all brought her the outside world and many, friendship, kindness, and loyalty.

The world of women in which she lived was late to recognize let alone adopt feminism. Prague was a provincial capital where conformity was rewarded and behavior governed by the question What will people think? Before the First World War, feminism was lampooned as a foreign idea that led to English suffragettes setting fires to gain voting rights and American girls riding bicycles in bloomers or skirts so short that they caused traffic accidents. Vestiges of that resistance to feminism are still evident in Prague today and are the product of the peculiar history of women in the Czech nation.

The leading Czech feminist of Pepi's time, Františka Plamínková, invoked in her speeches the founding myths of the nation, particularly the three daughters of Krok: Libuše, Teta, and Kazi. She argued that Jan Hus, Comenius, and the Bohemian Brethren educated women and that enemies like Pope Pius II wrote that "every old woman in Tábor knew the Scriptures better than an Italian priest." Feminists positioned their cause as part of the Czech national struggle against corrupt, militaristic, antifeminist Catholic Austria.

Women were the ones who taught Czech instead of German to their children at the beginning of the language revival. Two of the first Czech-language bestsellers were written by women. *Domácí kuchařka* — a cookbook — was calculated to win an audience because, as its author, Magdalena Rettigová, wrote, "unfortunately more people run after a good dinner than after the most

beautiful poem." *Babička* — a novel based on the author's grandmother's life in a Bohemian village — was written by Božena
Němcová, who in the manner of the Grimm Brothers also collected and reworked Czech folk tales.

Němcová and Rettigová cannot be viewed as feminists, but
they were followed by two feminist men. The first was Vojtěch
Náprstek, who spent a decade in the American Midwest and returned home amazed by the competence of American women.
Like many visitors to America, he was impressed not only by the
naturalness of relations between American boys and girls but by
local inventions that lessened the household drudgery that characterized women's lives in Bohemia. On his return to Prague, he
founded a women's library and an American Ladies Club in his
home.

Two of the club's lecturers in the 1890s were Thomas G.
Masaryk, future president of the nation, and his American wife,
Charlotte Garrigue. Mrs. Masaryk, raised with discussions of
feminism, morality, and temperance in a Unitarian home in
Brooklyn, was unwilling to be, as both the Czech and German
expressions went, a mere "priestess of the household." Masaryk
wrote and spoke for equality between men and women. "We
condemn our wives and daughters to household shelter, we narrow their horizons and deaden their energy while wasting their
talents," Masaryk wrote in 1904. "Why should a woman not earn
her living if she is capable of doing it?"

During the first decade of the twentieth century, the vast majority of the eighty-eight thousand women who worked in
Prague were still employed as cooks, nursemaids, salesclerks,
seamstresses, waitresses, prostitutes, and factory workers. Most
were Czech; some were Jewish; almost none were German. The
Czech feminist Karolína Světlá had been working since the 1870s
to educate girls and women and her colleague Eliška Krásno-
horská spent years trying to establish a school that would prepare
girls for university. The Minerva School finally opened in 1890
and the way it was received by the general public is evident in the
then popular saying, "Minerva girls, don't wreck my nerves!" Gisi
Saudek writes in her diary: "This morning Mother told me Min-

erva is only an experiment and that all the magazines make fun of women who are bluestockings."

The first doctorate earned by a woman in the Austro-Hungarian Empire was awarded in Prague in 1901; the first medical degree, in 1902. The first woman to hold an administrative position in a hospital did so in 1906. At a time when women composed 40 percent of American college students, they made up less than 5 percent of the student population in Prague, and were excluded from law, theology, technical sciences, arts, and agriculture. Although there were many women's publications — *The Czech Housewife, Women's World, Happy Home, The Czech Girl* — and social clubs and organizations before the First World War, an imperial law prohibited women from joining political organizations until 1912.

Pepi joined no club or organization. Nor was she preoccupied with the "women's question." Feminism came into her life, most surprisingly, at home. The widow at whose home she boarded served a daily dinner to paying bachelors of the neighborhood. One day, shortly after Pepi had moved in, she sat down beside Emil Rabinek, one of the regulars. A new girl was serving and, as she held a platter of vegetables out to him, Rabinek instructed the girl to serve Pepi first.

"But I've already served Mrs. Rabinek," she replied, and Emil Rabinek — who, my mother said, rarely missed a chance to display his wit — remarked that since their relationship was determined, he and Pepi might as well get acquainted.

Herr Ingenieur Rabinek, as he was addressed in the Austrian manner, was thirty-one years old. He too is listed in the Prague *Adresář* of 1910 — as an engineer and co-owner of Korálek & Rabinek, a firm dealing in electrotechnical supplies. Tall, trim, and elegantly dressed, he was the antithesis of Oskar Weigert. Although he was born in Moravia and bore a Czech family name, he had been raised in Vienna in one of those upwardly mobile, assimilationist Jewish families that had left the Czech countryside behind. He graduated from the Technical Institute of Ilmenau in Germany with high honors, then joined the imperial and royal army as a reserve lieutenant. He had come to Bohemia as chief engineer at the Kladno Ironworks and soon relocated to Prague. Although his name meant "little rabbi" in Czech, he presented himself as an atheist and citizen of the world.

It is from Reserve Lieutenant Rabinek's military dossier, preserved in Vienna since 1899, that I constructed a portrait of the man with whom my grandmother fell in love. When he was twenty-one, he had volunteered for the reserve program, which offered sons of the Austrian middle class officer's school, abbreviated military service, and, subsequently, reserve duty. In Prussia, which had the same system, antisemitism ensured that there were hardly any Jewish reserve officers. But in Austria-Hungary at the turn of the century, there were nearly two thousand, more than in any other European Army.

Reserve officers enjoyed such privileges as an audience with the emperor should they desire one, an invitation to a court ball, and a title of nobility after many years of service. But most important, officers were part of a brotherhood of equals. Anti-Semites might allege privately that Jews were cowards, and that their countless holidays and dietary laws made it impossible for them to soldier. But if they made these allegations in public to a Jewish officer in or out of uniform, they had offended his honor and were compelled to fight a duel. For Jewish men, the attribute of honor was a historically new phenomenon. They carried it with gravity and viewed it as a new measure of social standing.

My grandfather's military dossier records that while his character, in 1900, was "not yet fully formed," he was "honorable, ambitious, cheerful and courageous," a "gifted administrator, respectful and obedient toward his superiors, friendly towards his peers, and a good influence on his subordinates." Later on, the dossier mentions that Rabinek "keeps good company" (meaning that he did not frequent prostitutes) and keeps "his finances in order" (had no debts). In 1908, he was awarded the decoration of a Jubilee Cross. He was a good athlete — horseman, swimmer, skater, and cyclist — who liked to play the piano.

Beginning with that first dinner, Emil Rabinek and Pepi Weigert began spending their free time together. She learned he was one of five siblings who took for granted the freedom that had become available to Jews only thirty years earlier. Emil's father, Israel Rabinek, had been an engineer employed by the Austrian Railways. Over the course of his life he became one of those Habsburg bureaucrats who could, as Stefan Zweig wrote, "confidently look up in the calendar the year when he would be advanced in grade, or when he would be pensioned. . . ." Israel had died when Emil, his youngest child, was nine, just before the emperor was allegedly to have made him a baronet. His mother, Franziska, or "Fanny," Rabinek lived in a style that would have been fitting had the emperor delivered on his promise.

Fanny was Therese Furcht's contemporary. My two great-grandmothers had, for about a decade, lived in the same city — but in vastly different circumstances. While Therese all but starved, Fanny entertained in the tradition of those Viennese hostesses who had traded Judaism for the religion of high art. A woman of extremely strong will and strong opinions, she read extensively, attended concerts, the opera, and the theater, and cultivated a circle of assimilated Jewish friends. Emil Rabinek told Pepi he adored his mother but that his adoration was ensured by a decision to reside in Prague, six hours of train travel away.

None of the Rabineks attended synagogue, observed Jewish holidays, or viewed themselves as different from Christian members of Vienna's upper middle class. Emil's eldest brother, Gustav Rabinek, became an explorer and died in the Belgian Congo. His brother Leo was a *bon vivant* who expired in a Viennese coffeehouse. His sisters, Gisela and Gabriela, both married into the Viennese *bourgeoisie* and became Christians. Emil himself had converted to Catholicism in 1898.

Emil did not have to explain his reasons to Pepi. He had grown up with what one of his contemporaries called a "war against Jewish boys. In nearly every road there was a young hooligan who attacked and tormented the little 'Jew-boys' he knew and when we went home from our lessons in religion, still given outside the regular school hours, we were often ambushed by whole gangs. . . ." He learned early that Jewish quotas at institutions of higher learning, denial of appointments and promotions, total exclusion from some professions, and physical violence were ordinary features of life. At twenty, Emil was baptized.

Emil's conversion may have appeared bold and even romantic to the young woman from the Jewish Street who had just divorced her provincial Jewish husband. She may have admired his repudiation of Jewish tradition, now associated by modern, assimilated Jews with superstition and unscientific ideas. Throughout her childhood, Pepi had heard Aunt Rosa hold forth about Vienna's "apostates." About nine thousand Viennese Jews formally converted to Christianity between 1868 and 1903. Some, she said, claimed they had experienced religious revelation. Others, Aunt Rosa said, converted in order to pursue their artistic or professional careers, like Gustav Mahler. Whatever their reasons, they were derided by both the Christian and Jewish communities. After Mahler's appointment as director of the Vienna Opera was announced, two newspapers denounced "the frightening Jewification of art in Vienna" and questioned whether Mahler could adequately perform German opera even if "he had been baptized three weeks before." Jewish psychoanalyst Fritz Wittel believed that conversion meant adopting a false identity and showing moral weakness by capitulating to discrimination rather than struggling against it. In a similar vein Freud wrote to a friend, "The fact that things will be difficult for you as a Jew will have the effect, as it had with all of us, of bringing out the best of which you are capable." Theodor Herzl considered a pro forma conversion but concluded that loyalty to his father prevented it. "One does not desert the Jews," he wrote, "as long as they are being persecuted."

Emil Rabinek told Pepi that he viewed the question of loyalty as irrelevant. He had been raised in a secular family that ignored the Jewish calendar. In 1898, he had applied to a German technical institute and was refused — he inferred — because of its Jewish quota. He refused to be stigmatized by a past that had nothing to do with his present. While his older sisters may have been "true" converts, he, like Heinrich Heine, saw baptism merely as "the ticket of admission to European culture." His father was dead. His mother encouraged his conversion. The fact that his surname Rabinek identified him as a "little rabbi" or that his father's name was Israel did not concern him. I later read that a fifteenth-century Jewish convert to Catholicism named Jan Žídek (or "little Jew") felt the same way.

Pepi's own experiences of antisemitism as a child in Kolín as well as Aunt Rosa's endless preoccupation with ritual had made her ripe for rebellion against Judaism. In fact, as a girl living beside Kolín's cathedral, Pepi had experienced an obscure but persistent desire to become a nun. She had been afraid to confess this yearning to anyone before but Lieutenant Rabinek only found the idea amusing.

He regarded himself as a modern man and something of a maverick. Bucking the prevailing demographic tide of Jews who migrated *to* Vienna, he had chosen to leave it for what Viennese viewed as the provinces. In Prague, he retained an imperious snobbery. He did not learn Czech — viewing it as a language with no literature. He read the Viennese papers and was an active member of the German Casino, where he played bridge and attended lectures. He supported the idea of a sovereign Czechoslovak state because he thought the monarchy had outlived its usefulness and he identified himself with Stefan Zweig as a German-speaking·citizen of the world. He fancied himself progressive in everything from art to the "women's question" and found in Pepi an intelligent and eager audience for his views.

By the time he met my grandmother, Emil Rabinek had had his share of sexual and romantic adventure. His sexual initiation had most likely been with one of his mother's maids, one of Vienna's "sweet things," or, perhaps, with a married woman. He had conducted a prolonged and unsuccessful love affair with a daughter of Prague's German upper crust and been rebuffed, possibly because he was, despite his baptism, regarded as a Jew. He was on the rebound. Pepi was, like himself, of Moravian descent. She was a woman who had had the courage to sue her husband for divorce and who earned her own living. Yet she was anything but militant. Shy and fragile, she hung on his words. She had less formal education than he would have liked and knew little of high culture. But the idea of educating her himself suited his vanity. He thought her name too plebeian, chopped the first six letters off Josephina, and called her Ina.

I have no photographs of Pepi from this time, nothing that would tell me if she blossomed as she moved from being Pepi, the wife of a provincial syphilitic, to being Ina, the lover of a dashing man-about-town. My grandmother, who at twenty-eight was still a virgin, discovered the pleasures of sexuality with my grandfather. My mother told me that her parents had a very long and romantic affair, with Emil encouraging Ina to adopt the short hair, dress, and liberated attitudes of the "new women" of the time. Pepi continued to work as salon director for Moric Schiller, except that now she went on her buying trips with her employer and her lover. Rabinek liked to accompany her. Like his elder brother, Leo, he was a *bon vivant*, for whom first-class travel, excellent food, and a stimulating cultural diet were indispensable components of life. He introduced Pepi to the opera, took her to theaters, art galleries, and concerts. Since both of them earned good livings in those last years before the First World War, they toured the Alps and the Riviera, enjoying the luxurious lifestyle of the *belle époque*.

Neither one of them was in a rush to marry. He did not wish to have children, seeing them as an impediment to his personal comfort. His mother, the formidable Fanny, liked her son's bachelor status. An unmarried son who was a reserve lieutenant was a considerable asset in Viennese society. She knew him well enough to refrain from comment and hope he would get over "his little dressmaker." Such liaisons were natural, a Viennese tradition. But she made it clear that she would not welcome a marriage with a Jewish divorcée whose family name held no cachet among her friends.

Pepi, whose divorce came through in 1910, was also leery of family entanglement. Emil and Rudolf, busy with their own lives, did not press her to remarry. Aunt Rosa, now seventy-seven and living in an old-age home in Prague, did not either. I like to think that crusty Aunt Rosa took a secret pride in her niece. After all, it was Pepi who was the most successful of the Sachsel siblings and the one who was Rosa's financial support. Pepi probably did not tell her that Rabinek was a convert. So it happened that, nearly twenty years before Virginia Woolf published *A Room of One's Own,* Pepi had one.

That blessed state lasted four years, until June of 1914, when the Habsburg's Archduke Ferdinand was assassinated in Sarajevo. In July, an empire-wide mobilization was ordered. August ushered in the First World War.

When war was declared, most people believed that it would last for a few months at most. "We were a spoiled generation," Prague intellectual Max Brod later wrote, "spoiled by nearly fifty years of peace that had made us lose sight of mankind's worst scourge. No one with any self-esteem ever got involved in politics. . . . And now, overnight, peace had suddenly collapsed."

International relations had long been one of Emil Rabinek's interests and loyalty to the old emperor did not blind him to the new realities he observed in Prague. There, sympathies were with the Serbs, with France, with Russia. Most Czechs saw Habsburg Vienna and Hohenzollern Berlin as the enemy, as the centuries-old German oppressors of the Czechs. They had long viewed the French as the champions of liberty and the Russians as the Slav bulwark against the Germans. They saw the war as a long-awaited occasion to attain autonomy. Conscripted Czech soldiers sang Czech songs as they marched off to war. They shouted "Maria Theresa lost Silesia; Franz Joseph will lose everything!" Draft dodging became the symbol of Czech resistance.

Lieutenant Emil Rabinek shared the Czech antipathy to the war. He was thirty-six then, in the prime of his career, and viewed it as an unwelcome interruption in a very comfortable life. Duty obliged him to serve in the imperial army but his sympathies lay with Czech intellectuals like Thomas G. Masaryk, who had long been working for Czech sovereignty. He felt comfortable in Bohemia and thought Prague a far safer place for his mother than Vienna. With characteristic certitude in his own judgment, Rabinek announced to Fanny and his mistress that he was installing them together in an apartment in Prague. There they would live together until his return.

I have one photograph of them. Fanny is dressed in the black, tightly corseted women's dress of her generation. Her long hair is pulled back and up and she sits with the perfect posture of a woman who has been schooled to believe that a straight back is a social asset. My grandmother slouches in a way that I recognize as my own. Her hair is cut short in a boyish bob. She is close to scowling at the camera and she wears the loose skirt, white shirt, and man's tie that was the uniform of the working women of her time. A servant, the third member of the household, stands behind them.

For four years, these three women lived together in Prague. In my mother's account of the arrangement, Pepi went off to Schiller's salon six mornings a week while Fanny managed the household. Pepi found the mother she had never had, a woman as strongwilled as Aunt Rosa but firmly rooted in the secular world. Fanny found a daughter who came home with daily bulletins from the *salon*. Their only point of contention, my mother said, was the disparity in the number of letters they received from Lieutenant Rabinek, who favored his mistress over his mother by a margin of three to one.

That correspondence was among the family possessions destroyed by the Nazis and there is no way of knowing what mother and mistress truly felt and wrote about one another, or how they experienced the war. Ten million European men would die during its course; another twenty million be wounded. Every telephone call, every telegram must have triggered Pepi's anxiety. Faced with the prospect of her lover's death, she must have played and replayed her scenario of loss: her mother, her father, the disappearance of her two older brothers, the recent death of her Aunt Rosa.

But the war that transformed Europe did not transform Pepi's daily life. Not a shot was fired in Prague. Although her buying trips were suspended for the time being, she continued to discuss clothes with clients, taking their measurements, supervising fittings. As the death toll mounted and the Austrians imposed ever more stringent martial law in Prague, Pepi sewed and sold dresses. Censorship rendered Prague newspapers worthless. It was in Schiller's *salon* that she learned how other women were contending with their losses and the scarcity of food, milk, and soap. It was there she heard that thousands of Czech soldiers had deserted the Austrians and joined the Russians, that the French and British were being slaughtered on the western front, then that a revolution had taken place in Russia and that the Americans had joined the French and British. Through it all, even though they could not travel, women in Prague continued buying clothes. Rosenbaum and Hana Podolská — the *salons* that were to become the most prominent in the city — were founded right in the middle of the war.

Lieutenant Rabinek saw action on the front in 1915. His military dossier includes an application for decoration to reward his service in restoring Equipage #118 of Transportation Corps #3 "to complete fighting capacity and contributing to the successful crossing at Biecz and the crossing of the Ropa and Wisloka. There, he helped establish bridges in the face of enemy fire and has made himself worthy of high decoration." He spent 1916 and 1917 at a desk in the War Ministry in Vienna and was able to visit Prague once every month.

Fanny Rabinek died in September of 1918, just before the war ended. On October 28, Czechoslovakia became one of the new Central European countries to rise out of the defeated Austro-Hungarian Empire. In January of 1919, my grandparents were married in a brief ceremony at City Hall. She was thirty-seven and he was forty-one years old.

9

Just as I was pondering my grandparents' decision to marry after
ten years of conducting a satisfying love affair, I received an invitation to speak about my research before the Joseph Popper
Lodge of B'nai B'rith in New York. This was a branch of the Jewish fraternal organization my mother had belonged to, founded
by nineteenth-century Jewish immigrants to the United States
"to strengthen the spiritual and moral character of coreligionists,
to impress upon them the pure principles of love of mankind, to
support the arts and sciences, to bring relief to the poor, to visit
and care for the sick, and to render assistance to victims of persecution." Their idea spread to Europe and by my grandparents'
time, there were sixteen lodges in the Czechoslovak Republic,
with names like Veritas, Humanitas, and Menorah.

In Prague, the three B'nai B'rith lodges were elite, exclusive,
all-male clubs that included the city's most prominent scholars
and physicians. Applicants for membership were judged by rigid
social and cultural criteria and were elected or rejected by secret

ballot. In postwar New York, those criteria were dropped. The Czech Jewish intelligentsia were all but eradicated during the Holocaust and the Joseph Popper Lodge was forced into inclusiveness. Its members were all immigrants: those who fled Czechoslovakia before the Nazi annexation of 1938, those who fled Communism after 1948, those who fled after the Russian invasion of 1968. Women were now full-fledged members. By 1996, it was the only existing organization of Czech Jews in the United States.

My mother had always been among the younger members of the Joseph Popper Lodge and had always felt ambivalent about attending events at the only Jewish club she had ever joined. The current members ranged in age from their seventies to nineties. Some were raised in Czech-speaking homes; others in German-speaking ones. Most came from solid, traditional Jewish or Zionist families; a few, like my mother, became identified as Jews for the first time during the Second World War. They were the closest thing to the elders of my tribe. Some had rubbed elbows with my grandparents. They were the only group of people in the world who knew the world of my family and in a few years, they would be gone.

As the date of my speech drew near, I began to worry about what to wear. What would my mother want? What do they expect? Why is it an issue? What a question! What I wear will reflect not only on me but on my family, dead and alive. I ransacked my closet full of dresses and suits custom-made by my mother for me and, as usual, saw nothing I wanted to put on. My mother was one of the few members of the Joseph Popper Lodge who wore pants although I am not sure she ever wore them to meetings. I imagined the elderly members of B'nai B'rith inspecting me at the lectern and discussing my clothes over the telephone after they returned home. It is my uncharacteristic preoccupation with appearance before this group that shows me the close parameters of Pepi's society and makes her decision to marry Emil Rabinek self-evident.

I was so concerned about the way I would look to members of the Popper Lodge that I didn't begin to consider the effect they would have on me. It began in the elevator on the way up to the penthouse suite. The man standing beside me bent down to push the PH button. He was over six feet tall and looked to be in his eighties. He was dressed in the impeccable but unobtrusive style of Czech Jews: neatly pressed slacks, a sports jacket, white shirt, and tie. His hair was gray and carefully swept back off his forehead; there were thick glasses on the bridge of his nose and a hearing aid in his ear. Something about the way he held himself betrayed a former athlete and I felt the presence of my father, a former Olympic swimmer, who had been dead for over twenty years.

In Czech, I asked whether he was going to B'nai B'rith and when he said yes, I introduced myself as the speaker.

"I knew your father," he remarked in that heavily Czech-accented English that is, for me, the language of intimacy. I felt my professional self melt. I was suddenly seven years old and in pajamas, greeting my parents' guests who would all evening carry on agitated and mysterious debates in Czech over cups of coffee and plates of rich Viennese pastries.

The penthouse suite was like thousands of others set up on Sunday afternoons by American hotels: round tables, white table-cloths; a rectangular table with coffee and pastries; a podium bearing the hotel logo. But when I entered it, I felt as though I'd crossed into another country. Since my mother's death, there had been very few older people in my life. Here, I recognized decades of faces and names. Some were people who came to our home when I was a child, in the days when few members of the Czech emigré community could afford to invite guests for a full dinner and parties were arranged over dessert and coffee instead. Some were names in my mother's telephone book. Some were people whom my parents met at concerts or at the skating rink or beach or state parks during those weekends when they set forth on their eternal quest for fresh air.

"You look just like your mother," they said and shook my hand. One man just beamed at me without a word. He was my mother's lover for a time after my father died and I had not seen him for over a decade. This happened to me in Prague, with another gray-haired, carefully dressed man who was polite to a fault but could not stop drinking me in with his eyes. It turned out that he, too, had been my mother's lover before she married my father and had almost married her.

By the time I stepped up to the podium and looked around the roomful of people, I was rattled. With their carefully coiffed white and gray hair, in their modest but spotless clothes, the surviving members of the Joseph Popper Lodge looked, in my mother's approving phrase, very "well put together" for this Sunday afternoon lecture. They wore good but sensible shoes, good but unobtrusive jewelry, little makeup. No flamboyant Zsa Zsas here, no garish redheads. One of my mother's contemporaries later told me over coffee that, in Prague, her father had forbidden her to wear makeup. He was a typical Bohemian Jewish parent whose wish to avoid attention, I knew from my reading, dated back to the Middle Ages.

These elders of my tribe displayed the same understated style everywhere their diaspora took them, replicating in California, England, Israel, and Australia the tidy lives they were raised to live in Prague even as they lost their place in its social hierarchy. Most of the men had lost their professional identities. My father, an athlete and the son of a factory owner, became a factory worker in New York. Men who were lawyers or journalists drove taxicabs, became salesmen, or found work with other refugees. The women — many of whom had never worked for a living before — sewed, baby-sat, or found work in libraries. Their intellectual and cultural lives, however, were unaffected by emigration. They made good use of New York's public libraries, and — like their Viennese cousins — made up a loyal audience for piano recitals, chamber music, and symphony concerts, the opera, museums, and lectures. They viewed art as an indispensable element in their lives, just like my mother.

I was introduced by a man in his nineties, walked up to the podium and tried to begin my speech but choked. Then my glasses clouded up. Then, to my horror, I realized that I had begun to weep. Fortunately, my audience could neither see nor hear acutely and, also, there was a problem with the sound system. A few voices from the back rose to complain that they could not hear. I fiddled with the wires, tested the microphone a few times, and managed to attain a semblance of composure. Then I started telling them about my mother's death and my subsequent research into the history of Czech Jews. I ended by asking for questions and for any help they might be able to give me in my research. I was particularly interested in the First Czechoslovak Republic, founded after the First World War. Was it really as much of a Camelot as my parents recalled? Was it more of a democracy than the United States and were Czech Jews as assimilated as American Jews today?

There was silence, then a few hands were raised and a few comments ventured. It was apparent that caution reigned and that while some members of the audience were interested in speaking with me in private, none would do so before the group. I sat down at a succession of tables, sipped coffee, and talked with women whose mothers were contemporaries of my grandmother Pepi. They were far more interested in discussing her story than in the political or social features of the Czechoslovak Republic.

I told them how, between 1909 and 1919, my grandmother had enjoyed a love affair free of domestic routine, how she had enjoyed the rewards of meaningful work, how she and Emil traveled for business and for pleasure. How, at thirty-seven, Pepi assumed that her child-bearing years were over and Emil Rabinek was opposed to children. How he rarely lost an opportunity to point out to Ina, as he continued to call her, that children cramped the lifestyles of their married friends.

The sisters of B'nai B'rith listened and shook their white heads. Pepi was "very brave," said one. "Unusual," said another and I suddenly understood that, in Prague, my grandmother was seen by her society not as a free agent, certainly not as a heroine, but as an object of pity, a woman forced by circumstance to work and by a recalcitrant man to remain unmarried, outside respectability. For years I had gazed at the photograph of Pepi in my mother's workroom and identified her face with Anna Karenina, an association that now made sense.

I returned home trying to feel how much of an outsider she must have been. In Massachusetts, where I live, some women I know choose to live with other women; others choose to live or have a child alone. The exercise of choice is central to all our lives. We take choice so much for granted that we sometimes forget there are things we cannot choose.

In Prague of 1919, the notion of a woman controlling the circumstances of her life was all but nonexistent. Convention ruled and it was the assimilationist Jews who most closely observed the norms. They took care to behave "correctly" in the way newly enfranchised minority groups always do, to be more *bourgeois* than the old *bourgeoisie*. Jewish marriages were still being arranged during that long decade of my grandparents' affair. Dowries were still crucial on the marriage market and youth, beauty, family status, and money were still the salient measures of a woman's value. Pepi had no social status, no dowry, no sense of entitlement. She would not have been able to say, like British feminist Vera Brittain, "I felt sure I did not want to marry. . . . I loved my uninterrupted independence, and believed that I had outgrown all possibility of including children in my scheme of life." And, ultimately, even Vera Brittain chose to marry. It is more than likely that Pepi had wanted to marry Emil for years and that my grandfather, having reached the age of forty, decided it was time for him to settle down. For that, Pepi must have felt a debt of gratitude.

The Rabineks, unlike the Weigerts, did not have a Jewish wedding. They were married in a civil ceremony at Prague's New Town Hall. On that January day in 1919, the Rabineks were in tune with their times: secular, optimistic citizens of Prague embarking on marriage at the same time as the new Czech Republic embarked on its life. Elsewhere in Europe — in France, Great Britain, Germany, and Austria — the war had exhausted the populace and destroyed a generation. But while Czechoslovakia also had its wounded men and malnourished children, the war had brought long-awaited independence. The Czech national leadership, including sixty-eight-year-old "father of the nation" Thomas G. Masaryk, had survived intact. The capital had been spared.

While Vienna and Berlin were humiliated cities, Prague was jubilant and actively engaged in de-Austrianization, renaming its streets and monuments, revising its school curricula.

"The first year was a year of celebration," Olga Scheinpflugová, an actress and later Pepi's client, recalled.

> People were no longer irritated by the lack of food and goods; they knew that if they didn't have them today, they would tomorrow. . . . The map of Europe had changed; we were starting from scratch. . . . We celebrated new names of battles and people: the Marne, Wilson, Clemenceau, Štefánik, Beneš, Masaryk. The liberated Czech public had something to depend on. . . . German firms closed up. . . . The ones who stayed believed that they would be needed after the revolutionary fervor passed. . . . People straightened up and looked one another in the eye.

Journalists and diplomats traveling through the region contrasted the desperation and nihilism elsewhere in Europe with "earnest, energetic, self-satisfied" Czechoslovakia.

Herr Ingenieur or Pan Inženýr Rabinek, as he was now called, could have been characterized in the same way. He saw that of all the new countries to emerge out of the monarchy, Czechoslovakia was the strongest. It contained within its borders most of the monarchy's industries, including its coal and iron, chemicals, textiles, glass, and sugar. It produced almost all of its own food. Careful monetary policy curbed the inflation that plagued its neighbors and the new government was especially quick to take measures against unemployment. Rapid electrification helped Rabinek's wholesale business in electrotechnical supplies to boom. The firm of Korálek & Rabinek was soon doing so well that it added a shipyard on the Elbe River to its holdings.

My grandfather, who voted for the German Social Democrats, believed in the viability of the new state and disparaged those of his friends who viewed Czechoslovakia as a "geographical invention." Yes, the nation's 13.6 million citizens included three million Germans and 750,000 Hungarians as well as Jews, Gypsies, Poles, and Ruthenians. Yes, soldiers were returning to few jobs, little housing, strikes, and a lack of basic foods and services. Yes, the political situation was a chaos of political parties jostling for power. Yes, the end of the monarchy was accompanied by violent nationalistic excesses and the plunder and destruction of Jewish and German property, some of it with the tacit compliance of the police. But compared to pogroms in Poland and Russia or official elections in Austria, where antisemitism was public policy for some parties, they seemed to Emil transitory rites of passage into nationhood.

Czechoslovakia, he argued, stood out like a beacon in a sea of darkness. Speaking from Washington, D.C., Czechoslovakia's first president, Thomas G. Masaryk, had announced that Czechoslovakia would adopt the principles of the American Declaration of Independence, including an embrace of pluralism, separation of church and state, freedom of press and assembly, and the abolishment of aristocratic privilege, as well as gender equality. The Republic would become a "higher Switzerland" in Masaryk's phrase, a country that would aspire toward the integration of the Czechs, Germans, Slovaks, Hungarians, and Jews within its borders.

Thomas G. Masaryk had been born in 1850 to a father who was a coachman and a deeply religious Catholic mother. He grew up disturbed at the thought of other religions and afraid, he later wrote, of Jews. Apprenticed first to a locksmith at the age of fourteen, then to a blacksmith, his intellectual potential was recognized by the local priest, who sent the boy to a German-language *gymnasium*. He then attended the University of Vienna, where he studied history, political science, sociology, and philosophy, steeping himself in the writings of the Czech Protestant tradition and world literature.

In the late 1870s, Masaryk met and married American Charlotte Garrigue while both were studying in Germany. She, her family, and her country had a tremendous influence on her husband, who took the extraordinary measure of incorporating his wife's family name into his own. But Masaryk remained a deeply religious man who rejected the notion of one church, a man who carried on an intense correspondence with such moral philosophers as Leo Tolstoy. Among the leaders of the Czech national movement, Masaryk was always its voice of reason.

Twice while still a junior faculty member at Charles University in Prague, Masaryk had put his personal safety and professional life at risk to defend what he called "the truth" — first, when he contested the authenticity of two national epic poems that had allegedly been written in the tenth and thirteenth centuries but which turned out to be forgeries of Czech nationalists, and second, when he defended Leopold Hilsner against the accusation of ritual murder, beseeching his countrymen to dismiss superstition "because the belief in ritual murder casts disgrace on the Czech people."

When Masaryk became president of the First Czechoslovak Republic, the "Professor," as many called him, was sixty-eight years old. He addressed Czechoslovakia as he did his students, viewing the nation as an "ethical personality" that had been influenced by the Hussite movement in the way the French Revolution had influenced France. His marriage to Charlotte Garrigue offered a very modern model of marital relations: a husband and wife who were companions and intellectual equals. Together, the Masaryks had translated John Stuart Mill's *The Subjugation of Women* into Czech. As a young professor, Masaryk had been pleased to push his children's baby carriage in public. He even fed and diapered his children on occasion — unimaginable for a male in the universe of Kafka, Brod, and Kisch.

Emil Rabinek admired Masaryk and fancied himself a very modern man and a feminist in Masaryk's mold. For ten years, his mistress had worked for Moric Schiller. Now that Ina was his wife, that arrangement struck him as absurd. He insisted that she open a *salon* of her own. Schiller's had profited from her talents long enough, he argued. She should go out on her own. Her clients would certainly follow her.

Sure as always of his assessment of the situation, Engineer Rabinek rented a commercial space on the ground floor of a new apartment building on Spálená and Národní (once Ferdinand, now renamed National Street) midway between Wenceslas Square and the National Theater. Upstairs, he took an apartment large enough to accommodate his extensive German library with its beautifully bound translations from the French, English, and Russian, his piano, paintings, and the furniture he had inherited from his mother. His home was within easy walking distance of his office, of the German Casino, of the river. There, on the ground floor, Pepi opened Salon Weigert.

Her clients did, in fact, remain loyal to their dressmaker and new ones swelled their number. Czechs were now European citizens in their own right. Although "Clothes make the person" had originally been a German saying, the Czechs had adapted it and believed that clothes made a nation as well. Just as the belief that citizens of the new state needed new electrical appliances helped Emil Rabinek's business, the belief that female citizens needed new clothes helped Pepi's.

"Since people say clothes make the person," wrote journalist Milena Jesenská, "let's consider: what to wear?" In that first decade of independence, Jesenská wrote columns that read like a cross between Miss Manners, a social critic, and a fashion doyenne. Over and over again, she reminded Czechs that they were a people emerging from colonization who needed to discard many of their former ways. Over and over again, she reminded newcomers to Prague that they needed to abandon their rural habits. Her newspaper columns explained everything from the proper way to wash in the morning ("You need at least half an hour") to how and what to eat in public. The English were the most physically cultured people of Europe, she wrote, praising Pears soap, Atkinson's lavender water, and English bathrooms at a time when only new buildings in Prague had modern plumbing and most Czechs still washed in their kitchens.

Hygiene was only the beginning of Jesenská's personal improvement program. Dressing well was not only in the national interest but part of the feminist search for an appropriate way to live, to express personality, to facilitate freedom. She mocked the way any stranger could identify a Czech woman on a train. "Ten boxes," she wrote, "a cage with a canary, and a basket of cakes and cooked goose — that's the mark of a Czech. . . . Leave your straw hat with feathers quietly at home, along with your fancy shoes and lace blouse — and, above all, your jewels!" Czech women would do well to adopt the "English" habit of carrying everything in a suitcase, to wear a well-cut English suit with pockets, sensible English shoes, and a trench coat that would last for years.

Jesenská's columns of advice were part of a larger attempt on the part of Czechs to turn their nation toward non-German models of culture. French had long been attractive to Czechs and now every family that could afford it hired a French tutor for their children. Paris replaced Vienna as the arbiter of cultural life and Czechs were proud when their new capital was described as "the Paris of Central Europe." In fact, it had long been a meeting point for the crosscurrents of European cultural life. Now, it was a city hospitable to German Expressionism as well as French Cubism, to the emerging arts of film and photography, to the international literary avant-garde and to exiles and displaced people of all kinds. Russians fleeing the Revolution brought Russian literature and theater to Prague. Jewish refugees brought Yiddish culture and Zionism. Although there were few Americans, their culture arrived via the movies, and that most American of art forms, jazz.

It was in this newly cosmopolitan Prague that Pepi started her business and her married life. The Rabineks were among the first in Prague of what would much later be called "dual career" couples. Every morning, after breakfast, Emil would walk to his firm of Korálek & Rabinek and Pepi would go downstairs to open Salon Weigert. Both were absorbed by their work, and to Emil's Viennese niece, Lily, who stayed with them for six months in 1920, they seemed an ideal modern couple: prosperous and happy. Aunt Ina — as the family in Vienna called her — was plumper than the rule, but attractive and widely regarded as *tüchtig,* that approving German adjective meaning "capable" and "clever." She seemed to Lily the model of a self-made woman.

Her uncle, Herr Ingenieur, was elegant, charming, witty, and recognizably Viennese. Even after two decades of living in

Prague, he made no effort to learn Czech. There was no need. His Czech business partner spoke perfect German. So did the educated non-Jews with whom he socialized. Although in 1920, the number of Prague Jews who registered as "German-speaking" was a paltry 7,406 — the size of a small college campus — socializing within that tiny minority did not strike him as absurd. At least once a week, he attended a performance at the German Theater, which had a long tradition of brilliant programming. Every day, he read with pleasure the excellent *Prager Tagblatt*, the more liberal of the two German-language newspapers and perused other German-language journals at the Casino, an impeccably maintained German club on the former German promenade, with its private library, restaurant, and garden. Many Jews avoided the building because of some of its antisemitic members but Rabinek no longer regarded himself as a Jew and regarded the Casino's racists as the kind of idiots one was bound to encounter in every organization. There were anti-Semites even among his "brothers" in the Lodge of Freemasons, which held its meetings at the Casino and — like B'nai B'rith — selected its members by secret ballot from the Prague intelligentsia. Rabinek fancied himself an intellectual, and cultivated a circle of friends — Jews and Gentiles — who had long ago discarded such medieval notions as religion.

Between 1918 and 1930 nearly two million Czech citizens left Catholicism. About half formed a new Czechoslovak Church and the rest registered themselves as agnostics. Emil Rabinek's secularism was typical of much of Czechoslovakia's middle class and leadership. He applauded Thomas G. Masaryk for emphasizing the humanist tradition in Czech culture and treating Czechoslovak citizens to frequent philosophical musings. "Are we able to govern ourselves?" Masaryk wondered publicly. "Do we have enough ability, enough brainpower, enough perspicacity, enough will, enough resolution, enough perseverance?" Communism had won out in Russia, he liked to say, because "yesterday they believed in the priest; today they believe in the socialist agitator." The maturity of a nation, he said, could be ascertained by its freedom from antisemitism.

Masaryk had imbibed antisemitism along with his mother's milk. But — unlike any other European political leader — he confessed his childhood prejudice and analyzed its roots. When the president, in one of his articles or speeches, repeated his theme "We must break our ties with Rome. . . . We must overcome the Rome inside each one of us," Emil Rabinek would note that, just as Catholics were obliged to overcome the Rome within them, Jews were obliged to overcome Jerusalem.

His family of origin, the Rabineks, had been among those eager to "overcome the Jerusalem in themselves" one century earlier, during the time of the Josephine Reforms. By 1920, none were officially registered as Jews. With the rate of intermarriage in Czechoslovakia growing, synagogue attendance minimal except on the high holidays, and official membership in the Jewish community falling, Czech Jews were on their way to disappearing. Rabinek thought this a good thing and disliked the two groups that opposed this trend: the *Ostjuden* who arrived in Prague as refugees and the 5,900 Jews who registered neither as Germans nor as Czechs but as Zionists in the census of the new republic.

Like Gisi Saudek, he loathed the black-coated refugees who came to his apartment door selling pencils and other small items on a tray. Pepi — who had grown up with Aunt Rosa's conception of charity as economic justice — hastened to give them food and money before her husband realized that they were there. The Zionists were another matter. Sons of Bohemian and Moravian families like his own, they included in their ranks intellectuals and literati like Max Brod, well-dressed men Rabinek recognized as peers. These Zionists did not all argue that all Czech Jews should emigrate to Palestine. Rather, taking their cues from the cultural Zionism of Martin Buber, they proposed a reestablishment of a vital Jewish life in Prague that would reconnect with the lines of Renaissance Jews such as David Gans and Rabbi Loew. They viewed assimilation as immoral, a kind of national emasculation. Rabinek debated politely with them but dismissed their ideas as mad. Why would Max Brod choose the limitations of life as a Zionist? To be a German in Prague, Rabinek thought, was to enjoy the most highly developed civilization men had ever created.

It is very hard for me to like or even understand my grandfather as I try to paint his portrait. I dislike what I perceive as the Vienna in him, his snobbery, his entitlement and self-centeredness. I find his dismissal of Czech culture and his misreading of his German environment staggering. Even if I idealized German culture as he did, I think I would have noticed that the so-called island that was German Prague was really three islands — the university, the old German aristocracy, and the Jews — and that the first two were closed to the third. The aristocracy had always been a closed circle, a bastion of antisemitism. Its fraternities traditionally excluded and attacked Jews; professors like August Rohling had published tracts like *Der Talmudjude,* vilifying them, and Jewish scholars were expected to keep a low profile.

In 1922, a historian named Samuel Steinherz whom my grandfather must have known from the Casino broke that tradition. For twenty-one years Steinherz had taught medieval history at the university. His colleagues elected him rector and, rather than declining the honor as other Jews had done, Steinherz declared that he was a German and accepted it. German students, outraged at the notion of a Jew as rector, organized a strike, occupied buildings, and demanded his resignation. Their strike gained support throughout Austria and Germany. When Steinherz finally gave in and submitted his resignation to the minister of education, the minister refused to accept it. Antisemitism was illegal in the Czechoslovak Republic. In the end, Steinherz ended the impasse by going on leave.

The Steinherz Affair, as it was called in Prague, led the scholar, a historian of papal diplomacy, to change his field of research as well as his perception of himself as a German. He began to study the history of Bohemian Jews. He left the Casino to join B'nai B'rith. Steinherz was one of the many academics lecturing on the history of Czech Jews in the Terezín ghetto before he was murdered by the Nazis. Emil Rabinek, on the other hand, did not allow the Steinherz Affair to change his own self-image. He continued to believe he was a German.

Although Pepi did not observe any Jewish holidays, she visited Aunt Rosa's grave regularly and retained a strong, visceral sense of herself as a Jew. She was also far more sensitive than her husband to manifestations of antisemitism. Growing up in Kolín and even now, in Prague, she was aware that many Czechs still perceived all Jews as arrogant, German-speaking non-Czechs, former agents of Austria, Germanizers. That was why they boycotted Jewish stores or broke in and plundered them during sporadic strikes and riots. Unlike her husband, she read Czech literature and attended the Czech theater. She knew, as her husband did not, that Jews were still portrayed as outsiders, sly tavernkeepers in the countryside or shrewd secondhand dealers in the city, exploitative industrialists everywhere.

After the establishment of the new state, Emil Sachsel had joined his siblings, Pepi and Rudolf, in Prague, ending years of separation. All three had rejected Aunt Rosa's orthodoxy yet retained a sense of Jewish identity. Although they did not live by the Jewish calendar, their relations and circle of friends were made up almost entirely of people who had been born into Jewish families. And the continuing problem of Jewish "incidents" in the Republic, as well as the presence of observant, Zionist, or refugee Jews in Prague often raised the Jewish question at home.

Rabinek felt such conversation as an unpleasant intrusion into an otherwise gracious life. The war had not ended his *belle époque*. He was accustomed to living well and now that he was a married man, he wished to create a proper home in which he might receive friends whose hospitality he had enjoyed for a decade and had not, until now, been able to reciprocate. His days were marked by pleasurable ritual: his morning coffee, his office hours at Korálek & Rabinek, midday dinner, his afternoon nap, bridge at the Casino, the theater, occasionally a Sunday at the racetrack. He fully enjoyed his new, married life.

According to Rabinek's niece, Lily, Pepi enjoyed her new married life too. Aunt Ina suffered from some minor, unspecified nervous disorders — but so did most of the women she knew in Vienna. The fact that Ina regularly went for a "cure" with Dr. Lakatos in Baden bei Wien or off to Karlsbad or Marienbad for a few days of rest seemed to young Lily a perfectly appropriate thing for a successful businesswoman to do. It was during a spa stay in the summer of 1919 that Pepi was beset by unusual fatigue and nausea and wondered if she might be pregnant. Her physician first assured her that it was unlikely at her age, then confirmed her suspicion.

My mother told me that her father's response to the news was to demand an abortion, only to be told that it was too late. I have one photograph of them in 1919, a beautifully dressed, beautifully posed couple. Pepi looks sedate, filled by that fuzzy, hormone-infused cloud that I remember took over my being when I was pregnant. She is holding a puppy and is as close to smiling as she ever was before a camera. My grandfather stands a bit away from her, not handsome but compelling, as one of my mother's friends later told me — the kind of man you notice and look back at for a second time.

Pepi was almost thirty-eight when my mother was born on February 26, 1920. Emil, who had decided that the baby would be a boy and planned to name him Franz, merely adjusted the ending to Franziska. It is his reaction that informs my mother's account of her birth: *"When he stepped over to the crib of his newborn daughter,"* she wrote in her twelve pages, *"much of his shock over the undesired arrival had worn off. Studying the not too appealing features of the newborn he remarked that she was so ugly that her face would have to be covered by millions to ever find a husband."*

Her father's much-repeated response became a key feature of my mother's version of her childhood. So was his insistence that she be baptized — over his wife's objections — right there in the hospital. She was baptized Franziska Paulina Margaret Rabinek and called Franzi.

10

In most families, there are multiple versions of the family story; the larger the family, the more various the versions. In my family, as in many families of Holocaust survivors, it is difficult to construct even one. There are too few relatives. They possess few documents. Disaster has dispersed them. Moreover, each has designed his or her own strategy for coping with the destruction of the world into which they were born. One forgets, another attenuates, another denies key parts of the narrative. As I listen to Emil Rabinek's nearly one-hundred-year-old Viennese niece and my mother's three surviving Czech cousins, I must take into account not only their personalities and relation to my mother but also the way Nazism, Communism, and emigration affected their lives, their memory, and their outlook.

At ninety-nine, Emil Rabinek's niece Lily denies that there was ever any antisemitism in Vienna and, as I'm sure my grandfather would have, regards my interest in Jewish history as an unpleasant, unwelcome preoccupation. Lily lives in California, where her son is a well-known and successful scientist, where she hikes in the mountains and continues to play chamber music every day, just as she did in Vienna. I often feel that she continues to help me with my research only out of a sense of obligation toward my dead mother and those members of her family who were murdered in the Second World War. Lily's Viennese accent is so strong, her charm so rigorous, that when I am sitting in her living room, I forget the California light and think I am in Central Europe.

My mother's only first cousin — the son of Pepi's brother Emil Sachsel — is Peter Scott, who lives in New Jersey. Unlike Lily, he has never lost sight of the effects of Nazism on his family, and that inability to blind himself for a long time froze his emotional life. He left Czechoslovakia to study in France just before Munich. His mother, father, and younger brother, Heinrich, remained and were all murdered. His relationship with my mother was necessarily complex. They had been close as adolescents, so close that his father had warned him of the genetic consequences of having sexual relations with a first cousin. But their relationship was forever complicated by the fact that while Franci had survived a series of concentration camps, Peter had made his way from France to Cuba to the United States.

In New Jersey, Peter Sachsel changed his name to Peter Scott and married an American Jewish woman with a Boston accent. He did well. He had studied chemistry and developed a method for holding dye fast in cloth. His company was acquired by a corporation and he became our rich American "uncle" who periodically stepped in to bail my parents out of financial trouble. As a child, I liked to visit his big suburban house, to swim at his country club, to ride in his fancy car. Only later would I discover that in coming to my mother's financial rescue, Peter was repeating his father's role during the 1930s. When Herr Rabinek lost his money, Emil Sachsel had helped out his younger sister.

As a teenager, I resented Uncle Peter. I found him distant and unwilling to join our family activities. He never had time. He flaunted his European sophistication in suburban New Jersey, and as a child, I was annoyed by his snobbism and sexism — the qualities of the upper-middle-class Central European male that Arthur Schnitzler portrayed so well in his plays. My mother often said that family matters were difficult for Peter and that she represented a past he was trying unsuccessfully to forget. As Peter grew older, however, and particularly after my mother's death, he began to work at understanding his past. Therese's grandson and I became, to a degree, accomplices.

My mother's cousin Helli, on the other hand, remained aloof. A distant cousin, she could not remember how she was related to the Sachsels. Unlike Franzi and Peter, whom she considered spoiled children of the *bourgeoisie*, Helli was a serious student who opposed all national and ethnic divisions and supported the ideals of the Communist Party. She and her husband fled to England in 1938 and returned after the war was over. For a time, they lived comfortably in Prague. Her husband was a cardiologist; she worked at the Czechoslovak Academy of Sciences. Then, they and their three children became increasingly unhappy under Communism. In 1967, they fled and, with the help of two Jewish organizations, later emigrated to the United States.

Helli was grateful to those organizations but their help did not make her feel any more Jewish. She had discarded Judaism when she became a Communist. In Prague, her children had known only that they had had Jewish grandparents. Even in the safety of the United States, Helli rarely discussed family history. "Why do you have to write about your family?" she complained when I called her. "Why not something else?"

My fourth and best source, until she died, was Kitty, the other cousin my mother often described as her best friend and alter-ego. Their governesses took them for walks together when they were small children. They double-dated as teenagers. They survived Terezín, Auschwitz, and Belsen together and rode the same truck back to Prague at the end of the war. Kitty had wanted to emigrate to America but married a man who became an invalid and spent the next twenty-five years caring for him and their son, Miki, in a tiny flat where her bedroom had been the kitchen and the kitchen, a closet, and the few art objects from her family's prewar life looked sad and out of place. Like her cousin Helli, whom she rarely visited, Kitty told her son nothing about his family history, not even that his grandfather had been one of Prague's prewar Zionists.

Unlike Helli and Franzi, Kitty had no professional ambition. She wanted to fall in love, get married, and have children. From childhood on, she modeled herself on Hollywood starlets, chafing against the traditional modesty of Jewish Prague, dyeing her hair an improbable blond, batting her eyelashes at the bleak world of the socialist republic. My mother had played the role of older sister in her life. The fact that she had become a dress designer made her even more of an idol for Kitty and, in Prague, she liked to introduce me as her niece and insisted that I call her "Aunt."

A few months after my mother died, I flew to Prague with a suitcaseful of my mother's clothes. By that time, Kitty was a sixty-seven-year-old retiree but still blond. Just as improbably, she worked as secretary to the Chief Rabbi of Prague — to get out of the house rather than from any religious conviction, she hastened to assure me. Like Helli and my mother, she believed that there was something medieval about practicing Jews. But after the Velvet Revolution, tourism in Prague had boomed, the Jewish community was besieged by foreigners, and there were so few authentic Prague Jews left that she felt a call. Even her companion, Jaroslav — a Czech Protestant — was working at the Old-New Synagogue selling entry tickets. It supplemented their pensions, she said, and gave their lives structure.

But I sensed that Kitty got something more meaningful out of working in the old Prague ghetto. She liked being called on to interpret between German and French and Czech and English and typing up letters to addresses around the world. It reminded her of life before Communism and before the war, when she lived in a big apartment with beautiful things. I, just by my resemblance to my mother, evoked that world, too, and if I stood up straight, dressed well, and brushed my hair, she was willing to tell me anything I wanted to know.

It was Kitty who took me to the corner of Spálená Street and Národní třída in the bustling center of the city and pointed up to the windows of the apartment in which my mother spent the first years of her life. She showed me the balcony on which she and Franzi spent hours and once got into big trouble when they threw flower pots down onto the sidewalk below. My mother had dared her to do it. Franzi was often bossy, like her father, and Kitty once got so angry at her on that balcony that she declared that when they grew up and had families, her children would never play with Franzi's. "*Bohužel*," she said, "Alas," that was exactly what happened.

I took photographs of the building for my growing file of "documents" — photographs, photocopies taken from official registries, letters that documented the story on my mother's twelve pages. I tacked the photographs to the bulletin board above my desk and tried to imagine what went on behind the windows of that apartment where Pepi spent March of 1920 in bed.

Pepi was two weeks shy of thirty-eight years old when she gave birth and viewed Franzi as a miracle of what was then considered close to old age. I imagine that her delight was mixed with trepidation. The labor of childbirth had been long and exhausting and, in the end, the doctor had to extract her daughter with forceps. Although Franzi was unharmed in the delivery, Pepi's bladder and vagina were torn and required repair. For the first time in her adult life, she was unable to work and, for the first time, she was sexually unavailable to her husband.

Even an easy birth transforms a marriage and Emil Rabinek did not wish to have his marriage transformed. Rather than welcome the changes that fatherhood might bring into his life, he determined to insulate himself from them. A baby required a room: he had the bedroom farthest from his own converted to a nursery. A baby required care: he added a round-the-clock baby nurse to the household staff of cook and maid. Then he resumed his routine — his morning coffee, his office hours at Korálek & Rabinek, dinner at noon followed by a twenty-minute nap, coffee at the Café Elektra, back to the office, reading or bridge at the Casino until 7:30, dinner at 8:00 — as if nothing had changed.

The photograph of Pepi that hung over Franci's
cutting table

Women sewing shrouds for the Prague Burial Society, c. 1780
(Courtesy of the Jewish Museum of Prague)

DR. OSKAR DONATH,

BÖHMISCHE DORFJUDEN

JÜDISCHER
BUCH u. KUNSTVERLAG
MAX HICKL
BRÜNN.

A 19th-century Jewish peddler
(Courtesy of the Leo Baeck Institute)

The town of Brtnice c. 1905, with
the synagogue in the foreground
and the castle on the hill
*(Courtesy of the Jewish Museum
of Prague)*

The city of Iglau in the 1860s
(Courtesy of the Jihlava District Museum)

The plaque commemorating Gustav Mahler in Jihlava

Pepi Sachsel in Kolín, 1902

Kolín's Golden Lane

Kolín's wine and espresso bar
"At the Rabbi's"

Opposite:
Advertisement for
Moric Schiller
in Prague, c. 1905

Elegantní "novotiny" pro cestovní a lázeňskou sezonu

v prvním obchodním domě

se zbožím hedvábným a modním

MORIC SCHILLER

Příkopy, 9 a ll nové. * PRAHA * Příkopy, 9 a ll nové.

Vzorky franko.

Lieutenant Emil Rabinek in the early 1900s in Graz

Pepi (*standing*) and a friend in Prague

Emil's mother, Fanny Rabinek, her maid, and Pepi Weigert during the First World War

Pepi and Franzi in 1922 in Prague

Emil Rabinek in 1923 in Prague

Cousins Franzi and
Peter in Prague, 1923

Cousins Helli, Franzi,
and Kitty in 1926

Číslo 18. (Ročník VII.)   V Praze, dne 30. dubna 1927.   Jednotlivé číslo 1 Kč.

MODNÍ REVUE

Vychází každou sobotu. — Redakce, administrace Praha II., Karlovo nám. 15. — Řídí R. Jelenová.

Telefon 43.241. — Předplácí se na rok Kč 42.—, na půl roku Kč 21.—, na čtvrt roku Kč 10.50, na měsíc Kč 3.60. — Účet pošt. úř. č. 67.224.

Malá roba, sestavená z crepu imprimé a hladkého satinu. K tomu kabátek z otomanu, zdobený týmž materiálem, z něhož je sukně. Podobná kombinace, vhodná k přešití moderních šatů.

Malé roby.

Malé roby jsou toalety, nejužitečnější a nejpotřebnější ženám středních stavů; malé roby jsou šaty těch vlastností, které ženy průměrných a spíše malých, nežli velkých příjmů vyžadují, chtějí-li přes svoje přesně odměřené prostředky býti dobře oblečeny ke všem příležitostem. Jsou to tedy šaty především nenápadné, jak barvou a materiálem, tak střihem i výzdobou. Každá nápadnost se vymstí, neboť upozorňujíce příliš na sebe, nesmírně brzy se okoukají a omrzí nás snad po několika týdnech, zatím co je nezbytno, aby šaty dobrých vlastností, správně volené, těšily celou sezonu, případně celý rok a s malými změnami ještě v sezoně příštího roku.

Malé roby nesmí býti z příliš levného materiálu, aby nám nepřišly příliš draho. Je to paradox, ale pravdivý, protože levná látka nikdy nedá našim šatům a jejich střihu té jednoduché elegance, jaké potřebujeme, jdeme-li do společnosti, na návštěvu, do koncertu, účastníme-li se, ne právě sice slavnostních, ale také ne zase úplně všedních společenských událostí, při nichž dobré oblečení je nezbytností.

Vhodným materiálem je jemná vlněná látka, nebo dobré hedvábí. Z vlněných se hodí jemná ripsy, jež se dostanou ve všech barvách, nebo letošní francouzská novinka crépella (krepela), t. j. druh jemného, lehkého, vlněného krepu, také

Front page of *Modní Revue*, April 30, 1927, with an advertisement for Pepi's Salon Weigert
(Courtesy of the Prague Museum of Decorative Arts)

Helena Rissová at a PEN
Club party in 1938

Franci with
Leo Oppenheimer
in Prague in 1937

The last photograph
of Pepi, age 58,
in 1940

Franci at 19
posing for Salon
Weigert publicist

Franci and Joe Solar
on their wedding day, 1940

Jewish women sorting confiscated Jewish property in Prague, c. 1942
(*Courtesy of the Jewish Museum of Prague*)

Opposite: A transport of Czech Jews walk from the train station at Bohušovice to Theresienstadt
(*Courtesy of the Jewish Museum of Prague*)

Opposite, inset: Franci (*left*) and Kitty with British soldier in June 1945

Sewing machines confiscated by the Nazis in Prague warehouse, 1943
(*Courtesy of the Jewish Museum of Prague*)

KITTY

RADIOGRAM

RCA COMMUNICATIONS, INC.

A SERVICE OF RADIO CORPORATION OF AMERICA

RECEIVED AT **64 BROAD STREET**, NEW YORK 4. AT OCT 25 1945 STANDARD TIME

OLI/RY ZC210 *Via* RCA

PRAHA 35 24 1215

NLT PETER SACHSEL HOCHWALT NEWYORK

CABLE YOUR PRIVATE ADRESS STOP I AM THE ONLY ONE LEFT FROM
THE WHOLE FAMILY STOP PLEASE WRITE AT ONCE STOP YOUR
COUSIN FRANCES STOP FRANCES SOLAR PRAHA STAROMESTEKE 15

Telephone: HAnover 2-1811 To secure prompt action on inquiries, this original RADIOGRAM should be presented at the office of RCA COMMUNICATIONS, Inc. In telephone inquiries quote the number preceding the place of origin.

Form 112 TA 134-R

Telegram from Franci
to Peter, October 1945

Peter Scott in
New York, 1945

Franci Solar (*left*) skiing in the Tatras, January 1946

Franci and Kurt Epstein at their wedding, December 21, 1946

Franci and Helen Epstein in New York, August 1948

Pepi recovered slowly from her wounds of childbirth and cautiously felt her way back into active life. In just over one year, she had married, set up her own business, and become a mother. She had wanted to feed her baby herself but a breast infection obliged her to turn Franzi over to a wet-nurse. She must have been as unsettled as I remember being sixty years later by the unpredictable nature of motherhood, by the postpartum roller-coaster of hormones and by the simultaneous feelings of connectedness and isolation that attend maternity. She had no models for mothering. Therese Furcht was a faint memory, Aunt Rosa a model of religious fortitude rather than motherliness. The only other older woman she had known well, Fanny Rabinek, had been a *salonière*, preoccupied with her social and intellectual life.

According to all my mother's cousins but Lily, Emil Rabinek was an indifferent and sometimes hostile parent. At Helli's home, they referred to him as *rabiát*, which meant rabid or furious — always raving about something. Central-European culture is not now and never has been child-centered, like the American culture in which I became a mother. Parenting was not deemed a suitable subject for social conversation. It was considered neither intellectual nor creative. It fell into the private domain of women, not the public domain of men.

Emil Rabinek was representative of his generation in assuming that having children should not disturb the course of a man's life. It was Pepi who was atypical in thinking that she could have a child and then resume the course of hers. For a married, middle-class woman to give birth to a child and continue working was unusual if there was no compelling financial reason to do so.

But Pepi did not give up Salon Weigert. She had been raised by a woman who earned her own money and ran her own shop, whose frugal and satisfying life was organized around work. Pepi herself had been making clothes for nearly twenty-five years before she became a mother. Her work was central to her life. It was what had enabled her to leave Kolín's Golden Lane and move to the center of Prague. It was what had anchored her when Emil Rabinek went off to war, and what now eased her transition to motherhood.

That centrality of work and its value as an emotional as well as economic grounding for a woman was passed down from Pepi to Franzi to me, without a word being said. Implicit was the message that relationships change, men come and go, wars erupt, one may be forced to emigrate, but work is a constant. Perhaps sooner than was advisable for her health, Pepi returned to her *salon*.

From a late-twentieth-century point of view, Pepi had an enviable situation: twenty-four-hour childcare; a cook to do marketing and meals; a maid to launder clothes and clean the apartment; a workplace that she owned, one floor below her home. Moreover, the decade of the twenties — the Jazz Age — was a seminal time to be working as a dressmaker in Prague. The "take-over," as Czechs referred to their declaration of independence, had called for an overthrow of everything Austrian, for a new language, new ideas, and new symbols.

Yet the Great War, the take-over, and women's emancipation combined had not changed the importance of dressing well in Prague. Attire continued to be key and conformity was the rule. There were still dresses appropriate only for morning or afternoon or evening, for the coffeehouse, for the theater, for afternoon *thés dansants*, for the balls that continued to be held in the Republic. *Débutantes* still needed coming-out dresses; brides, large *trousseaux*. When Paul Poiret, the reigning monarch of *haute couture*, decided to stage his first show in Prague in 1924, it confirmed Prague's place on the postwar fashion circuit.

Most women of the Czech middle class could not afford a dress by Paul Poiret. But, as Milena Jesenská instructed her readers, a good local dressmaker was far more valuable than a famous Parisian designer. "A good dressmaker not only understands cut and material but understands the body, knows what it needs, what it can carry, what it can get away with wearing," Jesenská wrote. "She knows it objectively, like a sober professional who measures the immutable proportions of her subject." In the twenties in Prague, there were no star designers but hundreds of good dressmakers. At the bottom of the hierarchy were the "house" seamstresses called *Hausschneiderinnen* who, every fall and spring, came to the client's home for a week, made alterations in whatever clothes needed altering, and sewed new wardrobes for the women of the family. At the top were the *maisons* of Rosenbaum and Hana Podolská, modeled after the *maisons* of Paris.

In between were smaller *salons* like Salon Weigert, run by "little-known dressmakers," Milena Jesenská wrote, "who are technically just as adept as Mr. Poiret (it's some of these very dressmakers who sew for Mr. Poiret) and who ask for one-tenth of what he gets paid for a dress."

By the 1920s, photography and film had democratized the way fashion moved through society. More women saw what Gloria Swanson wore in a single film than had seen what Sarah Bernhardt wore in her entire lifetime. Dozens of international fashion magazines — *Vogue, Harper's Bazaar, L'Officiel* — as well as local Prague ones — *Erstes Prager Modenblatt, Elegantní Praha, Módní svět,* and *Nové pařížské módy* — reproduced the clothes and brought their details home.

Some of Pepi's clients now arrived at the *salon* with photographs. The older ones still ordered the somber, respectable fashions that had prevailed in Prague for years. The more daring took their cues from Chanel and the stylish movie vamps, flappers, and *femmes fatales.* They darkened their eyes with kohl, pulled their hats to their eyebrows, flattened their breasts, bared their arms, and wore flesh-colored stockings that made their legs look naked. During the 1920s, Pepi found that she could act on what she saw in Paris, add to her palette of colors, and widen her range of styles.

In my mother's account, Pepi viewed her *salon* as a place in which she enjoyed creative satisfaction and autonomy at a time when her home life was becoming tumultuous and unpredictable. As he approached the age of fifty, Emil Rabinek was no longer a dashing officer and bachelor-about-town. Korálek & Rabinek had made him a rich man and, in the process, transformed him from a liberal patriarch into what cousin Helli called a "social climber and despot." He came to regard his home as a private temple and expected his wife to tend it, ignoring the fact that Ina — as he continued to call Pepi — ran a business.

Herr Rabinek viewed his books, his carpets, his paintings, and *objets d'art* as testaments to his cultivation. They were proof of his belonging to a civilization he revered as the most highly evolved in the world. He was the kind of man who defined himself by the excellence of his tailor, by the location of his seats at the opera, by the brand of cigarettes — Egyptische — that he smoked. His piano was an altar that was polished till it gleamed. His dinner was sacred. It had to be perfectly cooked, accompanied by the correct wines, and elegantly served. When Emil found his roast overdone or his piano undusted, he turned his sarcasm on his wife. Was it really so difficult to manage a household? Was it too much to ask that he not be embarrassed in front of his guests?

It is a bleak and all too persistent marital scenario. During their long affair, Emil Rabinek and Pepi Weigert had dined out and at the homes of friends. When Fanny moved in with Pepi during the war, she had taken over the housekeeping. But marriage altered the equation of the Rabineks' relationship. Emil became by far the more powerful partner, the one who demanded and sulked and set the tenor of the couple's life. Every week, he upbraided Pepi for something that had gone wrong. Every few months, he fired one of the servants. Pepi, the charming, competent businesswoman, became an object of familial pity.

At Kitty's home, people said that Rabinek was killing Pepi. At Peter and Helli's homes, she was the object of much discussion and worry. "He terrorized his wife in a way that might have been common in Poland but was unheard of in a good Jewish family in Prague," said Helli, with particular vehemence. "He was nothing but a womanizer. You know why the servants had to leave? Because he molested them! He even tried to have affairs with Pepi's customers! I wish you'd write about something else."

Perhaps it is because I never knew my grandfather that I am able to absorb and ponder their characterizations as though Rabinek were a character in a novel. I feel for my mother, who had to cope with the pain and shame of having such a father, and for my grandmother, who had to live with him. Psychological abuse did not constitute grounds for divorce and, by all accounts, Pepi coped with it by taking refuge in her work. She was regarded by her extended family as a workaholic, an excellent dressmaker and saleswoman, and Helli's family even believed that Rabinek had married her because he knew she would always earn a living.

The plucky young woman who had set out alone for Prague from Kolín in 1904, the excited young buyer in Paris, the worldly young mistress of World War I were now history. During the first decade of her marriage, Pepi was undermined and bullied by her husband and transformed into a clingy, complaining wife. She was plagued by headaches and stomach troubles. Her recurrent attacks of agoraphobia — the malady that Emil had found so charming in his mistress — were now an annoyance to her husband. He took her to a hypnotist in Vienna and when that did not work, sent her away for cures at Bad Ischl and Marienbad. From the time Franzi was a baby, Pepi took her daughter with her.

During the twenties, when she was a little girl and long before she could understand what it meant, my mother became her mother's protector, best friend, and confidante, what therapists would later call "a parentified child." She also became the battlefield on which Emil and Pepi Rabinek fought.

Emil never got over his disappointment that his daughter was not a boy. He called her Franzi, or "Franky," rather than the more ladylike "Fanny" and took her to his barber to have her hair cut. He brought home pieces of electrical equipment from his office for her to play with rather than dolls and taught her how to splice wires. On their vacations in the Tyrolian Alps, he taught Franzi to climb trees, threw her into the water so that she would learn to swim, and bought her German *Lederhosen* — at a time when no respectable woman or girl in Prague wore pants and *Lederhosen* were a symbol of *Volksdeutsch*, or "ethnic German," identification.

Fatherhood also brought out in Emil Rabinek a passionate ambition for his child. As a young Viennese, he had grown up in a home that revered aristocratic titles as well as literary and artistic reputations and he wanted Franzi to be blessed with both. Like the Sleeping Beauty's father, who invited the fairy godmothers to celebrate his daughter's birth, he had invited prominent

Prague intellectuals of his acquaintance to her christening, including Max Brod and Egon Erwin Kisch. No child of his would ever suffer the handicaps he had suffered as a Jewish child. His two older sisters in Vienna — one a Lutheran, one a Catholic — were raising their children as Christians. Every Christmas, he bought and decorated a Christmas tree, ate the traditional Czech meal of fried carp and roasted goose, and exchanged gifts with his family. He insisted to Ina that his daughter be kept ignorant of any personal connection with Judaism even though Pepi's two brothers and their families remained nominal, if unobservant, Jews.

Pepi acceded to Emil's wishes. Although she rarely missed a visit to Aunt Rosa's grave on Yom Kippur, Pepi never went to synagogue and remembered her aunt's religious tradition as rigid and old-fashioned, hardly worth another battle against her husband. They were arguing regularly by the time their daughter could understand and reinforced their words with the traditional gendered gestures. Emil had angry outbursts; Pepi responded with tears. Emil walked out; Pepi retreated to bed. Franzi grew up watching her parents storming off into separate bedrooms, downing mysterious pills, brandishing the old army revolver that Emil Rabinek kept in his desk.

Apart from recalling those parental threats of suicide, my mother rarely talked about her childhood. On those occasions when I asked, she described herself — in a disparaging tone of voice — as "a spoiled little rich girl." The Rabineks did not belong to the circle of ultrarich Prague Jews who built themselves palaces in the Prague suburb of Bubeneč but Franzi grew up with her own room, her own nurse, then her own governess. Even after her father had lost his money, she was encouraged to think of herself as part of Prague's *zlatá mládež*, or golden youth, at a time when hunger and homelessness were prevalent among Prague's poor. I have had to piece together the picture of privilege from occasional, almost apologetic, references to riding horses and skiing in the Alps, but the visual documents I possess of my mother's childhood were captured by photographers in a succession of spa towns and by a painter in Prague.

His portrait, the only surviving piece of art from my grand-parents' Prague living room — hidden from the Nazis, smuggled out of Communist Czechoslovakia years later by my mother — shows a grave little girl with the family's lap dog. Neither Therese nor Pepi had been painted or photographed as children. They had grown up in a traditional Jewish culture that did not value art, where most people had no discretionary income, and where the only portraits on the wall were of the biblical patriarchs and philanthropists like Moses Montefiore. The portrait identifies my mother as an assimilated child. She lived on a busy artery of the capital and regarded the city — its river, bridges, castle, islands, churches — as her own.

In Brtnice and Kolín, under the continual surveillance of their small communities and bound by their traditions, neither Therese nor Pepi had ever set foot inside a church. In Prague, church was a regular stop on Franzi's daily outing, along with her walk in the park and her midmorning cup of hot cocoa. From the time she was a toddler, she watched her nurses — devout Czech girls from the countryside with names like Anna, Vlasta, and Mařenka — drop to their knees, cross themselves, and murmur their Paternosters and Ave Marias. Like so many children of Prague's Jewish middle class who had no religious rituals of their own, my mother came to love the vaulted church ceilings, the smell of incense, the stained glass, the Latin chants, and flowing priestly robes. Although Masaryk and most of the new Czech leadership wanted to rid Prague of Rome they could not expunge three hundred years of Jesuit influence in Prague. Catholicism was embedded in stone from the statues of the saints on the old Charles Bridge to the high towers of its cathedrals, encoded in the daily chime of church bells and the processions and feasts of the Christian calendar.

It was from her Czech nurses that my mother learned her first words, the words for food and toys and the people she loved. It was in Czech that she learned to say her prayers at night and heard the stories of the saints, original sin, and the Immaculate Conception. She attended mass, went to confession, celebrated her name day as well as her birthday, St. Nicholas Day, Christmas,

St. Stephen's Day, Epiphany, Easter, and Pentecost. Yet German was the language in which she usually spoke to her parents, since her father steadfastly refused to speak Czech.

When, in 1925, Franzi turned five, Emil Rabinek began to investigate Prague's schools. Although he viewed childcare as Pepi's responsibility, he — like almost every Prague patriarch — made all key decisions and education was important to him. Franzi was bright, precocious, like the women in his Viennese family, and likely to go to university. His cousin Berta was in the first sizable group of women to graduate from medical school; his cousin Greta was among the first group of women to become pharmacists. There were no private schools in the Republic, in keeping with the notion that all children should have an equal start in life. A Czech school was out of the question for Rabinek. But he realized that a German school would be retrograde in the new Republic. Besides, Franzi spoke German at home. The logical choice, he later told her, was the newly established *Ecole française de Prague.*

By the mid-twenties, France had become a political as well as cultural presence in Czechoslovakia. One year earlier, the two countries had signed an agreement that guaranteed French intervention in the event that the new state was attacked by Germany. The French government subsidized a school in Prague where the children of all French and Czechoslovak government employees and White Russian refugees were accepted tuition free and others could attend for a fee. It was coeducational, with small classes and bright, young French teachers who were thought more progressive than their Czech and German counterparts. Some families sent their children there because they were employees of the state. Some wanted their children to be educated in a "world" culture that was not German. Some were simply snobs who preferred the closest thing in Prague to a private school.

In the fall of 1925, Franzi entered the Ecole Française and, with the addition of some Czech language and history, received an education similar to one she would have had in Paris, complete with *dictées* and *explications de textes* and the *Fables* of La Fontaine. The idioms in which she couched her thoughts became

French. So did her grammar, her aesthetic sense, her perception of adults and children, of men and women, of the ways of the world. Her favorite books were soon Colette's Claudine series. Her favorite painters were the French Impressionists. The French orientation of her mother's *salon* reinforced the idea that French was best and, as a girl, Franci (as she now spelled her name) became a Francophile.

Franci loved the *école* and performed well, with never a poor report card until the third grade. It was that year, when she was eight years old, that religious instruction was introduced. Twice a week, the children were divided into two groups, with the Catholics receiving instruction from a priest and the Jews, from a rabbi. Franci was part of the Catholic group, which soon began to taunt the Jewish children with the antisemitic jingle:

> Jew, Jew, Jewish Jew,
> You have a poison tail.
> They'll hack it off
> and put it in a sock,
> Jew, Jew, Jewish Jew.

I imagine that she sang the ditty with all the glee of an eight-year-old. Although she looked more like her mother, Franci behaved more like her father: bossy, entitled, sure of herself. For days, she followed her classmate Margit, singing, so doggedly that Margit finally broke down in tears and told her teacher, who told her mother, who telephoned the Rabineks.

The incident and its aftermath evoked the only discussion of Judaism my mother remembered of her childhood. Emil Rabinek asked his daughter to explain what had happened, then required her to write an apology to Margit. He did not tell Franci, whose only personal link to Judaism was an occasional visit with her mother to Aunt Rosa's grave, that she herself was a Jew. In Rabinek's mind, Franci had been baptized a Catholic. For him, it was a simple case of misbehavior. But the issue of the ditty surfaced again when her uncle Emil Sachsel was told of it over dinner, and argued heatedly that this was a scandal, that such idiotic things could only happen when a child was brought up not knowing where she came from.

Fifty years later, my mother could still recall the violence of that argument between her favorite uncle, her father, and her mother, who tried to defend her daughter. That ditty, framed by the historical events that followed, haunted Franci and, fifty years later, she tracked down Margit — who had escaped the war by emigrating to Cuba — to apologize. Margit herself could not remember the incident but it loomed in my mother's memories, overshadowing the more customary ones that mothers pass on to their daughters. I rarely heard about Franci's piano or dancing or gymnastics lessons, or the games or foods my mother enjoyed in her childhood. It was as though the war had discredited all of that. It was not useful or valuable and she did not wish to pass it on to me.

An excellent student, she skipped fifth grade and went straight into *lycée*. She was confirmed into the Catholic Church along with her friends but, shortly after, told her father that she believed none of what she had been taught and wished to be registered on the census as *konfessionslos*, without religion. Emil Rabinek had no objection. Franci was baptized. She would face no professional obstacles as a Jew; that was the important thing. Following the procedures of the Republic, he wrote, in 1932, to the Prague municipality asking that his daughter's religion be formally changed from Catholic to agnostic and she was subsequently excused from all further religious instruction.

By the time children entered *lycée* in Prague, it was customary for them to join a youth group. Many joined a branch of Sokol, the national Czech sports association. Children of Social Democrats joined the Red Falcon. Children of Zionists joined Blau-Weiss or the Maccabi. Some joined the Young Communists, others the Scouts. My mother rode horses with the equestrian Sokol but otherwise joined no group. After school, she had piano lessons, riding lessons, gymnastics. During the summers, she traveled abroad with her parents until for the first time she went to summer camp.

Her father chose a German camp, located in the Sudetenland. That summer of 1932, she corresponded with her parents for the first time, writing her letters in the German she customarily spoke with them. Almost every one of her sentences contained a spelling error — a predictable enough phenomenon given that she had never studied German in school but an unpleasant surprise for Herr Rabinek. He was furious. How could he have allowed his daughter to reach the age of twelve without learning to spell? How would she write exams for university? She would have to transfer to a German *gymnasium*. No matter how logically Franci and Pepi argued for the *lycée,* for France, for seven years of friendships and belonging, his mind was made up. It was too late to transfer his daughter this year but she would continue her education in German.

Emil Rabinek had even less patience than usual during that fall and winter of 1932. The ripple effect of the American stock market crash of 1929 hit Europe full force. It was no longer possible to ignore the beggars in every street. Some of his friends at the Casino were facing bankruptcy; some committed suicide. Much of Czechoslovakia's international trade had collapsed or was in the final stages of collapsing, causing widespread business failures and unemployment. The newspapers were filled with accounts of starving, homeless people, people living in cellars, in abandoned train cars, in the cliffs outside Prague, and in the open air. In Germany, where unemployment reached five million, there was disturbing news of the success of the National Socialist Party and their leader, Adolf Hitler. During those weeks when my mother had written her first misspelled letters home, the Nazis had been elected the largest party in the German legislature.

Franci would later remember 1932 as the year her childhood ended. Although adults did not discuss current events with children and children did not read newspapers, she understood that things were going very wrong. First, Korálek & Rabinek lost its shipyard, then the partnership was forced to declare bankruptcy, then Emil Rabinek no longer went to his office. Once, in the mass of notes I have of interviews with my mother, she makes reference to her father's "nervous breakdown." What her cousins and the Prague telephone directory confirm is that the Rabineks could no longer afford their apartment. Sometime that year, they and Salon Weigert moved to a smaller one on Vodičková, next to the Lucerna Palace off Wenceslas Square.

In the fall of 1933, at the age of thirteen, Franci began attending the *Deutsches Staatsrealgymnasium* on Štepánská Street. She arrived angry and was treated with the indifference customary in a school where others have been classmates for years. In 1933, the only other new students entering the German high school were the children of German refugees, who could not speak Czech. Hitler was now chancellor of Germany; Prague had become a safe haven. Franzi (as she now spelled her name) fit in neither with the German Jewish students nor the increasingly pro-Nazi Gentiles — each with their own clubs and sports activities and dancing classes — and the only friend she made was a girl whose father was jailed in Berlin. She missed the *lycée* and began to spend more and more time assisting her mother in her *salon*.

Salon Weigert became the center of all the Rabineks' lives. Although it did not bring in the high income of Emil Rabinek's firm, Prague women continued to buy expensive clothes right through the worst of the Depression. Herr Rabinek, who had regarded the *salon* as his feminist indulgence, was now dependent on its income. He became Salon Weigert's bookkeeper and Franzi, its informal apprentice. Mother and daughter shared a fascination with fashion and Franzi soon became more interested in studying dress design than in studying for school. By the time she was in her fourth year, she decided that she would not complete *gymnasium*. Few girls did unless they intended to study at the university and university paled beside the *salon*.

Emil Rabinek had wanted his daughter to attend university but he recognized that she was passionate about fashion. The state of their finances spoke louder than words. The reserve lieutenant and electrical engineer with a higher education was now unemployed. Pepi, who had left school at fourteen, was supporting the family. She was now fifty-one and eager to pass on what she had learned to her daughter. Franzi jumped at the promise of eventually taking over the *salon*. It was agreed that Franzi would drop out of *gymnasium* but continue to study languages, adding English to French, German, and Czech. She would also take courses in fashion illustration and dress design and complete a formal apprenticeship at Salon Weigert. At fifteen, like Pepi thirty-eight years earlier, my mother entered the working world.

11

~

At fifteen, my mother said with sarcasm, she was a frivolous human being, interested in dancing, skiing, boys, and the *salon*. In *that* order. That was hard for me to imagine. The Frances I knew was sometimes an invalid, sometimes a soldier, but always intense, urgent, engaged with the world. There was not a trace of frivolity in her. Even her laugh — the laugh she claimed to have lost in the war — exuded tension. She studied the newspaper, voted in every election, was a serious reader. I never saw her entirely relaxed or carefree. But in 1935, 1936, 1937, while day after day fascism advanced in Europe, my mother claimed, she ignored the news and watched Fred Astaire and Ginger Rogers; ignored Hitler and hummed Gershwin and Irving Berlin; steeped herself in fashion and danced away the afternoons, oblivious to the greater world.

Her judgment of her younger self was unforgiving and verged on contempt. She had been naive, careless, unaware — the very opposite of what she was now. She had barely looked at newspapers, and when people discussed developments within Germany, she had paid little attention. Politics, particularly the politics of Czechoslovakia, had not gripped her in adolescence. She had embarked on an apprenticeship in fashion design and her mind was focused on clothes. After hours, she lived to have a good time.

It was from my aunt Kitty that I learned the rituals of their adolescence: long walks along the river; cocoa and cake in their favorite *cukrárna;* swim practice — Franci in breaststroke, Kitty in crawl — three or four times a week; sneaking into the movies by dressing in their most elegant clothes and putting on lipstick to make themselves look older. Together, the two girls raided Emil Rabinek's collection of erotic drawings from Belgium. Together, they learned to masturbate with candles. But it was not until I went through the album of photographs my mother had brought from Prague, poring over photo after photo of a laughing girl skiing or clowning with friends, that I began to see the person that my mother dismissed. Most of the small black-and-white snapshots were unmarked but as I examined each for clues to people and place, I found names my mother never mentioned. On the back of one, I found the notation "Robert Císař, First proposal, 1936." She was sixteen years old. It was the first I'd ever heard of it.

As I played back audiotaped interviews of Frances and mulled over my mother's brittle tone of voice when she described her prewar self, I realized that her years in the camps had transformed a normal, happy adolescence into something shameful. She had come to discredit her years as a teenager, to bury her memories of friends, boyfriends, adventures. It was shame that accounted for her silence in place of stories and she was not alone. Silence about "before-the-war" was widespread in her generation. Other people blamed them and they sometimes blamed themselves for not having seen what was obvious, for having denied or excused or delayed when action was required.

It is by now a truism that the victim is often blamed for the crime. Perpetrators tend to deny, repress, forget. Victims attempt to master trauma by assuming responsibility for it. That is the way I understand Frances's harsh judgment of herself as a girl. And there is another peculiar thing: although she knew almost nothing about Judaism, my mother seemed to have inherited an idea long ensconced in rabbinic tradition and passed down from Aunt Rosa to Pepi: that human misfortune is the consequence of sin.

By the time I was old enough to understand her, the narrative of her life that Frances told featured a spoiled, misguided, ignorant teenager for whom the concentration camps served as a kind of university. The war was what had transformed her into a human being. It was, I thought, a wild, irrational take on the Holocaust, one that depended on a portrait of herself as a careless dilettante. I did not believe it and, luckily, there was a living witness. Just as I had turned to Gisela Saudek for a window on Pepi's world, I turned to Helena Hartlová for a window on my mother's.

Helena had arrived in Franci Rabinek's class at the *lycée français* after being held in prison and expelled from school for participating in an anti-Nazi demonstration. She was fifteen then and, because she had been held back and my mother pushed ahead, the two girls wound up as classmates. They hit it off at once. Until then, my mother's most intimate friend had been her cousin. But where Kitty was two years younger than Franci, Helena was two years older. Where Kitty was Jewish *bourgeois*, Helena was Czech avant-garde. And while Kitty never did anything more provocative than throw a tantrum, Helena would soon become a secret courier and a connection.

During the war, my mother was classified a Jew and Helena an Aryan; Franci worked in concentration camps and Helena in the Czech Resistance. When I was born and my father wished to name me after his mother, Helena, my mother agreed because the name evoked her friend. They maintained their friendship even after Franci emigrated to America, while Helena had political difficulties and was placed under house arrest by the Communists. Every time I was in Prague I spent many hours with her, listening to a woman who was now an invalid but who retained a backbone of steel.

"Franci was immeasurably joyful," Helena reminded me. "She understood what fun was — you couldn't find a better companion. We didn't talk about books although we both read a lot. We didn't ask each other a lot of questions or have intimate discussions. We went to the theater. We went to the movies. And we went dancing. We liked to go to tea dances two or three times a week, not to meet men but because we loved to dance. The Spanish tango was popular. And the foxtrot, fast waltz, slow waltz, polka. You'd be surprised: your mother danced a fantastic tango."

Your mother danced a fantastic tango. The words ricocheted wildly in my brain: *Mother! Tango!* Helena lives in what was once her family's summer house outside Prague where, during the war, she hid fugitives. There is a constant tension in her that reminds me of Frances and the same impatience with imposters or fools. With Helena, there is an additional twist to the grueling generational story: her daughter, one year older than I and surely as bound to her mother as I was to mine, is dead. She hanged herself in the toolshed not far from where I was sitting when she was twenty, after she had been denied admission to university for "political unreliability."

Clara's suicide almost killed the woman who had survived Gestapo and Communist interrogations. Now in her seventies, Helena's health is gone. She cannot walk far or eat much. The highs and lows of twentieth-century Czech history have exhausted her. But when Helena laughs, it is easy to see the girl who was Franci's best friend: an intelligent, capable, mature young woman growing up in Prague during the First Republic, in that small window of time when the city was the centerpiece of Central Europe.

Like my mother, Helena was an only child. Her mother, like Pepi, suffered from recurrent depression and was frequently in sanatoria. Her father, who moved in government circles, was responsible for her upbringing. Antonin Hartl was an internationalist and freethinker who did not differentiate for his daughter between Christian and Jew. As was fairly typical of his generation of Czech Catholic intellectuals, he gave his daughter no religious education but insisted she learn languages. At home, he spoke to her in Russian and when Franci was sent to *gymnasium* to improve her German, he sent Helena to the Sudetenland to work on hers. In 1937, both girls' language-obsessed fathers enrolled them at the Prague English Grammar School.

Helena introduced Franci to the local art scene, to theater people, to cafés where intellectuals talked politics. Her father worked as a librarian for the Ministry of Foreign Affairs and also as an editor at a prominent publishing house. He was a member of the Společenský Klub, or Social Club, on Příkopy, a hub of cultural life where many of the most interesting figures of the Republic congregated. Helena had grown up among diplomats, writers, artists, and theater people. She knew Jiří Voskovec and Jan Werich, the satirical duo that performed the most sophisticated theater in Prague, and was especially friendly with their musicians.

Helena and Franci spent many hours at the thousand-seat Liberated Theater, which was located just down the block from the Rabineks' house, hanging out to watch rehearsals or running errands for the company. Voskovec and Werich were among Hitler's earliest critics and, in 1933, they produced a satirical play called *The Ass and the Shadow* that was based on a Greek fable but was a thinly veiled attack on fascism. When the ass was uncertain in the original, he spoke in a loud voice. In their play, the ass spoke with Hitler's voice. The German embassy filed a formal complaint, the right-wing German and Czech press began a campaign of denunciation, and the Czech fascist organization pasted their "Nothing but the Nation" stickers over the Liberated Theater's street posters. They created a countersticker and Helena and Franci were among the runners who pasted it up all over Prague.

In Helena's view, Franci was anything but frivolous. Unlike most of Prague's gilded youth, she worked and was focused on training to become a dress designer and take over Salon Weigert. When they went to the theater, Franci would critique the costumes and comment on the actresses who bought clothes from her mother. At the movies, even as she tried to grasp the witty American lyrics of "Let's Face the Music and Dance," she was preoccupied with Ginger's clothes: Was that collar made of fur or feathers? Was the sleeve cut straight or on the bias? Was the fabric studded with sequins or beads? On the ski slopes and in cafés, she noted the look of new fabrics or unusual colors.

Franci's approach to fashion as well as her expectations of work were very different from her mother's. For Pepi, fashion had been her only means of earning a respectable living; for Franci, fashion was a calling, a choice and an art. At the time she began to work in the *salon,* women composed one-fourth of *gymnasium* students, 15 percent of those at university, and — now that the teaching profession was open to women of all religious denominations and allowed for marriage — more than half the students at pedagogical schools.

Franci took for granted the predominance in the fashion world of women like Callot Soeurs, Madame Vionnet, and Lanvin. The reigning designer of the time was Gabrielle Chanel and Franci put her photograph beside those of Greta Garbo and Ginger Rogers on the walls of her bedroom. She knew every detail of her story: how Chanel had been an orphan raised by an elderly aunt, like Pepi, how her first boutique had been bankrolled by a lover, how she started out adapting sailor suits in Deauville. Chanel now ran a fashion empire employing four thousand people, but — more impressive to my mother — she was viewed as an artist.

A year after she left *gymnasium,* Franci was immersed in work at Salon Weigert, perfecting the basics of sewing and cutting, assisting her mother at fittings, learning the importance of patience, discretion, and tact when dealing with a variety of different bodies, different personalities, and different ideas about dress. In 1936, she took courses in illustration. The plan was, Helena told me, that Franci would finish her training in Paris.

Just as Helena drew her friend into the world of politics and the arts, Franci drew Helena into the world of fashion. Since Helena often attended consular receptions and parties with her father, she was ideally suited to become Pepi's *mannequin de ville,* a well-connected young woman who was provided with free clothes and accessories by a *couturière* and, in exchange, served as her walking advertisement. Helena wore dresses on short-term loan from Salon Weigert that were then returned and sold to other people.

"I remember Pepi in the *salon* as small, chubby, very, very smart, with penetrating eyes," Helena told me. "She employed maybe eight people at the time and it was clear to me that she enjoyed her work. But she was not as successful as she wished. The richest women in Prague would go to Hana Podolská, only a few houses away. Podolská knew how to get publicity. Your grandmother didn't. So I brought in business. I was the best-dressed woman in Prague and each time I had on something different. Women would ask where I had my clothes made and I would say, 'Here in Prague.' 'Not in Paris?' they'd say. 'Here in Prague?' and I'd say yes. 'And will you tell us where?' Well, I don't know, I'd say, and they'd all be terribly curious and badger me until, with a show of reluctance, I'd tell them your grandmother's name."

The game Helena played with the wealthy wives of Prague was but the beginning of what would become a far greater subterfuge. In 1936, when she was eighteen, she received a message from a man at the Czech Ministry of Defense who knew she held a diplomatic passport and that she was proficient at languages. At a meeting that she kept secret from my mother, Helena was asked to join a group that was forming to work against the Nazis. Improbably, training began in the basement of the building on Vodičková Street where Salon Weigert was located. There, a few floors below the workroom where Franci was learning to put together clothes, Helena was secretly learning self-defense, how to forge documents, how to handle interrogation. Her mission was to carry film and documents to Czechs in London who were trying to counter Nazi propaganda about the plight of the Sudeten Germans.

The three million Sudeten Germans were the descendants of those German colonists who had migrated to Bohemia since the twelfth century. Until 1918, they had enjoyed the benefits of belonging to the majority culture. Then, the founding of the Czechoslovak Republic changed the state language from German to Czech and transformed them from an elite into a minority.

Many Sudeten Germans felt they had become second-class citizens. Although Masaryk's Republic offered its minorities the most generous civil rights in all of Central Europe, Sudeten Germans felt victimized by the economic and political policies of the Czech government. In the twenties, most had voted for democratic parties but, by 1933, they were increasingly attracted to Nazism. When Hitler began demanding more "living space" for the German people, the Czechoslovak Supreme Court outlawed the Nazi Party in Czechoslovakia. Any political party that developed a program threatening the territorial integrity of the state, it ruled, must forfeit its existence. Many Sudeten Germans then switched their allegiance to the Sudeten German Party, headed by a photogenic former gym teacher, Konrad Henlein.

Konrad Henlein was careful to attenuate his admiration for Hitler and Nazism. While declaring his loyalty to the Czechoslovak Republic, he characterized his movement as an organization for Germans interested in national community and the Christian concept of the world. He made political capital of the second-class status of Sudetens. He railed against the indignity of having to deal with railway clerks and postmen who spoke only Czech; he claimed that German schools and hospitals were decaying while new Czech ones were being built. The border regions, he insisted, had never recovered from the worldwide economic depression. While Czech citizens in the interior were thriving, Germans in the border regions were living on welfare.

By the mid-1930s, Henlein had hundreds of thousands of followers. They tuned out of Czech broadcasts and tuned in to German radio. They painted swastikas on walls and fences and wore them in their suit lapels even though the symbol was banned by the government. Children and students wore the white knee-socks and gray shirts of the Sudeten German Party and saluted their leaders with an outstretched right arm and a *Sieg Heil*. Housewives hung portraits of Henlein on their walls and called him *Führer*. Jewish and Czech shops began to be boycotted in the Sudetenland. Czech and even ethnic German Socialists and Communists were regularly attacked in the streets.

In Germany, Nazi propaganda chief Josef Goebbels cranked

out hundreds of stories about the suffering of the Sudeten Germans in the Czechoslovak Republic. In Goebbels's propaganda, the Czechs were depicted as preparing a genocide of Sudeten Germans at a time when the Czechoslovak government was actually bending over backward to negotiate with Henlein. Goebbels aimed to make Sudeten Germans see Hitler as their protector and to arouse public opinion in Britain and France, where many people viewed Czechoslovakia as an island of democracy in an increasingly fascist continent. The documentation Helena would carry to London was designed to counteract Goebbels and to show the British press that Henlein was working closely with the Nazis, that the Sudeten Germans constituted a fifth column and a threat to Czechoslovak democracy. Unlike most of her generation and unlike most of the population of Prague, Helena's life centered around her political work.

Franci's life centered around Salon Weigert. She was her mother's business partner and fellow breadwinner in a family where the patriarch had abdicated. After losing his business, Emil Rabinek never worked for himself again. He kept the books for Salon Weigert but otherwise led the life of what Pepi's relatives disparaged as a coffeehouse Jew, who talked rather than worked and sponged off relatives and friends. He no longer frequented the Casino, since his club had been turned into a boisterous beer hall by Prague Henleinists. With no professional or social life to speak of, his womanizing became blatant. Within the family, Herr Rabinek was rumored to have propositioned more than a few of Pepi's clients and was known to be conducting a long affair with the wife of a local manufacturer. Every week, the two met at the racetrack, Kitty told me, at one of the fancy hotels that let rooms by the hour as well as by the week. It was impossible to keep the scandal a secret from Franci or Pepi. They tried to find refuge in their work.

As an apprentice to her mother, Franci studied the fundamentals of sewing, but learned the etiquette of doing business with fabric merchants and Paris *maisons,* and the strategies sometimes necessary for obtaining payment for her work. She became an accomplished saleswoman and, like Helena, a traveler to Paris, Vienna, Dresden, Berlin. There, in the evenings, she attended the theater and the best cafés to see what well-dressed women were wearing.

In the Czechoslovak Republic, as in Germany, France, and Austria, the fashion world was oblivious to politics. It had thrived throughout the First World War, through the Depression, through the inflation that followed. Now fashion went its way, impervious to Hitler.

So, for the most part, did the Czech nation. Emil Rabinek dismissed Nazism as a temporary phenomenon, as did most Czechs, whether they were cab drivers, scholars, or experts in international affairs. Before 1933, many Social Democrats like my grandfather declared that Germany was not Italy: it could never come under the sway of fascism. After Hitler came to power, they referred to Hitler as "that clown" and viewed Nazism as a temporary Prussian aberration, blaming the press for exaggerating his power. When Hitler left the League of Nations, began to remilitarize, and occupied the Rhineland, Czechs deplored its weakness but boasted of their army, one of the best equipped in Europe. In Prague cafés, there was more talk of the Spanish Civil War than of the danger looming just across the border.

Czech citizens took great pride in the fact that the Republic had mutual defense treaties with both the Soviet Union and France. Were France to come to Czechoslovakia's defense, they believed, she would be backed up by Britain. The Western powers were staunch backers of the only "beacon of democracy" in Central Europe. The Republic was a model of stable prosperity that had, in 1935, witnessed the smoothest of transitions from the government of its founding president, Thomas G. Masaryk, to the succeeding government of Edvard Beneš. Czechs felt nostalgia for the "Old Professor" and great sadness when he died two years later but their confidence in the security of the country he had founded was not in question. Hitler, said the Prague man on the street, was a lot of noise.

That's what Franci believed too. Although Helena was actively anti-Nazi, she said little about Hitler and nothing at all about her secret work. Franci did not follow the newspaper articles on disturbances in the border regions or Henlein's endless speeches and barely took note of the thousands of German refugees — Jews and non-Jews — who had fled Germany and were living in Prague. She would later remember not their presence in the cafés or their many émigré journals, but that her father had found their hawking of pens and matches a nuisance.

Pepi saw in the German refugees yet another version of Jewish victims when they rang the doorbell of Salon Weigert and always, my mother said, found something to buy from each. Franci, on the other hand, felt no identification with them or their situation. They were Prussian — not Czech. Their pronunciation of German betrayed a quality of sternness that she and her father found ridiculous.

Franci and Pepi still traveled regularly to Berlin, which had retained its status as a fashion center in those first years of Nazi rule. They were there during the 1936 Olympics, when Konrad Henlein was publicly awarded Germany's highest decoration and secretly met with Hitler. The city was festooned with swastikas and there were signs posted at the doorways of some shops that read Jews Not Wanted but Franci thought of herself as a Czech, not a Jew, and ignored them. Like so many first-generation Czechoslovaks, she took great pride in her citizenship. The Republic was just two years older than she was: its modern history began in 1918. Franci was taught in Prague's French school that democracy and freedom were precious and fragile states of being. The Czechs had been denied their freedom under the Austrians for three hundred years. Hers was a privileged generation.

Only years later would Franci recall that her uncle Rudolf Sachsel, who had accompanied them to Berlin on business of his own, had burst into tears after a detachment of soldiers marched by. She ascribed his reaction to senility. He was an old man, easily upset. She saw no atrocities, no smashed windows or Jews being dragged away by their hair. They were staying in a good hotel. They encountered no problems. Franci adopted her father's view that the press was in the business of selling sensation.

Several months later, Franci returned to Berlin to wrap up business for Salon Weigert. She was seventeen, a very young woman to be traveling anywhere alone, not to speak of Nazi Germany. Pepi liked to give her daughter all the freedom Aunt Rosa had denied her as a young woman but was concerned enough to arrange for Franci to stay in Berlin with friends of friends, the Josephs.

The Joseph family — two sisters and their mother — lived in an eight-room apartment. The father of the family had died and they told Franci that they were planning to emigrate to America. Since the declaration of the Nuremberg Laws, they said, Jews were not considered German citizens. All professions and positions were barred to them. Neighbors and former friends avoided them. Even the medieval miscegenation law had been revived: marriages and liaisons between Jews and citizens of German blood were once again forbidden.

My mother listened politely but did not take in the meaning of what they said. The Josephs were clearly very rich people, judging by their home. It didn't seem as though anyone was threatening them. The only peculiar thing about her stay was that when my mother suggested to Margot, the younger sister, that they go to the movies, Margot refused and insisted that she could not go because Jews were forbidden to attend the cinema. My mother tried to persuade her to go anyway and when Margot would not, Franci went to the movies alone.

"I was completely callous," she would later tell me. "I had no trouble in Berlin. I was a Czech doing business there. There were no signs that said Czechs Not Wanted at the movies. There was no religion on a Czech passport and if there had been it would have said that I was Catholic or an agnostic. I didn't relate to her when she told me she was Jewish. I went out and saw the German version of *Pygmalion* a few blocks away from their apartment at the Ufa Palace on Kurfürstendam. I didn't realize how terribly I behaved. I didn't realize it until camp, until years later. Then, it hit me: Who did I think I was?"

In some ways atypical, in some ways a typical sixteen-year-old, I think now, weighing her words sixty years later. What was *I* like at sixteen, when my mother encouraged me to go off alone into the world? I was almost as ignorant of politics as she had been in Germany, hitchhiking blithely through Europe and Israel, taking rides from any driver who stopped at the side of the

road. Like most adolescents, I believed I was invincible. No sense
of limits, of restrictions, of final endings. I was not so much in-
sensitive as heedless. Why should life have felt any different to my
mother? What was Hitler compared to adolescent willfulness and
a drive toward romantic adventure? It was at sixteen that I fell in
love with a kibbutznik. It was at sixteen that my mother fell in
love on the train home from Berlin. She seldom mentioned Leo,
but after my father died she made a trip to New Orleans to meet
someone she described as an old friend and when she came back,
she talked about the scent of his pipe.

"I first met your mother, together with your grandmother, in
a romantic manner," Leo Oppenheimer wrote me after her death
and I understood immediately why my mother fell in love with
him.

> I boarded an express train at Dresden, my home town,
> where I had been visiting my mother and sister. The train
> had come from Berlin and was very crowded, but I man-
> aged to find a seat in one of the compartments. After a
> while, I stepped out into the corridor to get out of the
> stuffy atmosphere and to look at the scenery which was
> speeding by very fast. The train was lurching heavily
> through some curvilinear railtrack. I was thrown off my
> feet and collided head-on with a young lady who had, at
> this very moment, tried to pass me.
>
> She recognized my embarrassment and after we had
> straightened up, she decided to remain standing in the rail-
> way corridor to look out at the lovely Saxon countryside.
> It was a pleasant afternoon in early fall. I explained to her
> some of the scenery and the small towns that were famil-
> iar to me. Eventually she asked me to join her in the com-
> partment which she occupied, where she introduced me
> to her mother. Before the train's arrival in the Prague-
> Žižkov station, we had exchanged addresses and tele-
> phone numbers.

Leo Oppenheimer was then twenty-three years old, a university student born and raised in Dresden and, like Franci, a thor-

oughly assimilated Jew. He had finished his studies at *gymnasium* in 1933 and had been planning to study law in Heidelberg. But because the Nazis had prohibited the study of law to Jews, he had gone to the University of Zurich. When the Swiss, in turn, introduced their own exclusionary system, Leo left for Paris, where he had an extended vacation but saw no future for himself. Because of the political situation and because Leo had always been interested in buildings and drafting, a family friend recommended that he study architecture in Prague. In January of 1934, he took the three-hour train ride from Dresden to Prague, rented a cheap room in a fifth-floor walk-up, and began his studies at the German Technical Institute.

For Leo Oppenheimer, Prague was what Paris had been for Hemingway a decade earlier. "Prague was my movable feast," he wrote.

> Because I had grown up in Dresden, I was sensitized to one of the most celebrated architectural environments in Europe. In Prague, I discovered equal excellence as well as a set of fundamental civic virtues: generosity, inspiration, sympathy, savoir faire, balance, enlightenment, spontaneity. Note that I listed generosity first: it was a generous community in terms of the maturity, the variety and the vigor of an inclusive cultural spirit. Some of the voices whose echoes I recall reverberating in the chambers and streets of Prague: Mozart, Janáček, Brahms, Dvořák, Stravinsky, Mahler, Čapek, Kafka, Werfel, Mann, Freud, Voltaire, Descartes, Hus, Le Corbusier, Francesco Borromini, Otto Wagner, Albert Einstein, Marx, Dostoyevsky, Felix Mendelssohn. It was a very generous city in terms of the spontaneity of free human exchange and associations, and in terms of its enlightened democratic polity. The grand old philosopher-gentleman, President Masaryk, was still residing on top of the hill across the Vltava and I felt assured that as long as he was on watch, things could not possibly go wrong.
>
> Prague never was a metropolis. It was not western or eastern or northern or southern. It was central. That was

what made it unique. Prague was not a city of extremes — not of size, climate or attitude. It reflected the most tempered and sanguine concerns and accomplishments of European civilization. Architects like to refer to the concept of "city" as a "large house" and Prague was a truly humane large house. That was why I fell in love with it. At the risk of being considered a naive, melodramatic sort of critic, I like to believe that the Prague of 1933–37 was like Periclean Athens.

Leo found my fashionable and multilingual mother a perfect companion with whom to explore this city. But although the way Franci dressed and looked allowed her to pass for twenty-five, Leo realized that she was sixteen — a full seven years younger than himself. A sexual relationship was out of the question with a Jewish teenager from a good family. In the tradition of Central European Jewish men of the assimilated middle class, Leo viewed women like my mother as potential wives — not premarital partners. That was the role of Czech girls. This did not prevent him, however, from escorting my mother and her cousin Kitty about Prague, from visiting the Rabinek household, and from establishing himself in my mother's imagination as the ideal man.

"You said you were curious to know how your mother looked to me and I will try to oblige," he wrote.

My general impression was of a serious, very intelligent, and determined person, mature well in advance of her age, in terms of substantial matters. However, she was emotionally adolescent. I believe your grandmother had a firm influence on her. She was a small woman, very calm but alert and observant and in command. She was the one who kept the family financially afloat and she knew her *métier*. I felt that her primary concern was to prepare her daughter for the rigors of this business and also to benefit from the contributions that Franci was already capable of at this time. Demanding, ambitious, dogmatic. A 100 percent businesswoman. Perhaps not the easiest of mothers to live with; perhaps she had to be this way in order to keep things going.

Your grandfather was a tall man, somewhat stooped, with a skeptical expression on his face, polite, reserved, and very quiet. Your mother mentioned to me that he had inherited a good amount of money and had lost it all in bad business dealings, combined with an irresponsible style of high living. He was retired and seemed to lend a hand in his wife's business. One got the impression that he was outmaneuvered by the two females of the small household and was an example of the Kafkaesque generation of German-Prague Jews of his time: the men caught and lost in the aftermath of the collapse of the Habsburg Empire, the period of severe economic inflation and cultural change, then the onset of Hitlerism. Franci must have been a late child and their only offspring. Altogether a familial setting conducive to neurotic events and conflicts.

The photograph which I am sending you with this letter, taken May 1, 1937, which shows us walking down Riegrovo nábřeží near the National Theater, conveys the image of a quite handsome couple. I have always been very fond of this photograph and the impression it gives. It's been a constant ingredient of my paraphernalia — ever since 1937! I am glad I kept it all these years so I can turn it over to you now. Who knows, given a different scenario than the one which evolved, your name might have been Helen Oppenheimer.

When I look at my mother's face in this photograph, I see an unfamiliar sparkle in her eyes, undoubtedly due to the touch of Leo's hand on her arm. Her posture and attire, even the angle of her hat, are perfect but relaxed. They are walking by the river, two young professionals of their time: the young architect, the young dress designer, very conscious of their style. They look like normal young people in normal times, concerned about appearing chic, oblivious to any danger. My mother believed that Leo had come to Prague because of its architecture. He did not dwell on the fact that, as a Jew, he had been turned away from law school. They sat in cafés, walked in the gardens of Prague. In the summer of 1937, Leo sailed from Cannes to Corsica. Franci and her mother embarked on their biannual buying trip to Paris.

They left Prague by car, with a friend of Pepi's whom my mother described as "a very conscious Jewess." The friend declared that she would not buy a single liter of gasoline in Nazi Germany and insisted on making a detour through Austria and Switzerland, entering France from the south. As they drove through Austria, Franci gazed out the window, tuning out the political discussion and thinking about her life. Pepi was now fifty-five and had decided to transfer the ownership of Salon Weigert to Franci when she turned eighteen. Franci's birthday was February 26 and the occasion called for a coming-of-age gift.

My mother loved to ski almost as much as she loved to dance. Most of the time, with Helena and other friends, she skied in the Krkonoše mountains northeast of Prague or the High Tatras, in Slovakia. Now, driving past the grassy slopes of the Tyrolian Alps, Franci decided that she would ask her parents for a ski vacation in Kitzbühel for her eighteenth birthday.

In February of 1938, while political pundits were taking bets on when Germany would annex Austria, Franci Rabinek set off from Prague to Kitzbühel. She did not change her plans when Austria's chancellor, Kurt von Schuschnigg, was summoned by Hitler and told that unless he appointed several Nazis to his cabinet, his government was doomed. She did not reconsider after conductor Arturo Toscanini, in a gesture of anti-Nazi protest, withdrew from the upcoming Salzburg Festival.

Six days before Franci's birthday, Hitler declared before the Reichstag, "There must be no doubt about one thing. . . . To the interests of the German Reich belong the protection of those German peoples who are not in a position to secure along our frontiers their political and spiritual freedom by their own efforts." It was clear he meant the seven million Germans living in Austria and the three million Sudeten Germans in Czechoslovakia.

One evening in Kitzbühel, a Viennese manufacturer with whom Miss Rabinek was eating dinner suggested gently that she return home. Franci ignored his suggestion. She planned to stay for two full weeks. There were movie stars on the slopes. She was having a great time. She was aware of the antisemitic atmosphere but did not, as she later said, "take it personally." She did not think of herself as a Jew. She was a Czech tourist on vacation.

Four days before Franci was scheduled to return, Emil Rabinek telephoned her hotel and asked her to take the next train home to Prague. But there was a ball the next evening, she argued. She wanted to go dancing. Her father insisted. Franci compromised. She would go from the ball to the train station and catch the early morning train back to Prague.

Just after she returned, Hitler invaded Austria.

12

~

Just how the Rabinek family reacted to the news of Hitler's annexation of Austria is missing from my mother's narrative, for her homecoming was quickly eclipsed by far more dramatic scenes. I see eighteen-year-old Franci brushing off family reproaches and briskly assuming charge of Salon Weigert; Pepi, exhausted by the crisis and estranged from her husband, ceding her business to her daughter and retiring to her bedroom; and Emil Rabinek covering his relief at her return with sarcasm as the German army secured its positions on three sides of the Czechoslovak Republic.

Nazi leaders repeated that Germany had no designs on Czechoslovakia, but it did not take a military strategist to know what would happen next. "London now regards it as only a matter of months before the swastika clasps Czechoslovakia in its arms," read the front page of the *New York Times* just after Hitler annexed Austria. But the Rabineks, like most of Prague's citizens, thought such predictions alarmist and unduly grim. Czechoslovakia was not Austria, they assured one another. It would not fall to Hitler.

Thousands of Austrian refugees now streamed into Prague. Like the German refugees five years earlier, they told what sounded like fantastic stories of beatings, suicides, arrests, and deportations to concentration camps. Prague's refugee organizations and philanthropists hastened to help and house the new arrivals. Newspapers publicized their stories. At the cinemas, newsreels showing elderly Jews being dragged into the street by their hair or forced to their knees scrubbing city sidewalks shocked Czech moviegoers.

The Rabineks worried about their Viennese relatives, even though almost all of them were baptized Christians. Emil's older brothers, Leo and Gustav, had died by then but his older sisters, Gisela Kremer and Gabriela Roger, and their seven children still lived in Austria. They were all working professionals and news of how they were responding to the annexation was confusing.

Although they were reportedly trying to obtain affidavits of financial support from relatives in England and America, Gisela Kremer's pianist daughter Erna was reluctant to abandon her concert career in Austria. Physician Berta, now the mother of twin daughters and newly divorced from a man who was now a Nazi, was also uncertain. Clara, who had once worked as an *au pair* in England, contacted her former employers and left for London. But Felix, an engineer who was in Switzerland the day Hitler invaded, returned to be with his mother in Vienna.

Gabriela's son, Kurt Roger, a composer and professor at the University of Vienna, fled immediately to Switzerland. His sister Greta, her husband, and their daughter, Margaret, waited. His sister Lily was married to Alphonse Hirsch, a German-Jewish investment banker who tried to obtain papers to leave immediately. But he and his family were being detained in Vienna by the Nazis while the bank's holdings were examined.

For my mother, news of her cousins was disturbing but remote. Since Korálek & Rabinek had gone bankrupt and her father had no professional reasons to travel to Vienna, the Rabineks had seen very little of their relatives. They had little knowledge of actual conditions in Vienna. It was easy for Emil Rabinek to conclude that his two older sisters, sixty-eight and seventy, were right in their decision to remain in Austria and that those of their children who chose to emigrate were cowards. He had been a reserve lieutenant in the Austro-Hungarian Army. He had been decorated. He was, he thought, a more authentic Austrian than Hitler. The violence would prove temporary. Of course the Viennese were anti-Semites. Hadn't Hitler learned all he knew in Vienna? But the Germans were basically decent, honest people. There were always hoodlums in periods of transition. But that was no reason to panic and to abandon one's home. If things were as bad as the press made them out to be, Gisela and Gabriela would have come to Prague.

My grandfather's thinking was typical of the men of his generation. In Prague, even Zionists called for solidarity with the Republic in the face of the Nazi threat. They had all served in the Czechoslovak army, many as officers. How could they desert at a time of danger? Between 1933 and 1939, before Britain restricted immigration, fewer than four thousand Jews left Czechoslovakia for Palestine. Apart from some prescient German refugees who began leaving for Paris and the very rich who began moving money to Switzerland, the vast majority of Czech Jews — like their Christian counterparts — remained calm in the face of the crisis. Kurt Weisskopf, then a young Prague journalist, would later describe how during that spring of 1938, people in Prague quoted the famous nineteenth-century Czech saying "We were here before Austria and we will be here after her," adding, "The same goes for Hitler." They disregarded the Nazi's "Horst Wessel" song celebrating the drawing of Jewish blood and sang instead, "The Russians are with us. Our enemies will be smashed by the French."

In the pubs and coffeehouses, pundits pointed to the civil war in Spain — now nearly two years old — as evidence of Nazi weakness. They argued that Hitler had no need for the Sudetenland, that its industries would compete with German ones. They refused to see that by the end of March, 1938, Czechoslovakia was already becoming three countries: fascist Slovakia, democratic Bohemia and Moravia; and the Sudetenland, where Henlein was terrorizing opponents and turning rule of law into a sham. Even in April, when Henlein addressed a roaring crowd in Karlsbad and declared "Like Germans throughout the world, we profess the National Socialist fundamental conceptions of life," the Czech government did not outlaw the party, choosing negotiation over force.

That May of 1938, Franci was thinking about clothes for her fall season: a more feminine figure was coming back into fashion, including a full bosom and longer hair arranged in complicated styles. For my mother and her generation, war was a subject that belonged to history, not to contemporary life. In school, she had been taught that there would be no more European wars after 1918. The League of Nations had been created to ensure peace and Czechoslovakia was one of its staunchest supporters. The major political issue for serious young people in Prague was social equality: whether or not to become a Communist. For a young dress designer, the answer was definitely not. She was now the family breadwinner, the sole support of her elderly parents. The salon was her world.

It was spring. Prague's thousands of lilacs had begun to bloom and lovers were once again strolling slowly along the river. Czechs spilled out into the parks, coffeehouses, and beer gardens to enjoy the sun after a long winter. People were preparing for the international Festival of the Baroque that was opening that summer to celebrate twenty years of the Czechoslovak Republic. At Voskovec and Werich's Liberated Theater, audiences left the antifascist comedy *Heavy Barbara* in the best of spirits, singing the sprightly finale, "We will advance against the gale — we will prevail against the foe." Few believed that fascism would soon move from the stage to their own streets.

The older generation, men who had fought in the First World War, agreed that the fascism of Spain, Italy, and Germany could never find fertile ground in Czechoslovakia. Franci's father usually had little in common with her cousin Kitty's Zionist father, but both thought Hitler a flash in the pan. They believed in Masaryk's democracy as fervently as their parents had believed in Emperor Franz Joseph's monarchy. Kitty's father, an "incorrigible optimist" according to reporter Kurt Weisskopf, published a bilingual periodical named *Most/Brücke*, or "Bridge," that scrupulously alternated the placement of the German and Czech words every issue.

Sixteen-year-old Kitty had no interest in her father's progressive biculturalism. She was interested in boys, clothes, and make-up. What had happened in Austria could not happen to Czechoslovakia, Kitty and Franci told one another, if a newsreel from Vienna managed to distract them from their favorite subject: what lines or gestures they might adapt from Greta Garbo's behavior in *Camille* for use in their own romances. Their fathers and boyfriends talked endlessly about a two-tiered Maginot Line that the Czech army had constructed along its borders with Germany. They said the Soviet Union and France were pledged to come to the country's defense in case of attack and that Great Britain would surely back up its ally France. But the two cousins discussed what kind of woman Leo Oppenheimer would eventually marry, the meaning of their double dates, and his best friend, Erwin, who had become Kitty's frequent escort.

The urgency of the political crisis first became real for all of them on May 20, when in response to German troop movements and troubles in the Sudetenland, the Czechoslovak army called a partial mobilization. Within a day, nearly two hundred thousand reservists had manned Czechoslovakia's Maginot Line. The presence of Czech army units in the towns and villages of the Sudetenland drove local Nazis into hiding and encouraged those anti-Nazis still living in the border area to assert their presence. Swastikas disappeared from view. Henleinists kept a low profile. In Prague, people read about the developments in newspapers that were censored by the government. They told one another that the call-up had given Hitler fair warning. Their troops were ready and eager to fight.

Emil Rabinek grew ever more ironic as Prague's German-speaking island became Nazi territory. He was, at sixty, an embarrassment to his family, an old dandy struggling to hold on to his dignity as he tried to learn proper Czech. Secretly, he was trying to find a way out of Prague for his daughter. In public, he repeated that as a baptized Jew and a decorated officer of the Austrian Army, he felt no sense of personal danger. He disparaged the notion of the Nazi threat to Czechoslovakia and belittled Pepi, who felt that a catastrophe was imminent. She had listened carefully to the stories of the German refugees of 1933 and she listened to the Austrian refugees of 1938. She listened to Salon Weigert's clients — Jews and non-Jews — who took the rise of Nazism seriously and to her brother Emil Sachsel, who now lived in Bratislava, just across the border from Vienna. The stories he told of the violence there evoked for Pepi the riots that accompanied the Hilsner Affair in Kolín. The influx of Jews into Prague reminded her of life on Golden Lane. But Pepi could not speak of her fears without evoking Emil's ridicule and Franci's impatience. Her sleeping and eating disorders worsened. Her agoraphobia returned in full force. She worried that they had no contingency plans, if not for themselves then at least for their daughter.

Franci adored her mother but viewed her as a classic neurotic. Pepi was fifty-six years old now and had been visiting *sanatoria* for as long as her daughter could remember. For Franci, an avid reader and amateur psychologist, the combination of Pepi's problems of aging, the handing over of control of her *salon,* and losing her husband's love had created a massive depression in her melancholic mother. Emil Rabinek only made matters worse by arguing that his wife's grasp of reality had been forever warped by a ghetto childhood. The Middle Ages were long over but she still thought as though she lived on a Jewish Street.

That summer of 1938, Franci tried to stay clear of her father's sarcasm and her mother's bouts of depression and have a good time. She was eighteen years old. The Festival of the Baroque was on and every night the churches and towers were lit with floodlights. Parks and gardens were crowded with musicians giving concerts and actors performing Shakespeare. The international writers' organization, PEN, was meeting in Prague and thousands of other tourists were in town. One Viennese refugee who arrived in July later wrote,

> We entered another world. Our relations behaved as if Austria was on a different planet and as if Hitler could never cross the divide between these worlds. My father's

brother took a flat for us, signing a five-year lease. Mother's brother sent an enormous flower arrangement to welcome us, unaware that we were penniless and in need of prosaic things like pots and pans. The ladies of the family gave a beautiful party. . . . The table was covered with a handmade lace cloth, shimmering silver, Bohemian crystal and dainty china. The fragrance of roses mingled with the smell of freshly baked yeast-cake. And my "tactless" mother had to spoil it all by telling the assembled ladies, "Get out while the going is good." A chorus of "It can't happen here" greeted her remarks and we were thereafter treated with the consideration normally shown to people suffering from a nervous breakdown.

Franci Rabinek shared the general imperviousness of the Czech citizenry. When she and her mother attended Festival of the Baroque events, they took in the art but also the attire of the internationally famous visitors who had come to the Festival. Mother and daughter discussed new lines and fabrics and designs for the fall season. They inhabited a world where women had nothing to do with war, where contemplating and choosing attire had always offered the illusion of power. During that summer of 1938, it offered an escape from reality as well.

Just before Hitler annexed Austria, Pepi and Franci had made a wedding gown for Helena Hartlová. Helena's husband-to-be was Jan Slavíček, the son of the beloved Czech Impressionist and one of Prague's best-known painters in his own right. Helena — unlike my mother — had little interest in getting married. Adventuresome and independent, she viewed men as necessary for dancing but not much else.

She thrived on her secret work as a courier and travel had only whetted her appetite for seeing more of the world. But even a young woman as unusual and headstrong as Helena was not immune to Prague's social constraints. She had been attending a diplomatic ball in one of Pepi's first low-cut strapless evening gowns when Slavíček spotted her across the room. He begged to paint her portrait in that gown, and as he painted, fell desperately

in love with her. "I didn't fall in love with him," Helena made sure
to point out to me. "It was his *paintings* I liked. And his milieu. Being with artists. But, of course, he never grasped that." Slavíček
was thirty-six, charming, and well connected. He pursued Helena until she agreed to become his wife.

Franci, still smarting from Leo Oppenheimer's decision to
keep their relationship platonic, felt more than the usual girlfriend's sense of loss as she supervised the preparation of Helena's wedding dress. Shortly after the wedding, the couple left
Prague for an extended honeymoon in Italy. There Slavíček
painted and Helena, with her artist husband as cover, was able to
continue working for Czech intelligence. Franci spent more and
more of her leisure time with her younger cousin Kitty.

They were a striking, smartly dressed pair: dark, independent
Franci, already running her own business; blond, flirtatious Kitty,
passing for older than her sixteen years. Both girls were hoping to
fall passionately in love like Anna Karenina or the heroines in Italian opera but, as insurance, were collecting a wide circle of ad-
mirers. Both worried that life was passing them by. Cousin Helli
had begun her medical studies and seemed likely to get married
soon. Cousin Peter was going to university in France. In June of
1938, Leo Oppenheimer finished architectural school and emigrated to America.

I don't know how my mother met Pepík Schön, the wise-
cracking, dapper young man whom she began to see as the most
likely candidate to marry. Pepík liked to speak English and to be
called Joe. He looked and dressed like the actor Rudolph
Valentino. He loved to go out on the town and always knew
where to go. His family, the Schöns, had been part of Kolín's Jewish community one generation earlier, just like the Sachsels. But
Joe knew nothing about Judaism and to underscore the fact that
he was a good Czech made a point of speaking terrible German.
He had no university degree and no profession. When my
mother first met him, he was finishing up his military service. He
loved nothing more than a good time. It was Joe's playfulness and
ability to make her laugh that attracted my mother and that re-
pelled her cousin Kitty.

"He was a spoiled coffeehouse Jew," Kitty recalled, "who did not work, who lived on his father's money, and ran after Franci." My mother, wounded by Leo, drank in Joe's attention. He rode horses, skied, and danced and took her to the hottest clubs. Whenever she was not working and he had military leave, Franci was out with Joe.

Like so many young men of his generation, Joe was cocky about Czechoslovakia's military readiness. Not only was his army the best equipped in Europe, he told Franci, but Czechoslovakia possessed the Continent's second-largest arsenal, and Europe's best state-of-the-art munitions. It was no surprise to him that Premier Daladier had declared that France's obligations toward the Republic were "sacred and not to be evaded." The Russians, too, had good reason to be allied to Czechoslovakia. They needed Czechoslovakia's military resources. Besides, Hitler was a lunatic, full of loud speeches but short on manpower and equipment.

Joe could not know that, for a full year, Nazi generals had been drafting plans for the invasion of Czechoslovakia. In June of 1938, when 85 percent of all Germans voted for the Sudeten Party, he dismissed the importance of the elections. In July, when the Petschek family — one of the wealthiest and most visible Jewish families in Bohemia — quietly put all its extended members and bank employees on a train and left Prague, he called them cowards. In August, when a Lord Runciman arrived in Prague to "investigate" allegations of Czech brutality against the Sudeten Germans for British prime minister Neville Chamberlain, he told my mother not to worry.

Franci did not worry. She loved spending time with Joe Schön, whose playfulness and solid Czech identity were a welcome antidote to her father. Emil Rabinek's inability to speak the native language had become a major liability. Belatedly he was trying to speak Czech with his daughter. Pepi was growing more and more withdrawn and depressed and Franci took to escaping both her parents by going out with Joe, who could make her laugh even at the worsening political situation.

In September, despite Hitler's repeated assertions that he had no territorial designs on Czechoslovakia, German radio stepped up anti-Czech propaganda, broadcasting a series of speeches by Hitler as well as other Nazi leaders. "A petty segment of Europe is harassing human beings," railed Goering in a typical speech. "This miserable pygmy race [the Czechs] without culture — no one knows where it came from — is oppressing a cultured people and behind it is Moscow and the eternal mask of the Jew devil. . . ." Armed Nazi gangs took over Sudeten towns. Thousands of new refugees from the border areas fled to Prague. Once again, the Czech army was called in to reestablish order. Konrad Henlein fled to Germany and, from there, issued a manifesto. "We want to live as free Germans again," Henlein repeated. "We want peace and work in our homeland once again. We want to go home to the Reich."

Neville Chamberlain met with Adolf Hitler at Berchtesgaden, not far from the Czech border. There, Hitler made clear that if Czechoslovakia did not cede to Germany all areas where Sudeten Germans made up more than 50 percent of the population, he would order his generals to take them by force. Chamberlain, who sought to avoid war at all costs, returned to London and relayed Hitler's ultimatum to his French counterpart, Daladier. They decided — without consulting the Czechs — that the Republic would have to cede its border areas to Germany. The integrity of Czechoslovakia would have to be sacrificed for peace.

When word of the Czech president's acceptance of the Anglo-French "solution" was made public in Prague, thousands of Czechs marched in Wenceslas Square shouting, "We are not Austria," "Down with the government of surrender," and "We want a military coup." The French and the British, faced with yet more demands from Hitler, advised the Republic to prepare to defend itself. Two days later, the Czechoslovak army mobilized and eight hundred thousand soldiers, including Joe Schön, were at their garrisons. Blackout regulations were published in the newspapers. Women bought dark fabric and black paper to put over their windows; older men dug trenches in Prague parks and registered for civil defense; everyone donated blood to the Red Cross. In a burst of communal energy, they prepared for a war that they might be fighting alone, while in London, Prime Minister Chamberlain equivocated.

"How horrible, fantastic, incredible it is that we should be digging trenches and trying on gas masks here because of a quarrel in a far-away country between people of whom we know nothing," he mused in a public broadcast about events in Czechoslovakia. "If I were convinced that any nation had made up its mind to dominate the world by fear of its force, I should feel it must be resisted . . . but war is a fearful thing, and we must be very clear before we embark on it, that it is really the great issues that are at stake."

After delivering this speech, Chamberlain received a new message from Hitler, offering to guarantee the new, reduced borders of Czechoslovakia if Britain and France agreed to his annexation of the Sudetenland. Chamberlain, Daladier, Hitler, and Mussolini met at Munich. Chamberlain conveyed their conclusion to Czechoslovak president Beneš: if the Republic decided to resist Hitler, it would have to go it alone. President Beneš, who later said he was incapable of leading the nation into suicide, recommended to his cabinet that they accept the Western verdict. Chamberlain returned to England and declared, "This is the second time there has come back from Germany to Downing Street peace with honor. I believe it is peace for our time."

In Germany, the army began crossing into the Sudetenland on the first day of October and occupied it without firing a single shot. On October 5, 1938, the Jewish Day of Atonement, President Beneš resigned from the presidency under Nazi pressure and sought political asylum in France.

For the world, the name "Munich" would become a synonym for political betrayal, self-delusion, and appeasement. For the Czechoslovak Republic, it was a catastrophic reality. The eight hundred thousand Czechoslovak men who had been mobilized were sent home. Their Maginot Line and armaments passed into the hands of the German army. The Sudetenland, containing one-third of Czechoslovak territory and population, became part of Germany. The country shrank even more when Poland seized the border district of Teschen and Slovakia demanded its independence. The Republic that had just celebrated its twentieth birthday became Czecho-Slovakia.

The political and economic losses were attended by the loss of national morale. Millions of citizens who had been geared up for war were now faced with the fact that their leadership had capitulated and that the Western democracies had abandoned them. France — the inspiration of the Czech national revival and the Republic's honored ally — had not honored its defense treaty. Great Britain had sold them out. A self-censorship almost as strict as that imposed under the Austrian monarchy now muted Czech media and cultural institutions. The old political parties were disbanded and one new Party of National Unity was formed. A new phenomenon — gangs of young fascists — appeared in Prague's streets.

All through my childhood, I listened to my parents and their friends in the Czech émigré community argue about Munich. What would have happened had Masaryk still been living? Had Beneš had any real alternative to capitulation? Should the Czechoslovak army have fought? How long would they have lasted? Would France or Russia have joined them? Could the Second World War have been averted? Shortened? How many lives could have been spared?

My mother would remain relatively quiet during the discussions of Munich. She had been disappointed by the role of the French and sympathetic to Joe's fury at demobilization. But, in fact, her own life had not changed because of Munich. September marked the start of her busiest season. Summer was drawing to a close, the theater season was starting, and women looking into their closets realized they needed new clothes. October was always busy at Salon Weigert and October of 1938 was no exception. A few of their customers had emigrated or were talking about it. But, apart from cousins Peter and Helli, none of my mother's extended family — two Sachsel brothers and their families, cousin Kitty and her family — left. Peter was studying chemistry in France. And Helli, in my mother's view, was an extreme case. Her fiancé was a prominent young Communist who faced arrest if he remained. Of course Helli had to follow him.

The Rabineks had no such reason. They were Czechoslovak citizens and both Kitty's cultural Zionist father and Franci's assimilated one prided themselves on their national allegiance. Hitler had declared several times that the Sudetenland was "the last territorial demand I shall make in Europe. I have no further interest in the Czech state." Great Britain and France had caved in on the Sudetenland but surely they would not back out of the four-power agreement that guaranteed the new borders.

In November, after hundreds of Jews in Germany and former Austria were beaten or killed in the national pogrom called *Kristallnacht,* another wave of refugees arrived in the city from the Sudetenland and more than five thousand people in Prague applied for exit visas. But most Czech Jews remained safe, unharmed, and unafraid. What was happening in Vienna and Berlin and the Sudetenland could not happen in Prague. There was little antisemitism in Masaryk's Republic and so little social discrimination that their intermarriage rate had grown to about 30 percent. Jewish rights as a minority group were guaranteed by the Czechoslovak constitution. Jews were better off than anywhere else in the world, not only an integral part of the nation's history but officers in its army, members of the civil service, nationally recognized artists, physicians, scholars. When, during dinner or a conversation in one of his favorite coffeehouses, anyone would raise the question of emigration, Herr Rabinek would declare that anyone abandoning the Republic now was an ungrateful and unpatriotic coward.

Even Kitty's Zionist father, Lev Vohryzek, argued that emigration was no sure thing and that life in Palestine was primitive, dangerous, and uncivilized. France was no safer than Czechoslovakia in the event of war. America was an unknown, far away, possible only if you had relatives there and could obtain an *affidavit.* Some people were investigating strange destinations — Chile, China, New Zealand — or running to Prague's Central Post Office to search American telephone directories for the addresses of families that shared their surname. Some wrote them beseeching letters. But although Emil Rabinek wrote a few letters to the Viennese branch of the family that had fled to England, he never mentioned it to his daughter.

The bottom line, my mother later said, was that they had no money. Emil Rabinek had turned sixty a week after Hitler's annexation of Austria and thought he was too old, too tired, and too poor to emigrate. For years, he had been clinging to an elegant lifestyle that he could ill afford. His apartment still contained his piano, his books and paintings, and assorted beautiful objects but the Rabineks' only income came from Salon Weigert. All their money was tied up in it and Emil Rabinek said categorically, "At our age, we are not emigrating without capital."

Franci and Pepi, like many people who remained in the country, tried to anchor themselves in their work and the routines of everyday life. They had a business to run, a dozen employees on the payroll, and a large clientele. That winter, as usual, they took their buying trip to Paris and did not even consider remaining there. "They were all so stupid, you cannot imagine how stupid they were," said Helli, who met them and tried to convince them to stay. "They were confident it couldn't last. Your mother and grandmother brought me my winter coat, conducted their business, and went back to Prague."

All authentic Czech politics and much of Czech culture had gone underground after Munich. Publishing houses and theaters were closely controlled. Many young people began to feel that Thomas G. Masaryk's "island of democracy in Central Europe" had been a mirage all along. Idealism became a joke; corruption reigned. The death of Masaryk's close friend, the country's beloved writer Karel Čapek, deepened the gloom: it was said that after Munich, he died of a broken heart.

Hitler leaned heavily on Czecho-Slovakia, forcing the new government to quit the League of Nations, reorient its foreign policy, adapt its economic policy to German goals, and take a new census of its Jewish residents. The flow of students and tourists to Prague stopped. Many foreigners who had been residing there returned home. The culture that Leo Oppenheimer had described as an Athens disappeared like Atlantis. Its architecture remained intact but its urbane, international spirit was gone.

It was raw and snowing when the Nazis marched into Prague on the morning of March 15, 1939. "Silent, mournful, abandoned, broken, Czechoslovakia recedes into darkness," Winston

Churchill had written after Munich, predicting the absorption of the nation by the Reich. Franci Rabinek had never heard of Churchill then but it seemed as though everything she had viewed as hers had slipped away like sand. She was just two years younger than the Republic itself. Czechoslovak democracy was the only reality she knew and, like so many people who grow up in political and economic comfort, she had always taken it for granted. Now, watching the German army take over the streets of her city, she was at one with the grieving people around her. She experienced the occupation of her country as a Czech. It would be months before she would be forced to experience it as a Jew.

13

The streets were empty at six o'clock on the icy March morning when the German army marched into Prague. Telephones all over the city had begun ringing at 4:30 A.M., when Prague radio began broadcasting a statement from the president urging calm in the face of invasion and discouraging resistance. The president said he had been forced by Hitler to sacrifice the state in order to save the nation. Units of the Czech army were being disarmed. All banks were closed. "A full blizzard was blowing and the snow was staying on the streets," wrote the American diplomat George Kennan. "For the rest of the day, the motorized units pounded and roared over the cobblestone streets: hundreds and hundreds of vehicles plastered with snow. . . . By evening, the occupation was complete." One year after newsreels had shown thousands of cheering Viennese welcoming the Nazis, they showed groups of silent or weeping Czechs.

Franci and Pepi spent March 15 standing at their windows in shock. Emil Rabinek had, by then, admitted that he was — by

Hitler's definition — a Jew but was still unwilling to admit that the situation was chaotic and their own prospects desperate. Joe Schön, on the other hand, suddenly tried to persuade Franci to leave the country with him. She would not consider it. She called him a coward and after a bitter argument, Joe left alone for the police station to stand in line for an exit visa. It was four in the afternoon when his turn finally came. He handed the German officer his passport. The officer looked him in the eye and asked if he planned to return to Czechoslovakia. Joe Schön stared back at him and replied, "Eventually." His request for an exit permit was denied and Joe returned to the Rabineks' apartment, where Emil was trying to persuade his wife and daughter that they would be all right.

That night, Adolf Hitler arrived in Prague and, in a gesture fraught with symbolism, slept in Prague Castle, home of the Czech kings and Thomas G. Masaryk. He summoned President Hácha to visit and forced him to enter by the servants' entrance. Henceforth, the president would be obliged to ask permission of the Nazi guard whenever he wished to use his presidential quarters. A postage stamp commemorating Hitler looking down over Prague would later be issued. With such dramatic symbols, Hitler aimed to humiliate the Czechs, obliterate twenty years of Czech independence, and incorporate Bohemia and Moravia into the German Empire.

The Czechs would long be ridiculed by other Europeans for capitulating to Hitler. Compared to the Poles or Yugoslavs or Greeks, the risks Czechs took were small and appear petty. Men wore the Czech tricolor in their jacket lapels. Women refused to hang Nazi flags in their windows. Crowds of young people gathered in Wenceslas Square to sing the national anthem. Parents kept their children home when schools required them to attend Nazi celebrations. But in the domain most pertinent to the Rabineks — the Nazi policy toward the people they defined as Jews — the majority of Czechs not only resisted but many took enormous risks.

There were many incentives for Czechs to turn against Jews: Prague was flooded with homeless and unemployed Czech refugees from the Sudetenland who stood to benefit from their losses. But both Nazi and anti-Nazi observers reported on a marked absence of Czech antisemitism. Czech leaders, apart from the fascist fringe, were so reluctant to create anti-Jewish restrictions that the Nazis gave up on trying to promulgate anti-Jewish laws through the facade of Czech government and issued almost all antisemitic decrees themselves. One third of Czech Jews were married to non-Jews. Most had assimilated to the point that they could not easily be distinguished from the rest of the population. In Prague, there was no anti-Jewish street violence, no looting of Jewish shops, and, apart from one bomb attack on the historic Old-New Synagogue, no burning of buildings.

The Nazis mounted a museum exhibit called "The Jews as Enemy of Humanity" in Prague and obliged schoolchildren and workers to view it. They made efforts to revive the myths of ritual murder, ordered the Czech police to reopen all unsolved cases of missing children and women, disseminated reams of the antisemitic newspaper *Der Stürmer* and other antisemitic literature. As elsewhere, they instituted penalties for Gentiles who fraternized with Jews.

Most Czechs, however, continued to do so. The Czech civil service had bowed to Nazi pressure in January of 1938, pensioning off its one thousand Jewish employees three months before the occupation. The Czech Bar Association had proved all too eager to transfer Jewish law offices to Czech owners. But the vast majority of professionals were resistant to anti-Jewish measures. When some hospital boards and insurance companies began to bar Jewish doctors, many Czechs protested and remained their patients. When newspapers and publishing houses came under pressure to exclude Jewish authors, others made it possible for some Jews to continue publishing their work under pseudonyms. The women who bought their clothes at Salon Weigert assured my mother and grandmother that, whatever the Nazis might think up next, they would remain faithful clients.

The Rabineks, like the vast majority of Czech Jews, felt their destiny was bound up with that of their country. They were not alienated from or fearful of their neighbors in the way of many

Polish or Hungarian or German Jews. They had become accustomed to regarding their state as a safe haven, a bastion of liberal democracy, an exception to the rules of Central and Eastern Europe. When, in April, a celebration was prepared in the Masaryk Stadium to mark Hitler's birthday, they were not surprised that three sides of the stadium remained empty. It made sense when wreaths appeared at the foot of statues of Jan Hus and the American president Woodrow Wilson. They were alarmed by the appearance of a native fascist movement but relieved that its demonstrations were largely ignored.

There was, despite the invasion, a spring season of 1939. Chanel was showing clothes with a strong peasant influence: full skirts, peasant blouses, checked kerchiefs at the neck. Franci and Pepi tried to adapt that look to Prague as they tried to sift out fact from fiction in the conversations of their clients and employees. They heard that the Nazis had marched in with prepared arrest lists and that hundreds of German émigrés, Communists, anti-Nazi journalists and politicians, and Jews had been arrested. They heard that many prominent people had fled or committed suicide, that thousands of Czechs were trying to obtain visas for exotic places like China, Venezuela, or New Zealand, that students and soldiers were escaping east over the border to Poland.

Emil Rabinek talked on the telephone and listened to the radio. His German had ceased to be of any service: the only news he trusted now came from the BBC. He heard that Great Britain no longer considered itself bound by the Munich guarantees to defend Czechoslovak territorial integrity because the Slovak Diet had declared the independence of Slovakia, thereby dissolving the Republic. How could one be legally bound to come to the defense of a country that no longer existed? France followed Britain's lead and did not contest Hitler's occupation. Stripped of the Sudetenland, Slovakia, and chunks of its eastern territory, the historic Czech lands of Bohemia and Moravia were declared a "protectorate" of Germany. A German aristocrat, Baron Konstantin von Neurath, was named protector. Czechoslovak citizens who had registered as German nationals in the national census of 1930 were now citizens of the Reich. Non-Germans were its subjects.

Franci listened angrily to the BBC broadcasts with her father and to Salon Weigert's clients with her mother. She had just turned nineteen. Helena had urged her to emigrate. Her cousins Helli and Peter were already gone. But, as an only child, Franci felt incapable of abandoning her parents. Nor could she abandon the *salon* she was so proud of managing and the thirteen people who worked there. Joe was another complication. He would not desert his country. In fact, she suspected that he was already involved in some kind of underground activity. They were thinking of marriage.

When Franci ventured out into the streets during that March of 1939, she was startled to see that almost all the shops — food stores, clothing stores, even bookstores — had been cleaned out by the soldiers of the German army. Signs were being taken down, their names painted over from Czech to German. Walls of buildings and the occasional balcony now displayed swastikas. There were new uniforms everywhere for new personnel. In addition to the protector, the German army, and the German police, there was the Gestapo, the Nazi secret police. In a gesture as symbolic as Hitler's spending the night at Prague Castle, the Gestapo had seized the Petschek bank for its headquarters.

But during that first month of life under the protectorate, Franci Rabinek still did not understand that the occupation had forever altered her existence. "Most Jews did not feel as if a gaping abyss had suddenly opened before them between yesterday and today," her Prague contemporary Ruth Bondy would later write.

They did not consider the situation as unprecedented or unparalleled. They saw it as a continuum, albeit a frightening one, a worrying one, fraught with danger, but not the end of their familiar world. In the first few weeks of the protectorate, life continued almost as usual, without any drastic changes, except for the overnight change in road traffic from left to right. Here an old German friend suddenly broke off relations; there an acquaintance quickly passed to the other side of the street. . . . Here and there, signs appeared marked "Aryan shop." But the pace of life had not changed.

Occupation or not, women continued to buy clothes. Every morning, Franci got up, dressed, and walked through the short hallway that led from the Rabineks' apartment into Salon Weigert.

The routine of opening up the salon, standing at her cutting table, then fitting coats, dresses, ball gowns, and traveling suits softened the impact of the German invasion. She listened to the wishes of her customers and suggested alterations, additions, accessories. She negotiated with her suppliers and supervised the work of her employees, trying to correct their mistakes without losing her temper. She argued with her father about billing and tried to keep up a running conversation with Pepi, who was slipping away into a silent, isolated world of her own.

"Your grandmother sat there in a corner and — forgive me for telling you this — she smelled of urine," Joe's cousin Vava Schön told me in Jerusalem. We were looking out at the Judean hills and I was glad of the blinding white light that kept me blinking. I knew, right away, that her unwelcome description of Pepi in 1939 was true.

We were sitting on a balcony in the ultraorthodox settlement of Kiryat Ya'arim where Vava's daughter lived. Her carefully coiffed white hair and the unobtrusive elegance of her dress stood out against the covered heads and shapeless skirts of the religious women in the town. Her destiny astonished Vava. In spring of 1939, she was beginning her career as a young actress in the Czech theater. Like Franci, she had been baptized at birth and brought up entirely ignorant of Jewish tradition. After protector von Neurath issued a decree defining as Jewish any person with two Jewish grandparents and banning Jews from all facets of public life, she was prohibited by law from appearing onstage. "I went to the *salon* every day after they kicked me out of the theater," said the actress, who later Hebraicized her name to Nava Shan for the Israeli stage. "Your mother was the boss and she behaved like one. I was very impressed with her. She was so young but she behaved like a big director. She gave orders. She was in charge. Her mother was depressed and listless, sitting by herself in the corner, an old woman who could not maintain control over her bladder. That happened to old women then. No one thought about going to a doctor and having it fixed."

She smelled of urine, I repeated to myself, trying to incorporate this unpleasant detail into my picture of Pepi. My grandmother was not even sixty then, fifteen years younger than Nava was now, hardly an old woman. But the pieces fit: that damage to Pepi's organs in giving birth to Franzi in 1920 had never healed. It marked the beginning of my grandfather's sexual indifference to his wife and his involvement with other women. Pepi had, since the suicide of her own mother, suffered from melancholia and psychosomatic illnesses. She, alone in her family, had charted the slow, inexorable rise of Nazism and her husband's dismissal of her "hysteria" had made her even more solitary. She had raised an unusually independent, confident daughter as well as a small, thriving business. But, as Nava remembered her then, Pepi was a silent, brooding presence obsessed with loss.

One month after the Germans marched into Prague, Franci had what she would later describe as her "first brush with reality." A tall, blond man appeared at the door of Salon Weigert, identified himself as a commissar appointed to "Aryanize" businesses owned by Jews, and asked politely for a tour of the premises.

My mother reciprocated his politeness. She led him through the workroom and *salon,* estimated the annual number of customers, income, and expenses, and answered his questions in her excellent German. The young commissar concluded that he would be unlikely to make money from Salon Weigert and said that he would not be "Aryanizing" her enterprise. But, in confidence, he told my mother that she had two options. Sell Salon Weigert to a non-Jew or, if she wished to keep it, sell *pro forma* to one of her seamstresses and stay on, ostensibly as an employee. He allowed that his wife could use some new clothes and left.

As soon as the commissar had closed the door behind him, Franci briefed her mother and father about the situation. Then they called together their staff. Their twelve seamstresses and one tailor were all young Czechs, many of whom had apprenticed at Salon Weigert. Most adored Pepi and had watched her daughter grow up. They had few complaints about their employers and no wish to lose their jobs. The Rabineks, for their part, were so startled by the commissar's visit and so certain of the character of their employees that they recounted his message word for word.

The thirteen young Czechs in the workroom did not seem surprised by the problem facing them. Similar things, they all knew, were happening all over Prague, to all kinds of businesses. A lively discussion began, centering on which one of the seamstresses would be the best qualified to "buy" Salon Weigert. It ended with the agreement that they would all think it over and decide the next day. That evening, Franci tried to persuade her parents of the necessity of the plan but Emil and Pepi Rabinek were nervous. How could they be sure to get the business back? How could she hope to run the business as an employee? Who would deal with suppliers? Who would sign the checks? How could they be sure that no one would inform on them?

Franci said there was no other choice. Their only legal alternative was to close down the *salon* and live on their savings until the Nazis were driven out of Prague. The Rabineks did not stop worrying but, as had become their habit, they accepted Franci's view of the matter. At nineteen, their daughter was now in charge of their collective destiny. She was the new generation. They could no longer make decisions.

The following morning, the seamstress who had been at Salon Weigert the longest volunteered to become its official owner. My mother asked a non-Jewish Czech lawyer who, she knew, had already arranged for more than one such transfer to draw up a secret contract. Marie would buy Salon Weigert. Franci would become her forelady. The two would draw the same salary and divide any additional income. A copy of their contract was buried in the garden of the lawyer's country cottage and a sign painter was hired to put Marie's name at the entrance door. The other seamstresses began to call Marie "Miss Marie," and several of Pepi's old customers asked discreetly if Franci had managed to sell for a decent sum. Similar transfers and renamings of firms were occurring all over Prague. They had become a fact of life.

In June, protector von Neurath issued a decree that eliminated Jews from virtually all economic activity in the protectorate. Part of it called for Jews to register any platinum, gold, silver, or precious stones with a special agency and it was Joe's mother's response to this decree that led to Franci's first encounter with the Gestapo.

Mrs. Schön had decided to safeguard some of her jewelry with her son's friend and former commanding officer. She wrote the major's name and a description of the jewelry on a slip of paper, the paper was discovered at the home of Joe's brother, who was under surveillance by Gestapo agents, and they arrested him and his mother. When they asked Mrs. Schön where Joe might be, she directed them to Franci and all three Rabineks were also arrested.

During her first encounter with the Gestapo in June of 1939, Franci must have been terrified but her identity was still intact. She was still a young, entitled Czech citizen, a professional woman secure in her civil rights. Recalling her first interrogation years later, my mother said in that peculiar language I had grown up trying to decipher that she had not been "mistreated." The Gestapo agents had not hit her. They had just alternated offering her chocolate and threatening to shoot her if she did not answer their questions. She had been "unwilling" to tell them anything. She was worried about her parents and that the Gestapo might discover the fictitious arrangements at Salon Weigert. She told her interrogators that she knew nothing about the major or her boyfriend's mother's jewelry.

That night, after their separate interrogations, all three Rabineks were taken to Pankrác Prison. There they were lined up against a wall, then taken to different cells. Franci was put with two middle-aged women, neither of them Jewish. Ludmila introduced herself as the wife of a Czechoslovak army officer and Sokol official who had fled the country; Marianne, as an Austrian and former actress. When Franci introduced herself by saying that she had been arrested by mistake, Ludmila turned over to go back to sleep while Marianne burst out laughing. Franci, whose customers ran the gamut of Prague's women, pegged the first as a dowager and the second as a *femme fatale,* the kind Greta Garbo might portray.

The stately Ludmila had been a prisoner for three months, suspected of withholding information about the underground of former Czech army officers. She had been married to the same man for twenty-five years and exuded the stolid, reassuring air of a Czech matron. The red-haired, witty, and flamboyant Marianne, my mother gathered, had married or lived with many men. The most recent was a Viennese Jewish journalist who, like Ludmila's husband, had fled his country. Marianne had divorced him, citing racial grounds, then went to work on behalf of their Jewish friends. She had smuggled money and jewelry into Switzerland while carrying on an affair with an SS officer stationed in Vienna. When he was transferred elsewhere, she moved to the protectorate and became involved with the Czech Resistance.

In other circumstances, my mother thought, Ludmila and Marianne would never have shared the same room. Ludmila thought Marianne's stories of sexual escapades too risqué for the ears of a nineteen-year-old daughter of the Prague middle class and her involvement with an SS officer repulsive. Franci, of course, was fascinated by every detail of Marianne's erotic life and so impressed with Marianne that she began to listen to her lectures on Nazism.

Ludmila and Marianne undertook Franci Rabinek's long overdue political education. They instructed her never to admit to anything her interrogators suggested, never to display interest in any reward, and never to volunteer any information on her own, especially names. For hours, the two older women explained to Franci Hitler's vision of Europe and the day-to-day workings of the Nazi machine. They tried to make her understand that what she had seen in the newsreels was true. The Nazis were butchers, they argued. Under Nazism, Jews were subhumans and she, Franci Rabinek, would be treated just like any other Jew, whether or not her father had been an Austrian army officer, whether or not she had been baptized.

Marianne described the brutal humiliation of the Viennese Jews, their arrest, the confiscation of their property. She argued that Franci should make every effort to leave the protectorate. She insisted that it was foolish for the Rabineks to continue living adjacent to the *salon*. Their presence endangered Marie and a large, modern apartment right in the center of town would sooner or later be confiscated by the Nazis. Franci should move somewhere less central now, not wait to be thrown out.

Ludmila agreed with Marianne. Their opposition to Nazism was stronger than their strongest personal differences and their spirit of resistance fired up my mother's own. Franci would remember Pankrác as her first classroom in the university of the war and Ludmila and Marianne as her first professors. Until then — with the exception of her mother and her friend Helena — Franci had regarded most women as helpless and mostly uninteresting people. Emil had never hidden a certain contempt for the feminine that undermined his so-called feminism and Franci had absorbed that contempt, adding on to it her own observations from the *salon*. Her two cellmates gave her a new perspective on women.

When Franci was released from Pankrác, she returned to a silent apartment and *salon*. There was no message from Joe; no note from Marie, no sign of her parents. She rummaged through her father's desk, where Emil did the bookkeeping for the business, looking for a hidden message and found instead an unlabeled vial of tiny pills.

It was clear to her that the pills were poison. Both Rabineks had threatened each other with suicide for as far back as their daughter could remember, in a ritual that was, by now, less frightening than routine. But since the occupation, suicides had become common, often public, expressions of despair. In one incident, four Jews had jumped, one after the other, from a building in the center of the city. She did not want her father, so volatile, so sure of his view of the world, to have such easy access to death. That day, she took the pills to a pharmacist, who replaced them with saccharine.

When Emil and Pepi Rabinek returned one day later, Emil was furious at Joe, whom he held responsible for their imprisonment. He paced about the flat railing against Mrs. Schön's stupidity for keeping lists that sent innocent people to jail. Pepi was pale and ten pounds thinner. She had worried herself into believing that Franci had been deported and could not stop weeping and clinging to her daughter. Joe himself, although apologetic, was feeling even cockier than usual. He told them he was responsible for their release. He had managed to bribe the Gestapo.

Joe told an intricate story of how he had recruited a Czech lawyer friend who had obtained their release for the paltry sum of twenty thousand Czech crowns stuffed into a copy of *Mein Kampf.* The Gestapo had not arrested the major. They had confiscated the jewelry and let him off with a lecture on the danger of being a "Jew-lover." Joe's conclusion was they had nothing to fear. Nazis could be bribed like anyone else: all you needed was money.

When Franci responded by telling them what she had learned from her cellmates in Pankrác, her father and boyfriend answered in one disparaging voice. How could Franci be so naive as to believe what she was told in a cell? Didn't she know that there was always one collaborator planted in a cell? Wasn't Marianne a *provocateur* planted by the Gestapo? What kind of woman boasted of an affair with an SS man?

The Rabineks' two weeks in Pankrác had also made them more optimistic about Nazism. Joe was right when he said the Germans could be bought and every prisoner they had met had expressed eagerness to fight Hitler. "There is probably no country in Europe where war — and war at the earliest possible date — is so universally desired as in the protectorate of Bohemia and Moravia," wrote George Kennan in a dispatch to Washington. The Czech army had gone into exile and underground to regroup. Apart from a small Czech fascist movement, the entire nation was resisting the Germans. The resistance was laughable, in the good-natured, obstructionist tradition of the Good Soldier Švejk, rather than of a heroic nature, but a feeling of solidarity against a common enemy was cheering all the same. In the darkness of movie theaters, Czech audiences hissed during German newsreels; in coffeehouses, Czech waiters handed German patrons their newspapers upside down. Telephone wires in German offices were mysteriously cut or crossed; hammers and sickles were painted on German cars and wherever and whenever a German asked a question, Czechs replied, *"Nerozumím,"* "I don't understand."

Kennan described that summer of 1939 to his State Department superiors as one of strange weather and electric storms, "grimly symbolic of the rapidly alternating hopes and fears in the minds of the people.

"Everything is in suspense," he wrote.

> No one takes initiative; no one plans for the future. Cultural life and amusements continue in a half-hearted, mechanical spirit. Theaters and public amusements attract only scanty and indifferent crowds. People prefer to sit through the summer evenings in the beer gardens or the little parks along the rivers, to bandy the innumerable rumors in which they themselves scarcely believe, and to wait with involuntary patience for the approach of something which none of them could quite describe but which they are all convinced must come and must affect all their lives profoundly. The near future should show whether this waiting attitude is the result of a sound instinct or whether it merely expresses the natural reluctance of a people which has just awakened from a twenty-year dream of independence to accept again the status of a nation of servants.

Franci Rabinek, however, began investigating outlying neighborhoods of Prague to which her family might relocate.

August brought the first wholesale exclusion of Jews from Czech cultural life. The protector decreed that all Jews living in Bohemia and Moravia were required to relocate to Prague. There, they were prohibited from entering all restaurants, coffeehouses, playgrounds, museums, theaters and concert halls, swimming pools, bathhouses, hospitals, and nursing homes. Jews Not Wanted signs were posted at all entrances. Franci and Kitty, accustomed to escaping the summer heat at their swim club and in the coolness of movie theaters, found the scope of their lives reduced. "You knew you were worthless because you were a Jew,"

Kitty told me suddenly one day in Prague. "All those restrictions added up to a total erosion of your self-esteem."

For the two cousins, the imposition of a Jewish form on their identities felt like a punishment dreamed up by a lunatic. Franci had never set foot in a synagogue and had never said a Jewish prayer. She and Kitty had always celebrated Christmas with beautifully decorated trees, carp soup, stuffed goose, and wonderful cookies. They were typical Prague girls who had, for several years, been examining their faces in the mirror and redrawing the lines of their eyebrows and lips according to Hollywood specifications. Now, Nazi propaganda had seized the initiative, idealizing "Aryan" looks and making Jewish physiognomy a matter of public discussion. Kitty decided to lighten her hair; Franci's was so dark that it was a lost cause. They could do nothing about their brown "Jewish" eyes, so their attention turned to their noses.

Kitty's was small, straight, and unremarkable but Franci's was long and slightly hooked at the end: the stereotype of a "Jewish" nose. Its length and shape became the focus of all her frustration with the Nazi restrictions. "I thought if my nose were different," my mother later told me, "I could go to the movies." During that strange prewar summer, my mother talked her boyfriend, her parents, and one of Prague's few plastic surgeons into helping her obtain a nose job.

When, on September 1, Hitler invaded Poland and the Allies declared war on Germany, my mother perceived Czech jubilation through the haze of a postoperative headache. Her doctor had urged her to avoid looking in the mirror for a few weeks. Her new nose was enormously swollen. But he assured her that the operation had succeeded: the nose would be short and straight with a slight upturn, very much like her mother's.

I imagine that Pepi tended her daughter sadly, understanding the futility of straightening a nose when it was the whole world that was askew. In Paris, Gabrielle Chanel closed her *maison*, declaring that wartime was no time for fashion. The Rabineks, like so many other families in Prague that September, listened for news of an attack on Germany by the armies of the British and the French. Surely they would crush Germany and put an end to

Hitler by Christmas! But instead of being crushed, the German army crushed Poland. Instead of fighting, the French sat waiting for the Germans to attack them. The British were unprepared for war. The Americans were sticking to their policy of neutrality.

In Prague, disappointment with this "Phony War" fed the resistance movement. Protector von Neurath sent nearly two thousand members of the Czech intelligentsia to concentration camps as a warning against political dissent but the deportations helped solidify a mood of passive resistance. On September 30, after a rumor was circulated that the day's tramway proceeds would be collected by the Nazis for their Winter Fund, Czechs boycotted public transport and walked. On October 28, Czechoslovakia's Independence Day, so many thousands of people demonstrated that the German police were called in. In November, the funeral of a medical student who had been shot during that demonstration touched off another wave of student demonstrations and, on Hitler's orders, a second attack on the Czech intelligentsia began.

The SS troops broke into student quarters throughout Prague, killing nine student leaders and deporting twelve hundred students to concentration camps. All Czech institutions of higher education, serving some nineteen thousand students, were forcibly closed. Czech libraries, archives, and laboratories were vandalized. In yet another symbolic action, the Charles University Law School was declared an SS headquarters.

The random selection of victims and the reign of terror had a galvanizing effect on the population. Rumors made the rounds of Prague: the Nazis were planning to sterilize all Czech women; chlorine and lead were being secretly added to cigarettes to poison the population; all Czech marriages were to be prohibited. Parents refused to take sick children to German doctors. They avoided German shops and refused to serve Germans in their own. The Nazis upped the ante: They closed Czech high schools throughout the protectorate. They required all Czechs to take off their hats as a sign of respect for the swastika or face arrest. They prohibited all demonstrations of Czech nationalism. They banned listening to foreign radio broadcasts. Jews were subjected

to additional restrictions and were obliged to carry special identity cards marked with the letter J. They were no longer permitted to own radios. They were obliged to observe a nighttime
curfew of 8 P.M.

Franci chafed at the restrictions. As 1939 became 1940, all the
Rabineks still worked at Salon Weigert but Pepi had become a
shell of a woman. Emil still kept the books but now that the Rabineks had been forced to turn in their prized radio, his life was
organized around the four daily broadcasts in Czech from the
BBC. He walked several miles a day across Prague to listen at the
home of a former Czech employee, then returned home to up-
date the elaborate war maps he had put up on the walls of his
bedroom.

Joe Schön, who had become Franci's fiancé, was there every
evening, moving the pins with their carefully labeled tags over
the map of Europe, discussing military strategy and the latest
news. Joe had never held a job. His military service remained the
most meaningful experience of his life and now several of his former army buddies were engaged in helping Czech men escape
from the protectorate and join the Czech Free Forces in England.
He had also changed his family name from Schön to the Czech
"Solar." A Jewish name spelled trouble not only for himself but
for everyone with whom he worked.

Franci celebrated her twentieth birthday without fanfare. I
see her in a quiet but steady rage, furious that the Rabineks' survival now depended on their continuing good relations with
Marie, furious at the restrictions on her life, furious at the loss of
most normal pleasures of adulthood. Her new nose had not
bought access to the movies. Pepi was so terrified by the
Gestapo's periodic sweeps through movie theaters that she fell
apart whenever Franci expressed a desire to see a film.

In April of 1940, Denmark fell to Germany, followed by Nor-
way. Joe decided that the time had come to stop helping other soldiers escape across the border and to join the Czech army abroad
himself. There was a long and tearful leave-taking in the Rabinek
household, with even the testy Emil moved to tears. Then Joe
disappeared, arranging for two baskets of flowers — one for

Pepi, one for Franci — to be delivered on the day after his departure.

Franci was just becoming accustomed to her fiancé's absence when, one week later, Joe reappeared unshaven, filthy, and smelling of manure. His group had been intercepted by a German patrol. Some of his companions had been shot; others taken into custody. He and a friend had made their way back to Prague, mostly on foot, with the aid of Czech farmers who hid them in their barns. He was dangerous to anyone he stayed with. He would have to go into hiding for a few weeks.

In May, Holland and Belgium fell. In June, the German army took over Paris. In July, all Jewish children were barred from attending school in the protectorate. Franci felt the world closing down. She insisted to her parents that the time had come to move out of the city. They relocated Salon Weigert and found a small apartment for themselves in Barrandov, the Czech film colony on the outskirts of Prague. Many of Emil Rabinek's cherished possessions, including his piano, were sold. The remainder of the Rabinek's books, paintings, furniture, and clothes were crammed into the tiny space.

Although it was a rational and necessary move, Franci hated it. All her life she had lived in a large apartment in the very center of Prague, a short walk from any coffeehouse or movie theater she might decide to go to at the last minute. Now she was stuck in an outlying neighborhood where the streets were all but empty, where movie stars were chauffered into town but ordinary people like herself had to use a bicycle or wait for the bus that transported hundreds of film technicians and extras back and forth from the film studios. The only bright spot in her world was Joe, now a hero because of his narrow escape from death, who brought her flowers, who bought her a puppy, who could still make her laugh.

There were no more Jewish marriages permitted in Prague's City Hall, where Emil and Pepi had been married. Instead, in August of 1940, Joe and Franci were married in a small district court. Jews were no longer allowed to ride in taxis, so the wedding party arrived by tram and one of her apprentices brought her bouquet to spare the bride public embarrassment. Because Jews were no longer allowed to frequent restaurants, the owner of Père Louis, the French bistro that the newlyweds had long frequented, closed his establishment "due to illness" for the reception.

The wedding photographs that survived the war show Franci Solar in a black wedding dress and a silly hat looking like a reasonably happy bride. Joe Solar looks like Rudolph Valentino. They honeymooned in Zlin, a town primarily known for the production of shoes, because Jews were prohibited from staying in all but a few protectorate hotels and Joe had a friend there.

After their four-day honeymoon, the Solars returned to the Rabineks' tiny flat in Barrandov to begin their married life.

14

I grew up thinking that ordinary life stopped during the war. I conceived of it as six long years when all color drained from the world and left only the gray of battlefields and concentration camps. But, of course, it was nothing like that, not for my mother and not for Czechoslovakia's Jews. The segue from prewar life to deportation took more than three years and it was gradual, marked by ever shrinking circles of permitted movement. Even that process of forced constriction was not as obvious then as it is in retrospect. Ordinary life continued independent of and impervious to Nazism. The weather might light disaster with sunshine or rain out a triumph. Habit, temperament, and chance continued to exist under occupation, as did sex, illness, birth, and death. In October of 1940, six weeks after her daughter's wedding, Pepi Rabinek scanned her daughter's face and ventured the guess that she was pregnant.

The physician's confirmation set off a furor in the Rabinek-Solar household. Pepi, remembering her own unexpected pregnancy, became teary and sentimental. Joe Solar was delighted with the news of his impending fatherhood. Emil Rabinek went into one of his rages. He railed about sexual carelessness and the irresponsibility of bringing a child into the world. In 1919, he had demanded that his wife have an abortion. Now he demanded one of his daughter.

Franci agreed with his arguments. Having a baby was out of the question. She was twenty years old and the only member of the family to hold a paying job. Joe had no work. He spent his time with his army buddies, engaged in activities that he said were too dangerous to speak about. The elder Rabineks were unemployed. After they moved to Barrandov, Marie had let Franci know that her parents were all but useless and that serving as a front for three Jews was no longer possible for her.

"Marie had undergone a subtle change," my mother would later write.

> *Being the owner, in name, of a thriving business, had given her a status she had previously only maybe dreamed of and the incessant antisemitic propaganda in the newspapers had given this simple girl an idea of the risk she was taking and even a justification of our reversed roles. For the moment, the Germans were winning and there was not the slightest sign in the air that the status quo would not go on for her lifetime. She decided that one person of our family was enough to keep the old clients coming. This put my parents out of work.*

There was no question in Franci's mind about the necessity of an abortion. She had always told Helena and Kitty that she wanted children but not right away. Her husband was himself a large child; she could not take seriously the notion of his becoming a father. The continuing stream of Nazi edicts clearly delimited the life a Jewish baby would have: Jews were barred from public parks, gardens, and the boats on the river, prohibited from attending schools, cinemas, and theaters.

Abortions were illegal in the Czechoslovak Republic but the law had often been circumvented. Under Nazi occupation, Jewish doctors were closely watched and Christians were forbidden to treat Jewish patients. But one of Joe's army buddies found a Czech gynecologist willing to perform the operation. His wife would serve as nurse; there could not be much anaesthetic; and Franci would have to leave the office immediately after the procedure. Until the last moment, Joe begged his wife to change her mind but she remained resolute. Afterward she was bundled into a friend's car and taken home, where Pepi sat by her bed, checking her temperature. One day later, Franci was riding her bicycle to work.

In the scholarly literature on the Nazi protectorate, all of 1940 and most of 1941 are described as a period of relative calm. Unlike other countries Hitler conquered, the protectorate was not bombed. Its soldiers lost their honor and arsenal but they retained their lives. For a time, because Hitler needed Czech labor, Czech foodstuffs, and Czech arms, rations in the protectorate were better than those in Germany. Although life for Czech Jews was more difficult than for the rest of the population, it was infinitely better than life for the Jews of Poland, Germany, and Austria.

One year after the Germans marched into Prague, the Rabineks and Solars were living quietly in their small apartment in Barrandov. Every morning, Franci rode her bicycle into the center of Prague, changed her clothes, and assumed her role as director of Salon Weigert. She had finally grasped the meaning of the occupation: they were utterly powerless. Accepting this state of affairs came hard to Franci. It was not fair. It was outrageous. Here she was forced to defer to a former employee and subjected to innumerable indignities because her grandparents happened to have been Jews "by race," that is, registered members of a Jewish community.

At home, Franci forced herself to avoid criticizing her parents. At work, she forced herself to rein in her resentment of Marie, to maintain a relationship with her that was cordial, if not warm. Several of the *salon's* customers, upset by Pepi's disappearance, took pains to inform Marie that they would take their business elsewhere if Salon Weigert did not retain its real owner. Still,

Franci could not be sure how long her "front" would last. Every morning as she began her work, she would look into Marie's face and try to read her mood. How much time did she have left? A week? A month?

In Barrandov, Pepi Rabinek became a full-time housewife. The business of keeping house had become increasingly difficult for Jews. In August, stores had been ordered to limit shopping hours for Jews to two hours in the morning and one and a half hours in the afternoon. In October, another edict barred Jews from receiving ration cards for clothing. Black-market prices of clothing, as well as food, coal, and soap were soaring and trading in family heirlooms was useless as the market became glutted with jewelry and art. Pepi worked hard to establish good relations with her neighbors, the storekeeper, and her husband.

The occupation had forced my grandparents to mend their marriage. Emil Rabinek was now sixty-two and, for the first time in many years, obliged to share his bedroom with his wife. He lived far away from his former mistresses and could no longer indulge his expensive habits. He curtailed his visits to the barber and, instead of frequenting the Casino, began to reread his favorite German classics at home. He helped his wife with the shopping and together they walked Tommy, Franci's terrier, in the woods and fields. He played chess with his son-in-law and kept his extensive war maps up to date. His life was still organized around the broadcasts of the BBC.

The highlight of those broadcasts was Jan Masaryk's *Volá Londýn!* (London Calling!) announced by the opening bars of Beethoven's Fifth Symphony. Jan Masaryk, the former Czechoslovak ambassador to Great Britain, was the son of the founder of the Republic. He had remained in London when Hitler declared the protectorate and joined the Czechoslovak government-in-exile as foreign minister. Following the homey model of Franklin Delano Roosevelt's fireside chats, Masaryk spoke to his country in a personal vein, maintaining a link between the growing number of Czechs in London and those trapped in the protectorate. He delivered the latest war bulletins, told jokes, encouraged Czech solidarity, and gave first-hand accounts of what the war was like for the British.

"The people of London are very angry," he said on October 16, 1940.

I have been to have a look at the districts in which poor people have been deprived of everything by the Nazi savages. Calmly and of course sadly they look at the ruins of their little houses and an old woman says, "We shall never forgive them, we shall fight until the end, even if they destroy half of London." The English are a queer people. They are not fond of giving expression to their feelings, and a great provocation is needed for them to burst out. The Germans have succeeded in making them properly angry and their anger will be long lasting. . . .

I learn that some sort of extorted manifesto of Czech writers is being prepared which would . . . attempt to show to a skeptical world that our intellectuals have reoriented themselves and have become Greater Germans. . . . These are base and naive deceptions. . . . I know and I know joyously . . . that the vast majority of our people at home stand as firm as they did on March 15, 1939. For Hitler's men have proved a thousand times that they mean well with no one except their own people. And I beg you not to forget this even for a moment. Deception, lies, robbery, and sadism — those are the philosophical foundations of your temporary tyrants. Believe nothing they tell you!

And on October 23, just before Czechoslovak Independence Day:

I know with equal certainty that the final victory will be a victory of those ideas which inspired our beloved nation for a thousand years and fortified it through good and evil. I urgently warn you to keep calm in face of provocation. Stay at home. Do not wander about the streets. Do not assemble in groups. At home you have your books and these will serve to fortify you. There are books in sufficient number. It may well be that the Nazis will try to provoke you. Take no notice — it would only end in futile arrests and massacre. This time the motto must be Silence!

Although listening to foreign broadcasts in the protectorate was a criminal offense and the Nazis tried to make short-wave parts unavailable, hundreds of thousands of Czechs tuned in regularly to the BBC. Hunched over a radio set with others listening to the foreign minister's voice, Emil Rabinek was able to feel as though he were still a citizen. Just as Thomas G. Masaryk had successfully used his presidency to set a humanistic tone for the First Republic, Jan Masaryk successfully used his broadcasts to influence moral behavior under the occupation. "The Czech nation is probably as solidly opposed to its present form of rule today as it was a year and a half ago," George Kennan wrote back to Washington that fall. "There is simply no real National Socialist sentiment in Bohemia and Moravia except among the Germans themselves."

The Solars felt the restrictions on their lives more than the elderly Rabineks. When they wished to go out after the 8 P.M. curfew, they had to sneak past Herr Lachmann, a German informer who kept close surveillance of "Jewish activity" on his street, and who was outraged that Jews were still permitted liberties such as the right to keep pets. Eluding Herr Lachmann in order to visit friends down the street became one of the Solars' regular pastimes. Christmas arrived. Then New Year's Day of 1941. The Rabinek-Solar household tried to keep warm despite the scarcity of coal, to celebrate the holidays, to keep busy as the number of their "privileges" was inexorably reduced.

In January, all residential telephones belonging to Jews were disconnected except for a small number necessary for the remaining Jewish physicians and officials of the Jewish community. Then Jews were denied ration cards for apples. Then ordered to turn in all stamp collections. Then prohibited from buying any fruits, nuts, cheese, candies, fish, meat, poultry, onions, or garlic. Leisure activities shrank to reading, walking, and listening in secret to the radio.

"Well, here is another Wednesday," Jan Masaryk broadcast in mid-February.

The tinder is burning in the Balkans. . . . Bulgaria may well be the next victim of the German gospel. . . . Rumania has drunk almost to the dregs the cup of German friendship. . . . And Turkey, the most exposed but also the most prepared of the Allies, is standing ready to defend its so dearly purchased freedom. . . .

In May, he reminded his countrymen of the need to resist Nazi measures against the Jews:

We had a rather unpleasant raid. Westminster Abbey was damaged, a very unmilitary objective. . . . Our Red Cross also received a blow from the Germans and the building was gutted. . . . Jews and Christians were doing rescue work and it never occurred to anyone that there were differences between them of race, religion, class, or property. So it should be even when bombs are not falling and so it was in the first Republic. Let us bear that in mind.

In July of 1941 Jews were barred from walking in any wooded area in Greater Prague and, in September, from entering or using any public or private lending library. That month, in the protectorate as throughout the Reich, all Jews over the age of six were ordered to wear a yellow star marked *Jude*.

Pepi Rabinek sewed the three stars allotted to each Jew in her family carefully onto their coats and jackets. A few Prague Jews wore the yellow badge with pride; others with a sense of humiliation. Many Prague Jews, ignorant of its history, made light of the Nazi-generated symbol. They dubbed the Jewish Community Offices where the stars were distributed as "Place d'Etoile."

Franci viewed the yellow star as a personal insult and often left home without it. She found her mother's quiet acceptance of the badge disturbing and ascribed it to Pepi's religious upbringing in Kolín and her abandonment of Aunt Rosa and the tradition of her ancestors. Whenever Pepi, afraid that her daughter would be arrested if she went out without the star, insisted that she wear it, Franci compromised by placing her large shoulder bag over it. She was not alone. Many young Czech Jews of her generation, wrote Ruth Bondy, "still stole into movies, took walks in the park, and ate pastries at the bakery with the lightheartedness of youth, its boldness in playing with fire, its anger at its own helplessness."

At the end of September of 1941, the indignity of wearing a Jewish badge was dwarfed by a catastrophe. Hitler replaced Reich protector Baron von Neurath with the former head of Nazi security police, Reinhard Heydrich. The new protector's mandate was to eliminate continuing Czech resistance, the Czech intelligentsia, and Czech Jewry.

Upon his arrival in Prague, Heydrich declared a state of emergency, imposed martial law, and established a set of summary Nazi courts staffed by the Gestapo. Within three months, more than five thousand members of the Czech elite were arrested and over four hundred Czech generals, university professors, lawyers, journalists, business leaders, and heads of the Sokols, the Czech national gymnastics organization, executed. Remaining Czech cultural institutions and churches were severely restricted; agriculture was tightly controlled; Germanization of the school system was enforced; Czech political autonomy became a fiction.

In a gesture as calculatedly symbolic as Hitler's spending the night in Prague Castle, the Czech Tomb of the Unknown Soldier was demolished. "The Czech people still do not have enough common sense to realize the consequence of their existence in the middle of a Europe led by Germany," wrote the official German daily Der Neue Tag. "Therefore they will have to learn what realism and loyalty mean."

From London, Jan Masaryk urged his countrymen to avoid provocation and maintain their faith during the reign of terror:

> When news began to come in of mass executions in France, Norway, Yugoslavia, and elsewhere, I waited intently to see when Hitler would remember us too. Well, he has remembered. Heydrich has come to Prague to break your spirit and intimidate you all. In that, of course, he will not succeed.
>
> I am a little ashamed to speak to you today from here, where I am in safety. . . . Please, do not let yourselves be

provoked into the actions for which Heydrich's bloody hands are waiting, and go about your own business calmly. Do not give Heydrich this opportunity now. . . . Therefore no strikes, no hasty demonstrations and manifestations. It is difficult for me today to wish you a good night.

In mid-October, the first deportations of Prague Jews began. A transport of one thousand left for the ghetto of Lodz, Poland, quickly followed by four more. To the Rabineks, who had been hearing accounts of Jews being forcibly resettled into what had been the medieval ghetto of Prague, three or four families sharing one kitchen and one toilet, these transports did not, at first, seem sinister. *"Only the wealthiest families were taken,"* my mother later wrote, *"and, to us, it did not seem too different from being forced to relocate to the old ghetto where Jews lived one family to one room."* Then the transports to Poland stopped. Rumor had it that Czech Jews were to be given a town of their own, a garrison town called Terezín. In November a special transport of able-bodied young men was called up to make the garrison ready for a civilian population.

Out in the film colony of Barrandov, the Rabineks were buffered from the catastrophic changes in the life of Prague Jews. Thanks to the prescience of Franci's cellmate, the red-headed Marianne, they still had some control over their lives. Emil Rabinek could still spend an hour shaving or reading undisturbed. Pepi could persuade the local shopkeeper to sell her sugar and lard under the table and bake cookies and cakes when she wished. Because soap was so expensive, she dyed sheets and clothing dark colors that did not show stains. She went through her family's clothing piece by piece, repairing what needed to be repaired.

Joe was spending more and more time in secret activities. He knew the ins and outs of the black market and brought home not only money but such articles as duffel bags and knapsacks that were packed so that the two families could be ready to move at twenty-four hours' notice. He reveled in smuggling family valuables to the homes of non-Jewish friends under the nose of the street's informer, carrying out his father-in-law's library, his paint-ings, and the photographs that appear in this book.

Franci's life remained the most "normal," strangely dissoci-ated from the overall situation for Jews in the protectorate. She was able to continue working. Every morning, she placed her shoulder bag over the yellow star and pedaled off toward Wen-ceslas Square, inconspicuous in the traffic of bicycles that flowed back and forth between the film colony and the city. I see Franci, twenty-one years old in February of 1941, willful as ever, furious at life, wearing invisible blinders as she rode through Prague, ig-noring the men in uniform, refusing to acknowledge the swastikas.

The image of Franci Solar riding to work in those winter streets — her bag over her star over her heart — is a new and haunting one for me. My mother often said that she had discov-ered the protective device of psychic numbing in Auschwitz, after she had been tattooed with a prison number and, staring at it, watched her forearm become two forearms, her body, two bod-ies, her self, two selves. But I think that protective mechanism of splitting off happened much sooner, long before she saw the in-side of a concentration camp.

Czechs who lived through the occupation all describe the or-ganized insanity of daily life in the protectorate. One anonymous witness wrote,

> Everything you look at has the hand of occupation upon it. You are ordered about by notices in the street. Every time you pass these inscriptions you are forced to realize afresh that you are no longer master in your own country. . . . If you turn on the radio or open a paper you are shouted at or stared at by insults and outrages . . . all the details of normal life become abnormal. You are under a permanent pathological tension. You cannot get rid of it . . . you cannot wash it off. . . .

Franci and her entire generation learned to switch their senses on and off, to tune out the protectorate. Once inside Salon Weigert, she tuned back in. In Paris, Madame Vionnet and Mainbocher had joined Chanel in closing down their operations but about sixty *maisons,* including Schiaparelli, remained open for business, continuing to determine the lengths of hemlines, the width of shoulders, the placements of waists. Fashion magazines contin- ued to come out on schedule and, in the *salon,* they represented the ultimate authority.

At work, Franci immersed herself in details. She kept an eye on the books, ordered what was needed from suppliers, corrected her employees, tried hard to preserve relationships with her cus- tomers. The concentration she brought to her work combined with her need to escape must have been such that, at times, I imagine she actually forgot the reality of the protectorate. But she could not allow herself to forget too often. Informers had be- come a scourge of life in the protectorate and the fashion busi- ness involved so many people that any one of them — a client, a worker, or a supplier — could report her to the Gestapo.

Toward Marie, Franci felt bitterness and confusion. Reflecting on her role as my mother's front under Heydrich half a century later, I see that Marie was risking a great deal. But Franci saw only her usurpation of power. She came to view Marie as her enemy and the clients as her allies. The German customers, she said, used to assure her of their friendship and sent their best regards to Pepi, but the Czech clients were, my mother later wrote, "*a ray of sunshine. Many an heirloom from our house found its way into theirs. They also very forcefully kept Marie aware of the fact that I was the reason they kept coming to Salon Weigert. They and my friends from school and sports kept my faith in the human race.*"

In December of 1941, following the bombing of Pearl Harbor by the Japanese, the United States finally entered the war. "This is another Christmas gift for you at home from those abroad," de- clared Jan Masaryk in his Christmas Day broadcast from the United States.

The American nation is today united and the defeat of Hitler is today much nearer . . . though I warn you again that it will not be very easy. Many trials are awaiting us still and much blood will flow. The outcome is sure but don't wait for miracles and above all don't think that somebody else will win this war for us — your resistance today is very important. . . .

Russia is our ally and an ally that is doing great work. Here in America the government and President Roosevelt are watching your heroic fight against the Germans with sympathy and with admiration. In Russia and England they count upon you and they know that sabotage and the preparation for settling the final accounts are increasing and will increase still further. And we believe in you and love you very much. . . .

I am homesick today, very homesick. Good night.

An exultant Emil Rabinek made new flags on his wall maps for the Americans, who would surely end the war. On their second New Year's Eve in Barrandov, the Rabineks and Solars drank to a German defeat in Russia, an American and British invasion of Europe, to the deaths of Heydrich, Hitler, the protectorate, and Nazism. But as 1941 became 1942, the news broadcast by the BBC was anything but good. The Americans were unprepared for war; the British were exhausted; the Germans were advancing in Russia; their allies, the Japanese, were advancing toward India.

In the protectorate, the barrage of anti-Jewish edicts continued: any employer could terminate the employment of a Jew at any time. The prohibition barring Jews from libraries was extended to include museums, exhibitions, galleries, archives, and auctions. In January, Jews were forbidden to buy newspapers and periodicals. In February, they were barred from using all laundries and cleaning establishments. Every week, trains deported Jews from Czech cities and towns to the concentration camp of Terezín and, from there, to other destinations in the east. Whatever possessions they could not carry were seized by the Nazis. Other people moved into their homes. In Prague, forty-five warehouses were packed with furniture, typewriters, binoculars, cameras, paintings, religious objects, musical instruments, that had once belonged to Jews.

During those first months of 1942, Franci Solar was still riding her bicycle to Salon Weigert every morning. It was now a crime punishable by death to hide a Jew or to conceal Jewish property and Marie was growing increasingly nervous. The restrictions mounted: Jews were required to register all cameras, typewriters, adding machines, skis, ski boots, and ski poles. They had to give up all pets: cats, dogs, and birds. Franci turned in her canary but refused to give up her terrier, Tommy. Then, just before Franci's twenty-second birthday, Joe was caught black-marketeering. He was arrested, tried by the Gestapo, and sentenced to five months in prison.

Although Joe managed — from a prison cell — to arrange for a four-foot-high lilac bush to be delivered to Franci on her birthday, he proved far less stalwart than the Rabineks had been in 1939. He had heard about the stepped-up beatings and random shootings under the Heydrich regime. He knew that the execution chamber in Pankrác boasted a guillotine that was regularly used. He was not the kind of man who could survive a long period of time in prison, he told his wife when she came to see him on her weekly visit, and begged her to get him out. His desperation met with the contempt of Emil Rabinek, who said he found it unmanly to beg a woman for help.

Like so many other men of his generation, Herr Rabinek had remained — apart from his listening to the BBC — a law-abiding subject, if no longer a citizen. He had been raised to believe that without law there was chaos and he followed the law to the letter even when it was promulgated by Hitler, when it was unjust, and when it had disenfranchised him. He loathed the black marketeers and believed that his son-in-law got only what he deserved.

Franci was astounded at her father's attitude. Like most of her generation, she flouted the laws of the protectorate. She did not claim that her husband was a hero. Maybe Joe was even, as her father claimed, a coward. But he was her husband and he had been judged by a kangaroo court. This was not justice but repression. Pepi tried to mediate and, for her pains, became the brunt of both her husband's and daughter's anger. Joe's arrest had turned back the clock: once again, Franci was an only child, a battleground for her elderly parents. Joe had entertained and diverted them all. Now Franci had no companion and no place to go.

One month became two, then three, and despite intensive efforts, Franci could not — as Joe had two years earlier — gain access to anyone within the prison system. Then, on May 27, all efforts became impossible. Members of the Czech Resistance — paratroopers flown into the protectorate from England — fatally wounded Reich protector Heydrich. He would be the only leading Nazi to be assassinated during the Second World War and Hitler was so outraged at his murder that he threatened to execute thirty thousand Czechs if the culprits were not found.

Martial law was declared in the protectorate. All Czechs were required to appear at special offices to have their identity cards stamped. Anyone who failed to register and anyone sheltering a person without a stamped identity card was to be executed. All Czech movies, sports facilities, and theaters were closed. More than four million Czechs in thousands of cities, towns, and villages were subjected to the exhaustive search for the perpetrators. There were, officially, 1,331 executions. Some of the victims' names appeared in the newspapers and were broadcast over the radio; others simply disappeared. Over three thousand more people were thrown into prison, beaten, tortured, shot at random. A huge reward was posted for information about the perpetrators. Anyone found concealing information or failing to report persons engaging in activities hostile to the Reich would be shot.

After Heydrich died on June 4, the Nazis leveled the mining village of Lidice, shooting 173 of its men on the spot, deporting its women and children to concentration camps, knocking every building to the ground. One of every ten Czechs would be shot every day, it was rumored, until the assassins surrendered. Fourteen days later, on June 18, the two assassins and five other Czech parachutists were cornered in the Church of St. Cyril and St. Methodius in Prague. After a gun battle, they committed suicide but their deaths did not end the reign of terror. The Orthodox Church was dissolved; its bishop executed; all family members and associates of the seven parachutists arrested and, later, killed. On June 26, the village of Ležáky was destroyed.

By that time, Franci Solar was unemployed. *"Marie informed me early in June that she found the situation too precarious,"* my mother later wrote, *"and as of that moment I could not anymore set foot in the business. In my hurt pride, I did not even ask her for a small share of the profits."* That was all my mother wrote and almost all she ever said about the matter. In time, Franci must have realized that she owed her last three years to Marie, that Marie had taken enormous risks that far outweighed the benefits she received. But during that June of 1942, Franci felt only that the center of her life — her work — had been taken away. Her husband was in prison. Given the current political climate, it was anyone's guess whether and when he would be released.

Restricted from all normal channels of leisure, forced into domesticity, Franci began to learn housekeeping. In Barrandov, Pepi had recreated much that she had learned from Aunt Rosa. She now taught her daughter how to make potato dumplings and potato goulash, and cakes sweetened with carrots and other root vegetables, resulting in my mother's horror when carrot cake became a fashionable dessert in America. She turned her energy to scrubbing floors, polishing furniture, and — illegally — taking long walks with her dog.

Barrandov still maintained a patina of prosperity. Heydrich planned to transform the Czech film colony into a center of Nazi art and culture. Nazi propaganda chief Goebbels, wanting to build a film industry to rival Hollywood's, supported the expansion of the film studios and the construction of the largest sound stage in Europe. Film technicians as well as movie stars lived in Barrandov, some of them in luxurious villas with swimming pools copied from those in California. Barrandov was still producing Czech films in 1942 and, although the film colony actually hid a pocket of anti-Nazi activity, the Germans viewed it as secure.

Every day that summer, Franci Solar walked with her dog, Tommy, through the fields and into the woods. She had little else to do. Despite her nose job, she had not been inside a movie theater for two years. She had not been to the theater nor to a single concert. After an initial spurt of household cleaning, she had become listless and depressed. Every week, she heard about friends and relatives who had been deported to Terezín, the old Austrian army garrison built in 1780 by Joseph II and named after his mother, the empress Maria Theresa.

During the First Republic, Terezín served as a garrison town for the Czechoslovak army, with an array of cheap restaurants and pubs. It was lackluster. It was in the sticks. But it was nearby, in the familiar terrain of Czechoslovakia, not somewhere in Poland. Her cousin Kitty's family was there already. So was Joe's actress cousin, Vava. Every Jew in Prague was preparing for deportation, trying to guess the best combination of food and medicine and clothing and books to include in the allotted 50 kilograms of luggage, worrying about what to take and what to leave behind.

Franci argued endlessly about these preparations with her parents, then sought refuge in the company of her dog. With Joe still in prison, Tommy had become her only playmate. One July day, she attached one of her yellow stars to his collar, telling him that he was a Jew too. They set out for their walk and, once in the fields, my mother took him off his leash. Tommy disappeared into the tall grass as was his habit and did not come back. It was very hot standing in the summer sun and, after whistling and calling his name for a while, my mother decided to let him get back to the house alone, as he often did. When he was not home by dusk, all three Rabineks went out to search for him. No one had seen Tommy. Franci returned when it was dark to find her mother in tears: Herr Lachmann had been out hunting and, supposedly mistaking Tommy for a rabbit, had shot him dead.

All three of the Rabineks mourned Tommy but for Franci, the shooting of her pet was the last straw. She stopped going out of the house and waited to be deported with everyone else. She was not even able to muster much excitement when, toward the end of July, Joe completed his five-month sentence and was released from prison. Two weeks later, he received his summons to what was now called Ghetto Theresienstadt.

Franci sank ever deeper into depression. For years, she had been suffering from recurrent sore throats. Several doctors had recommended that she have her tonsils removed to avoid later complications but she had always been frightened of surgery and used her professional obligations as an excuse to keep postponing it. Now, with the prospect of deportation and dubious medical care ahead, she and her parents agreed that it would be wise to have the tonsillectomy. Emil Rabinek walked to the Jewish Community Offices to ascertain whether there were any transports scheduled for the following two weeks. When he was assured that none were planned, he made arrangements for his daughter to have the operation in the one remaining hospital in Prague where Jews could be admitted.

Franci's tonsils were taken out at eight in the morning on the third day of September. That afternoon, a friend of Joe's appeared at her bedside with the news that a transport had been scheduled after all, that she and her parents were on the list, and that she, Franci, could receive a medical exemption but her parents would have to leave as directed.

My mother later said that, for a few minutes, she stared at the hospital ceiling and weighed the burning sensation in her throat against the prospect of taking the train the next day to Terezín. There was not much to consider. She felt she belonged with her parents. She wanted a change. What would she do in Barrandov without Joe or her parents, all alone? That thought was more frightening than being deported with an unhealed throat. She spent the night in the hospital The next day, against the advice of her doctors, she checked out and went home to help pack.

On September 4, 1942, dressed in several layers of winter clothes and weighed down by their 50 legally allotted kilograms of luggage, Franci Solar and her parents took the tram from the center of Prague to the Trade Fair Hall, where Korálek & Rabinek had customarily rented a stand and where Franci had often come to spend the day, returning home with balloons and coils of electrical tape and wire. The Trade Fair Hall was now serving as a processing center for the Jews of Bohemia and Moravia. The tram crossed the river, affording its passengers a beautiful view of Prague Castle, the Charles Bridge, the rooftops and spires of Prague.

I rode that tram fifty years later, amazed at the shortness of the distance, at how quickly it arrived at the Trade Fair Hall. There were geraniums in the window boxes of the buildings it passed, laundry drying on the balconies, the last vestiges of normal life for Franci, who would probably not have noticed them. Her throat was raw and burning. When they arrived at the Trade Fair Hall, she collapsed on the floor. She would not see Prague again for three years.

15

When she was in her mid-fifties, my mother decided to write a memoir of the three years she was in Theresienstadt, Auschwitz, Hamburg, and Bergen-Belsen. She gave it the title *Roundtrip,* in part because she conceived of her journey as beginning with her deportation from Prague and ending with her solitary return, in part because irony was her defense against pain. *"Why do I feel compelled to add my voice to the great chorus of statistics, learned reports, psychological studies, fiction and drama already written?"* she wrote.

> *There is no one answer, but perhaps my first and foremost concern is with my children and their generation who seem to me almost as troubled or even more than I was at their age. . . .*
>
> *Considering that children tend to be strangers to the inner life of their parents . . . and having no fortune to bequeath, I can only try to give them an honest and true picture of their mother in her youth and of my way of dealing with the perplexities of*

*existence. It might possibly give them some understanding of the
diversity and often puzzling behavior of the human animal in
addition to the corrupting force of power in the hands of a few
individuals who usurped it with the help of an indifferent, in-
timidated, and dissatisfied population.*

One of my mother's clients, a literary agent, sent *Roundtrip* to
a dozen New York publishers before giving up. There was no
market, some of the rejections read. Or, she lacked an angle. Or,
they did not publish Holocaust memoirs. Not many writers are
able to separate rejection of their work from rejection of themselves and Frances Epstein was no exception. The rejections
wounded her and confirmed her suspicion that no one was interested in her experience. She gave the manuscript to me, to use as
I saw fit. After all, she had written it for me and my brothers. After all, I was the professional writer in the family.

The last thing I wanted then was my mother's book. I had
lived with it all my life. It was her story, not mine. I wanted to get
away from, not into it. Even though I was then in my mid-
twenties, I had neither been able to rebel against my parents nor
truly leave home. I was in the process of writing my own book in
an effort to separate what was mine from what was hers.

I found it far easier to reread *Roundtrip* after my mother's
death, to look at it with my own eyes in a way that would have
seemed to me disloyal while she was alive. I could compare my
mother's narrative with hundreds of other survivor memoirs —
many by women, some by women she knew — and check it
against the current scholarship on every facet of her journey. She
was occasionally inaccurate about names and dates but her story
was so compelling that I understood how *koncentrák,* the single
Czech word my mother used for all the concentration camps,
eclipsed her family history and become the center of rather than
the interruption in her life. Frances often spoke of it as her university, a place where she had received her higher education.

The hierarchy of the Rabinek family was overturned at the
Trade Fair Hall. Every few hours, a new order was broadcast over
the loudspeakers. All house keys were to be turned in. And iden-

tification cards. And cash. Herr Rabinek and hundreds of men like him made their way through the vast beach of bodies to the appropriate table. Most had never been treated with such contempt. Bereft of their documents, polishing their eyeglasses with their handkerchiefs, they wandered back to their families, disoriented.

Pepi, on the other hand, grew stronger. It was Pepi who staked claim to a patch of floor space, organized their possessions, insisted that Franci drink, Emil eat, and all of them get up and move their limbs every few hours. It was Pepi who dressed Franci in her beautiful camel hair coat that was a part of Salon Weigert's spring collection of 1939 and coaxed her to her feet. Then the three of them, each tagged with a number on a string around their neck, joined the long procession of Jews walking to Holešovice Station in the early morning. There they boarded a special passenger train to Bohušovice, the train station closest to Terezín.

September, in Czech, is *Září*, or "glowing" — and that September of 1942 was particularly golden, hot and sunny. The transport of Jews to Theresienstadt did not pass through a gray fog as I had always imagined but through fields freshly ploughed under and piled with yellow haystacks and newly dug potatoes. The leaves on the trees were still a bright green. The sky was blue. *"Our humanity was still intact,"* Franci later wrote. She was still thinking and feeling like a free person, acutely uncomfortable in the several layers of clothing she was wearing to save space in her luggage. She was appalled at the behavior of the SS guards who herded them off the train at Bohušovice, and worried that her father would yell back and be shot.

During the two-mile walk to Terezín in the noonday sun, Franci was still able to note the strangeness of the long procession of city people in the Czech countryside, to be astonished that her mother managed to carry her 50-kilo allotment of luggage and shocked when one of the Czech guards told her that anything they could not keep their hands on would be stolen. She was puzzled by the deserted streets and ramparts of the former garrison town — later she would find out that the Czech population had been evacuated and that a curfew was ordered every time a transport arrived — and shocked by the "quarantine" in a former horse stable where "processing" included a body check and pilfering from their carefully packed luggage. Her throat felt like sandpaper. She had been looking for her husband's face and had not found it. Now she lay down on the floor, closed her eyes, and refused to move.

It was Pepi who organized a patch of dirty straw for her family, who sent Emil to fetch water for their daughter, who coaxed her into drinking it, and who tried to think where, in this teeming, unfamiliar place, Joe Solar might try to make contact. Familiar with the ingenious ways of her son-in-law, Pepi guessed that he was waiting for them in the latrines. She coaxed Franci to her feet and toward the row of primitive toilets, where they found her husband hiding behind a partition, waiting for them to appear.

Even in this squalid place, Joe was glib and self-assured. The Rabineks, he explained, had arrived on a "transit" transport that would leave within forty-eight hours, for rather than being a settlement, Theresienstadt was really a way station to camps in the east. But because he, Joe, was an "essential worker" extending the railway track from the station at Bohušovice to the concentration camp, they would be "exempted" from further deportation. Once they got out of quarantine, things would improve. They would adjust.

When Pepi relayed what he had told them to Emil Rabinek, he discounted it as another of his son-in-law's empty promises. Franci counted as her husband's immediate family, he said. Her parents did not. In the mass of terrified people, Emil found a former Casino friend who promised to do something for the Rabineks. Joe managed to get word to them that he was pulling strings. But a few hours later, when paper slips were distributed to the Jews in the stable, Franci was ordered to remain; her parents, to continue on the transport.

It was then, my mother later wrote, that Emil's sarcasm, his sense of entitlement, and his self-control all disappeared. He had known it all along. Joe talked a lot but he was a little nobody. In a situation like this, one's only hope was connections to the top people. Franci should look at the families around them. Other daughters were not letting their old parents go off into the unknown by themselves.

Emil Rabinek burst into loud sobs and began speaking with unfamiliar difficulty, using startling, unfamiliar words. His daughter was the center of his universe, he said. He could not live without Franci. He would not get back on the train with the transport. He could not go without her.

Her father's weeping and torrent of words stunned Franci. The father she had known for more than twenty years had rarely expressed feelings of affection, let alone love. Emotion was Pepi's domain. On those occasions when Herr Rabinek went away on business, he left with a perfunctory kiss to his daughter's forehead and some instructive farewell. Franci was so stunned that she no longer heard anything but her father's voice, no longer saw nor smelled, no longer felt the burning of her throat.

Finally, Emil Rabinek mastered his outburst of feeling. He sat up straight on the straw-strewn floor of the stable and a defiant expression appeared on his face. He announced that he refused to allow himself and Pepi to be murdered on a schedule conceived by the Nazis. He had made his own plans and provisions. He patted his breast pocket and told them that inside were enough deadly pills to end both their lives.

My mother was far too disturbed to be able to think. Instead, she blurted out that he did not have what he thought in his pocket, that she had discovered the pills three years earlier, after they had been arrested by the Gestapo, when she had returned home first and searched his desk. A pharmacist had replaced the pills. They were not poison but saccharin.

It was the sudden whiteness of her mother's face as much as her father's all too familiar rage that made clear to her the enormity of her mistake. *"It dawned on me that she too had known about Father's secret escape hatch and was now as lost as he,"* she wrote in *Roundtrip.* *"Instead of being protective, I had deprived my father of the last possibility to decide his fate as a free man. I wanted to explain. I wanted to tell them that I exchanged the pills only because I could not face the idea of being left alone. I wanted to tell them how much I loved them. I could not utter a word."*

The three of them spent the rest of the day and another night on the straw on the stable floor alternating bouts of silence with agitated argument. All around them were other families who would be leaving on the transport together the following day. There was no need for Emil Rabinek to point out to Franci, as he did, the number of daughters who were accompanying their parents into the unknown. Franci was beside herself with guilt and grief. She knew that her connection to Joe was not half as deep as the connection she felt to her parents. And despite two generations of baptism, Judaism's moral code, particularly its Fifth Commandment — Honor thy father and mother — had not disappeared from the family's ethical culture.

Once again, in my mother's account, it was Pepi who was strong. That night, while her husband was sleeping, she held her daughter in her arms and urged her to try to disregard Emil's anger. She, Pepi, understood why Franci had taken the pills to the pharmacy and had them replaced. She, Pepi, would have done the same thing. As for their impending separation, Franci was now bound to her husband — not to her parents. She and Emil had lived full lives. They had both celebrated their sixtieth birthdays. Franci was twenty-two. She had most of her life still to live. Calmly, with a prescience that Franci could not understand, Pepi told her daughter that she would take only a small bag of food for the transport and that Franci would keep the rest of the Rabinek luggage.

More than half a century after this separation was forced on my mother and grandmother, I cannot recount it without the blood draining from my face. My mother was separated from her parents in the doorway of that stable in Theresienstadt, sobbing, restrained from joining them by two of Joe Solar's friends. The last she saw of them was their backs as they walked away, toward the train station at Bohušovice, each holding a handle of their small food bag. Neither one of them looked back.

That September of 1942, the population of Ghetto Theresienstadt included about 58,500 Czech, Austrian, and German Jews, about 40,000 of them too old, too young, or too sick to work. Twenty-two and able-bodied, Franci was immediately assigned to the work usually given newcomers, a twelve-hour night shift in a hot attic of aged, terminally ill prisoners dying of scarlet fever, jaundice, typhoid, dysentery, or starvation. Nearly 4,000 people died in Theresienstadt that September, more than 100 every day. Touted as a "model ghetto for the Jews," Theresienstadt was more like an enormous waiting room of a railway station where thousands of people died before their train arrived.

Franci reported to work sobbing and, as she later recalled, all but useless. Ordered to bring water or bedpans to the people lying half naked in the September heat, she could not discern the dead from the living and began to hallucinate, seeing her mother's and father's face on every skeletal, dying body. She would not know until decades later where her parents had been taken. She could not know what happened to them when they arrived at their destination. But she felt that she should have gone with them, and that she had been prevented from doing so by her husband.

Joe Solar, who congratulated himself on rescuing his wife from deportation, became the object of Franci's contempt. His wife did not want him to touch her. She did not want to hear his voice or look into his eyes. From the very beginning of their marriage, Emil Rabinek had not disguised his dislike of Joe's slickness, his smart-ass remarks, and his penchant for the black market. Joe had always come third in Franci's attachments, after her parents and after her business. Now he had lived up to her father's view of him. His boasts of being able to save her parents had been hollow. Joe had failed and Franci blamed him, not the SS, for her loss.

Like other young Czech Jews who had been there for a few months, Joe had already adapted to life in Theresienstadt. He had carved out a niche for himself in its social system and was, my mother believed, happier than he had been for the previous year in Prague. Working outside on the railway track every day, Joe had created a network of Czech workers and policemen through whom he contacted his "Aryan" buddies back in Prague. They had established an illegal mail service that smuggled letters between the ghetto and the city and brought in food and tobacco.

Smoking was officially prohibited in Theresienstadt but cigarettes were its unofficial currency. Unable to stanch his wife's flow of tears in any other way, Joe finally forced a cigarette into Franci's mouth and ordered her to inhale. Franci began smoking.

Nicotine proved an effective drug, so effective that except for the nine months that she was pregnant with each of her children, my mother was never able to stop. Smoking numbed her senses sufficiently that first week in *koncentrák* that she could bring herself to talk to her husband, force herself to eat and wash, and notice that the society in which she now lived was not unlike the society she remembered from before the protectorate.

Franci Solar was assigned the second tier of a three-tiered double bunk on the second floor of the all-female Hamburg barracks, in a room that included every stream of Central European Jewry. The double bunk above her was home to an odd couple: a Catholic convert who, my mother noted with amazement, never failed to recite her prayers, and one of Salon Weigert's former customers, who talked only of her lost possessions. In the double bunk below, a ribald storyteller from Frankfurt shared the bunk with the modest sixteen-year-old granddaughter of the Chief Rabbi of Bohemia. Franci's own bunkmate was Margot Körbel, a strikingly beautiful woman of thirty with prematurely white hair, whose husband, Arthur, worked with Joe Solar on the railroad.

It was Margot who unpacked the blankets and dyed green sheets that the Rabineks had left with Franci and who arranged her luggage on the wooden plank that served as their bed. Each of the bunks had been transformed by the women who lived and slept in them into miniature homes and their barracks into a microcosm of the world they had left behind. Margot introduced Franci to her new neighbors using the honorifics of their husbands, as in "Frau Professor Stein" or "Frau Ingenieur Baum." She also introduced her to the camp's workings.

Although Theresienstadt was called a "model ghetto for the Jews" by the Nazis, Margot told her, it was nothing like the Jewish ghettos that existed in Central Europe before 1848. Those

were rooted in religious tradition, with genuine political autonomy. Jews left them every morning and could leave them forever
by converting to Christianity. No Jew could leave Theresienstadt
and prisoners were forbidden any contact with the outside world.
It seemed like an autonomous political entity because it was run
by Jews but, in fact, this too was a mirage.

The woman in charge of their room was called their "room
elder" because Jews were forbidden to use the title "commander"
or "leader." She reported to a "barrack elder" and so on up to the
council of elders, who were Nazi-appointed officials. Moreover,
Margot told her, the population of this "ghetto" changed on a
daily basis with some people dying, some being deported, and
new groups arriving without notice. Every strong, young new-
comer, like Franci herself, had to be welcomed and viewed as
having been saved from deportation. Illness was a constant
threat, as were the scarcity and contamination of water and food,
the infestation of lice and other vermin, and, of course, deportation. Franci would have to learn to inure herself to the sight of
old-fashioned hearses, drawn by human beings, hauling corpses
out of the ghetto and half-rotten potatoes back in. She would
have to forget any choosiness she might once have had about
food. And she had to force herself to wash every day even if there
was no soap and the water was cold as ice. Margot was scrupu-
lous about washing not only the face that was visible but what
she primly called her "other" face.

My mother later viewed Margot as the person to whom she
owed her life, a second mother, older sister, and friend combined.
She was fortunate, Margot explained to Franci, that Theresienstadt was not somewhere in Poland but in her own homeland.
Margot herself had been raised in Breslau, Germany, and had fled
to Prague with her husband in the mid-thirties. Her knowledge
of Czech proved essential to her and Franci should realize that, as
a Czech, she was among the camp elite. Some of the Czech men
had performed military service with the Czech guards. They not
only had access to the outside, where they could speak the native
language, but because they had been the first prisoners, the ones
who had adapted the garrison for use as a concentration camp,

they ran everything: the hospital, the kitchens, the warehouses, central administration.

In Theresienstadt, Margot said, Czech Jews were the officials, quartermasters, cooks, and elders. German Jews like herself were second-class and most of the older Germans who had arrived here thinking they were coming to a place of privilege could not get over their shock at having to barter all they possessed for food. Just how critical Franci's status as a native Czech was became clear when, that first week, the former owner of a large Prague *salon* recognized her in the street. The woman was now the head of one of Theresienstadt's clothing workshops. Few of her workers had any professional training and, seizing Franci by the hand, she had her reassigned from nursing to sewing.

Making clothes again, even cheap dresses for Germany, stabilized Franci. The ten-hour-a-day work shifts cutting and sewing were easy compared to tending the ill and elderly at night. Like Joe and Margot and Kitty, who had been quarantined with scarlet fever when Franci arrived, and Joe's cousin Vava, who had preceded her to Theresienstadt, she adjusted. In February, the deportations to the east suddenly stopped and an illusion of normalcy settled in. Franci learned to be blind to the emaciated figures picking through garbage in the street, to ignore hunger, filth, noise, lack of privacy, sickness, death, and the fear that deportations would resume. Over the course of 1943, while 15,126 Jews arrived and 12,696 died in Theresienstadt, Franci sewed. After hours, she earned chunks of salami and cigarettes for repairing other prisoners' clothes or converting blankets into skirts and coats, while Vava performed poetry readings and plays for audiences who valued theater more than bread.

"The corpses are piling up," the young writer Julius Fučik, imprisoned in Pankrác, wrote in his diary. "They no longer count them in tens nor in hundreds but in thousands. . . . But even in this horror, people still live. It is unbelievable but people still live, eat, sleep, make love, work, and think about a thousand things that have no connection with death. . . ."

Franci contracted the mumps and had repeated infestations of lice. She attended Saturday afternoon soccer games in the courtyard of the Dresden barracks and tried to take in the lavish cultural menu of music, cabaret, opera, and drama. Artists painted and drew on anything they could find, and created puppets out of scraps and stage scenery from garbage. Entire plays and scores of music were reconstructed from memory, copied out and performed by people who, in the protectorate, were prohibited from entering a theater or concert hall. Franci heard the Verdi Requiem performed by singers and musicians who were deported after their performance.

There was also a palm reader in Theresienstadt whom Margot and Franci consulted one evening in a room housing old people. As she held Franci's hand between her own hands, the palm reader said that her young and handsome husband was engaged in activities that would cost him his life. She, Franci, would be widowed. After the war ended, she would marry a man she had met in her childhood and leave Europe to raise her family. When Franci questioned her about the Rabineks, the palm reader would say nothing and turned to Margot's palm. "Too many widows, too many widows," she murmured, telling Margot that she would live but her husband would die before the war was over.

The two bunkmates did not tell their husbands of their visit to the palm reader. For her twenty-third birthday that February of 1943, Joe Solar had surprised his wife with two outrageous gifts: a vial of French perfume and two pork chops, smuggled into Theresienstadt in hollow shoulder pads. One year earlier, sixteen prisoners had been executed for expediting letters, the crime of engaging in illegal correspondence. But the executions had not dissuaded Joe from smuggling. He loved nothing better than outsmarting the Germans under their very noses. Even in camp, his exploits managed to entertain my mother, who was both appalled and thrilled by the risks he ran. In Prague, his black-marketeering had made him a criminal. In *koncentrák*, he was a hero. What was he? And, as the chief beneficiary of his smuggling, what was she?

Margot, thirteen years older than Franci, was the person with whom Franci discussed the ethics of ghetto life, the shifting definitions of moral behavior. The proximity of the dead and dying,

the daily routine of trade in stolen goods, and the continual
threat of transport "to the east" transformed people. Old marriages fell apart. Old friendships died. Total strangers formed
steadfast bonds. Sex was a form of currency as well as escape. But
Franci could not find much sexual feeling in herself, not for her
husband or anyone else.

She compared herself to Margot, who had fallen in love at
first sight with her husband, Arthur, ten years earlier and who behaved as though it had been yesterday. She compared herself to
Kitty, engaged to marry a Christian in Prague, but infatuated
with her boyfriend, a member of Theresienstadt's Jewish police.
Kitty had arrived in Theresienstadt just after her nineteenth birthday, on one of the first transports, and lived in a small, relatively
private room in the Hamburg barracks. She and her three roommates had worked out a schedule to accommodate their three
love affairs and one marriage and Kitty now offered her cousin
the use of the room for a few hours as well. Franci reproached
herself for not being able to match Kitty's enthusiasm.

Just as Pepi had redirected to her daughter the emotional energy that should have gone to her husband, Franci, too, sought
out a child. Many of the children interned in Theresienstadt had
no mothers or fathers. The parents were imprisoned elsewhere
or had already been murdered. Couples like the Solars were encouraged by the council of elders to "adopt" such an orphan. Because they were in their twenties, they were advised to choose a
toddler but when the day came to choose, Franci was drawn instead to a tiny, dark-haired girl with enormous eyes who looked
about nine.

Gisa turned out to be twelve. Her parents had been taken
away from their home in Karlsbad when Hitler annexed the
Sudetenland. Then seven, she had been placed in an orphanage
with her older brother, who was the only person in camp with
whom she spoke. Gisa reminded Franci of a mouse or, perhaps,
of herself. She insisted on "adopting" Gisa, spent much of her
free time walking with her, feeding her, trying to elicit a smile. A
gift of chocolate that Joe smuggled in for her had no effect: it
turned out Gisa did not know what chocolate was. She nibbled at

the bread the Solars brought her, then tucked it away to share with her brother. And she began to speak only after hearing Franci say a few words of English to Joe during one of their silent walks.

Franci spoke *English!* Could she teach her? Could they start right away? Franci began to teach her on the spot, English grammar, dialogue, and songs from the Fred Astaire movies she had seen with Kitty. Phrases such as "dancing in the dark" and "when we're out together dancing cheek to cheek" became her bridge to Gisa and a bridge to her younger self. Franci began to sew clothes for Gisa and to teach the girl, who had never been to school, other subjects besides English. Gradually, the tiny twelve-year-old began to talk about her childhood and what she remembered of her parents.

Perhaps because of Gisa, Franci became interested in learning. One of the subjects she chose to learn about was religion. Like so many other Jewish children in Prague, she had been nursed by a Catholic woman who told her stories of the saints, took her to the yearly Christmas markets, and brought her colored eggs at Easter. Franci had been drawn to the rituals of Catholicism and was fascinated by the jeweler's wife in the bunk above her, who followed her prayer schedule as strictly as though she were living in a convent. On her first Christmas in Theresienstadt, Franci attended midnight mass with her but was unable to connect to the people assembled in an attic reciting the liturgy.

Her attempt to come closer to Judaism met with the same result. Margot had been a member of the Blau-Weiss Zionist movement in Germany and had even been in Palestine for agricultural training. She was attending secret evening lectures on Zionism, which she summarized for her bunkmate upon her return. Joe's cousin Vava, who had been baptized as a baby, was also studying Judaism, with a Viennese rabbi. Franci attended a Sabbath service with her and watched a group of old men covered in prayer shawls praying in Hebrew. Vava said she felt a kinship with them but, try as she might, Franci felt she was a stranger. Nor did she feel close to any of the secret Communist cells that had sprung up in camp. Her identity, even after three and a half years of Nazi occupation, remained that of an unpoliticized, secular Czech citizen.

It is because she felt so Czech that I feel all the more satisfied reading the speech that Jan Masaryk broadcast from London on September 29, 1943. No prisoner in Theresienstadt was able to hear that speech but some of the Czechs who guarded the camp could and some undoubtedly did.

"Yesterday," Masaryk began,

we recalled St. Wenceslas and Munich. Today we should remember the Jewish New Year. The Jews are entering on their year 5704. In America, Britain, Russia, and Palestine, the Jews are in their synagogues praying for those most wretched of the wretched whose synagogues the German barbarians have destroyed and whom they have slaughtered in millions. The Jews have experienced much throughout their eventful history but none of their sufferings have been so terrible, so intolerable, and on such a mass scale as today.

Like ourselves, the Jews cannot live freely under a totalitarian regime. . . . We soon discovered that the Jews would be followed by Social Democrats, priests, and scholars, and when Hitler had finished with these representatives of freedom and progress he hurled himself at the rest of us, Poles, Belgians, Dutch, Norwegians, French, Yugoslavs, Greeks, and Russians. It began with antisemitism and it ended in a world war. . . .

After the war we shall all be poor and the Jews poorest of all. Those who manage to escape the frenzy of the Nazis will start from scratch like everybody else. And I should like us to be able to say to our children and to the whole world after the war that we helped the Jews with everything that lay in our power and that throughout the horror of the German regime we remained decent people. I know you will agree with me and that you will act accordingly. May God help you. Good night and a better New Year to the Jews.

There was little hope of that. Although the balance of power was now against Germany and the Allies had made a landing in Sicily, the more immediate news in Theresienstadt was that the railway line linking Terezín to Bohušovice had been completed. The number of men "protected" by working on the project was cut and although Joe Solar managed to hold on to a job, his work was mostly inside the ghetto. A new Nazi commander kept close tabs on the Czech guards. Interaction between prisoners and members of the outside world became riskier than ever.

Under the new commander, changes occurred whose significance would only later become clear. He ordered the naming of streets that had been marked previously by letters and numerals. Evocative names were painted on street signs: Post Office Crescent, Park Street, Riverside Road. He ordered the three-tier bunks removed from all the barracks in camp; the town park to be beautified; the evacuation of six thousand prisoners in a barracks that was fumigated, whitewashed, then readied as a warehouse for archives of the Reich. The deportations that had stopped in February resumed.

On September 6, 1943, three weeks before Masaryk's broadcast, some five thousand Czechoslovak Jews were sent "to the east." About six weeks later, Kitty turned twenty-one and lost the protection she had received for two years as the daughter of Lev Vohryzek, a house elder and Zionist leader, just at the time a transport of Danish Jews arrived, creating an urgent need for space. Franci was shocked when her cousin's name appeared on a deportation list in December and amazed at Kitty's lightheartedness. Kitty was convinced they were going to a new ghetto and ecstatic that her boyfriend was going too.

Her transport left Theresienstadt in the midst of the beautification program. Rumor had it that the deportation of Jews had aroused such outrage in Denmark that their Red Cross had demanded to inspect the camp to which they had been taken and that, fearful of antagonizing neutral Sweden, the Nazis had agreed. An international delegation of the International Red Cross would be visiting Theresienstadt.

Franci Solar now worked in a warehouse where she repaired

confiscated Jewish clothing to be sent to the Reich. On January 15, the barracks where she had been living was evacuated, fumigated, whitewashed, and the first floor turned into a reception center. Six days later, a train filled with Dutch Jews pulled into the railway stop in Station Street. The transport included several prominent figures from the camp of Westerbork and their arrival was filmed. The following month, the commander of Theresienstadt was once again replaced.

The new one hastened the "embellishment" of what the Nazis were now calling the "Jewish Settlement of Theresienstadt." He determined what route the visiting delegation would take from the station and set about improving its facade. Lights were fixed, shops were built and their windows were stocked with carefully selected items from the warehouse of confiscated Jewish clothing. Everything visible got a new coat of paint. A ghetto currency was introduced. A community center appeared, containing a stage, a prayer hall, and a library stocked with confiscated Jewish books. Prominent Dutch prisoners were assigned to large rooms with real furniture. New regulations were published in a "Bulletin." It had been an offense not to salute and get off the sidewalk when spotting an SS officer: now the reverse was law.

The change in protocol did not, however, change the reality of *koncentrák*. One evening in early March, Joe told Franci there had been a breakdown in his network. The next morning, he was arrested and taken to Theresienstadt's Small Fortress, where political prisoners were kept and often murdered. Franci berated herself for not feeling more than she did. She later wrote that she worried less about the way Joe was being treated than about his fear of torture. She was afraid he would divulge the names of all the other men — Jews and Czechs — involved in his smuggling operation.

Joe's friends rallied around Franci. Two of her male friends came to visit every evening. Both had Christian fiancées back in Prague, both were aware of the absolute camp taboo on sex with the wife of a jailed friend, but each suspected the other of designs on Franci. A Czech policeman, the brother of the guard who had arrested Joe, looked after her as well. Every week, he came into the warehouse, ordered her outside, and locked her into the guardhouse to eat a lunch of sandwiches and pickles prepared by his mother. After fifteen minutes, he led her back with a loud warning to work harder. He told her that Joe was working with a detachment of prisoners loading coal. Once he brought a scribbled note that said Joe was well and loved her.

On May 12, Theresienstadt's council of elders was ordered to prepare three transports of twenty-five hundred people each. All the unsightly inhabitants of the mental ward were to be deported, as were all the orphans. The remaining number of places on the list would be filled by other prisoners. Although friends tried to pull strings, Franci Solar's name and the names of all the families of men in the smuggling network had been placed on the list. On May 18, 1944, wearing her camel hair coat from Salon Weigert's spring collection of 1939 in which she had arrived, Franci Solar left Terezín for the "east."

16

~

A few months before she was deported, my mother wrote, she had a nightmare. She was alone in a place she had never seen before where the ground had an unusual, almost yellow color. There was a forest of barbed wire instead of trees. The sky was a dark purple shot through with lightning. Franci awoke screaming. For days, she asked Margot and Joe and everyone else she knew whether they had ever seen yellow ground and a purple sky. No one had. It was only when she was hustled out of the train and into the night on a road between two walls of barbed wire that she recognized the landscape of her dream.

Arrival at Auschwitz has been well documented. My mother, too, described the shock, the stench, the searchlights, the noise, and the march down a seemingly endless barbed-wire corridor. She had not heard the name Auschwitz in Theresienstadt and believed, as all the Czech Jews did, that they were going to a family camp called Birkenau from which they had recently received postcards.

"A few striped figures flitted back and forth in the dark carefully keeping out of the way of the SS," she wrote.

> One of these creatures materialized next to me at one end of a stretcher with a covered corpse and said "Nazdar," Czech for "Hi." I tried to see who it was and recognized to my delight our friend Tommy Schwartzkopf, who had left Terezín in December. He looked old and hungry, explained hurriedly that everything of value would be taken from us, to give him whatever I wanted to save and he would smuggle it into camp. I had very little. My own and Joe's old wristwatches, a fountain pen, a toothbrush, a comb, some stockings. Pushing this under the cloth with the corpse, Tommy disappeared into the dark without being noticed.

The women were separated from the men and lined up for registration. After the SS left, another of Joe's friends, Honza Pollak, pulled Franci into a tiny room where he gave her a bowl of soup. Transports were kept under strict quarantine, Honza said, but he was block elder of this barracks; this was his room. Honza was in his early thirties, a lawyer by training, and a well-mannered, proper man whom Franci had considered something of a prig in Theresienstadt. Now, in the eerie surroundings of Birkenau, she found his propriety and methodical way of speaking reassuring.

Honza explained that Auschwitz was divided into three sections: Auschwitz I, Auschwitz II, or Birkenau, and Auschwitz III, where the factories were. He said nothing to her about the gas chambers but explained that the family camp in Birkenau had been created for the five thousand prisoners who arrived from Terezín in September of 1943. Unlike other prisoners in Auschwitz, they had been allowed to keep their children, their civilian clothes, and their hair. Their camp elder was a German criminal prisoner but all other officials were Jews, as had been the case in Theresienstadt. "Registration" in Birkenau included a body search, a tattoo on the forearm, and assignment to a barracks. In Theresienstadt, almost all the prisoners had been Jews; the most powerful had been Czech Jews. In Auschwitz, it was dif-

ferent: there were Jews, Gypsies, homosexuals, a spectrum of political prisoners from various countries, and common criminals.
Most of the *kapos* were drawn from the German and Polish criminal contingent, Honza said, and behaved just like the SS.

Honza left out several key details. He did not tell Franci that
on March 7, exactly six months after their arrival in Birkenau,
members of the September transport from Theresienstadt had
been ordered to write postcards, then murdered in a gas chamber. Nor did he explain that, despite the family camp's special status, living conditions were subhuman and about a thousand of
the five thousand members of the September transport had died
within six months. He said he had sent Tommy to hide her valuables so that if Franci got dysentery — as she surely would — she
could barter them for medicine. He told her that little Gisa was
living in his barracks and Kitty, too, was safe.

Honza said she needed to be strong and that she could count
on his help. Then he let her out into the quarantine room, where
the last remnant of women was being tattooed. The Polish
woman "scribe" etched the number A-4116 into her forearm. Exhausted, Franci fell asleep on the crowded floor.

The following day, block elders arrived to look over and
choose the incoming prisoners for their barracks. One of them
was Renée, a striking blonde who had worked as a cook in Theresienstadt and for whom Franci had made clothes. Renée was
block elder of a barracks of old women and promised Franci a
choice corner bunk near the only barracks window, extra rations
of bread, and soup from the bottom of the pot. Franci understood that this was not altruism, that Renée expected her to sew
for her. She accepted, much to the dismay of her cousin Kitty,
who came racing into the barracks as soon as she could. Franci
could not remain there, she insisted. Didn't she know if she
stayed with these old women, she would go straight up the chimney? Why had she come here anyway? Why hadn't she run away?

How could she have run away? What chimney? Franci asked,
frightened. In place of the lovely girl who had left Theresienstadt
six months earlier with her boyfriend stood a gaunt and haunted
madwoman. Her eyes darted wildly in her face. Her hair was

matted, her body unable to remain still. Didn't Franci see the smokestacks? They gassed people here. Then they burned them.

Franci told Kitty to calm down. Honza had met her and told her everything. He had said nothing about gas.

Kitty stared at her older cousin with despair. All their lives, Franci had known better.

Listen to me, Kitty said. Every six months they take ten thousand people and put them in the gas chambers. Look at the chimneys. Can't you smell it?

When she sniffed the air, Franci became aware of a peculiar odor, the way hair smelled when the hairdresser left the curling irons on for too long. This is a big camp, she told Kitty. People die. Especially old people. You know Germans are obsessed with cleanliness. Of course they have a crematorium.

But Kitty did not back down. She started all over again. Gas. Smoke. You came in September; you went in March. Kitty came in December; she would go in June. What did Franci think happened to the five thousand Czechs who came in September? Where were they? They wrote their postcards. Then they walked into the gas singing the Czech national anthem. The national anthem!

Something had broken in her cousin. She was a robot, repeating the same words over and over again. Came in September, gassed in March. Came in December, gassed in June. There was less than a month left. Why was Renéc still alive? Because she had a boyfriend in the SS. In the end, they would all go to the gas.

Franci tried to be strong. She heard herself telling Kitty that she wanted to go outside for a walk. Although it was May and the air was warm, there was not a patch of green in sight. The main road stretched straight and yellow-brown between rows and rows of barracks and barbed wire and, as they walked and Kitty chattered, Franci saw how five months in Auschwitz had transformed not only her cousin but everyone else she had known in Terezín. They were all much thinner, with matted hair and sickly skin. Except for the *kapos,* they were all dressed in rags. Kitty said that some of the women were trading sex for food and that ordinary people had become different. One of Theresienstadt's star soccer players was now a block elder who beat his men. Kitty's block elder, a former model who had been Franci's classmate in Prague, treated her women like servants. The only elder who seemed not to have been corrupted was Honza. He had chosen to accompany his mother on transport and walked arm in arm with her every evening. The children in his barracks worshipped him.

Although Kitty begged her cousin to move into her block, Franci decided to remain where she was. She could not imagine herself playing court to a woman she considered a birdbrain. Renée treated her as an equal. Honza's and the children's barracks were just across the way and Gisa was living there. She was assigned to the clothing workshop. There, once again, she sewed.

In the summer of 1944, there were gaping holes in the German army uniforms she held in her hands and dark stains that she recognized as blood. The war was clearly not going well for the Germans. But, unlike Terezín, where their Czech guards had carried news from the BBC to the prisoners, news in Birkenau was unreliable. Rumors were rampant: the Germans were fighting for their lives; a great rebellion was being planned; they would set the camp on fire with gasoline from the sick bay; at least one thousand prisoners could escape before a second group of Czech Jews would be sent to the gas.

When Franci asked Honza why he had not told her the truth about the crematoria, he said only that he knew she would find out soon enough. Honza believed, against all reason, that something would happen, that no more of the Czech Jews would go into the gas singing their national anthem, that they would somehow see the end of the war. Franci found his faith admirable but unconvincing. In Theresienstadt, she had been known as an outgoing person. In Birkenau, she withdrew into a world of her own. She knew that Kitty missed her, that Gisa was in need of her attention, but she could not bring herself to resume English lessons or even see her regularly. She had discovered a distant cousin of her mother's in the camp but talking with her evoked the image of Pepi and was so painful that Franci stopped seeing her too. She ignored the old ladies in her room. She saw less of

Honza. Although hunger plagued her and he did not expect sex in exchange for food, Franci Solar did not wish to beg. She had developed the ability to mute the signals of her senses.

She lived in fantasy. Like thousands of prisoners before and after, Franci planned her escape. It was summer: the best time to survive outdoors. She would not need warm clothing. The forests were thick. There were berries in the woods and fruit in the orchards. She would locate and steal some insulated wire cutters, cut a path through the barbed wire, get to the railway station, and hide under a cattle car until it left Auschwitz.

She spun fantasies about Leo, the student she had met when she was sixteen on the train back from Berlin. She imagined that she had been able to persuade him to become her lover and devised a seduction drawn from operas she had seen and novels she had read. She relived the walks they had taken together in Prague, their conversations about art, the smell of his pipe. She did not allow herself to speculate on his life in America, whether he had married, become an architect, fathered children. He remained in her mind as he had been before the occupation, a handsome, ambitious young man aiming to rebuild the world.

She did not daydream about her husband, her business, or her parents. She did not know if the Rabineks had been brought to Auschwitz or elsewhere. She did not know if Joe was dead or alive. It was all she could do to keep herself strong as Honza told her, clean as Margot had insisted, and able to get from one day to the next.

Three weeks after her arrival, June 7 came and went without incident. There was no selection. Nothing. Then, in the middle of the month, Kitty — who had never stopped trying to draw out her cousin — told her that the Germans intended to select a group of people between the ages of fifteen and forty-five for a labor transport to the Reich. The people selected would not be gassed.

Everyone began to discuss the possibility of a transport *out* of Auschwitz. Girls younger than fifteen tried to find ways to make themselves appear older. Older women tried to obtain peroxide from the sick bay to dye their hair. On June 20, SS officer Josef

Mengele, Birkenau's chief physician, arrived to select the first group of male prisoners.

The pessimists maintained that the selection was a ruse, that the Germans had heard of a planned rebellion in camp, that they were identifying those young men likely to organize such a rebellion and eliminating them. For hours, the women took turns watching the railway tracks and wept when the first transport of their brothers, lovers, and husbands left Auschwitz. Next, the women were ordered to appear for selection. Naked, holding their clothes over their left arm, they waited for their brief interview.

Franci stood on line for several hours, long enough to learn that most of the women around her were planning to tell the doctor they were dressmakers. A summer thunderstorm had been brewing all day and the onset of lightning made the hall, with its line of naked women, its cluster of SS men, and its elegant presiding officer, look like the creation of a surrealistic painter. Franci observed that Mengele sent all old or weak women, all women wearing eyeglasses or bearing any kind of scar on their body, to one side; the young, healthy women to the other.

Not much past twenty-four and starved in Birkenau for five months less than Kitty, Franci was worried less about her health and more about her appendectomy scar. She had noticed that he asked some women questions and, certain that whatever professional claim she made would get lost in the massive operation of the war, she decided to lie. When Mengele asked her age, her marital status, and profession, she replied, "Electrician."

Electrician? Was that true? Did she know how to fix wires and such things?

Jawohl, she replied resolutely.

He told a scribe to make a note: A-4116, Electrician.

That evening, the women selected for work took their leave of those to be gassed. Franci said farewell to Pepi's cousin Hella. Then to Gisa. The small, silent girl was barefoot and holding in her hands the pair of Franci's shoes that Franci had given her in Theresienstadt. Gisa was thirteen, too young to be selected for work but old enough to know what it meant to remain behind.

My mother would later write that she regained interest in life on the July morning when she left Auschwitz. The sun was shining in a blue sky. The cattle cars into which she and Kitty were herded were relatively clean; their floors strewn with fresh straw; and there were only about fifty girls to a car so that they could spread out or lie down. The doors were left open and they saw farmers working in their fields, cattle grazing, people walking along dusty roads. One of the girls started to sing and soon the cattle car was ringing with the cabaret songs of Voskovec and Werich, Czech folksongs, and pop tunes from America. They rolled around the car, tickling one another and screaming and laughing like children. At night, when the doors were locked, they curled up on the straw and slept more comfortably than they had since they had left Prague. They did not know where they were going — only that they had left the gas chambers behind and were heading west through the Reich.

Finally the train entered a city, slowed down, and halted before a row of buildings with huge sliding doors. They were unloaded into what looked like an enormous warehouse, one side facing the railroad tracks and the other side facing a canal. Beside it was a similar building whose second-floor windows were filled with men waving and shouting. There were no dogs and only one, elegant SS officer, whom they nicknamed Petrovich, after a then popular German movie star. The guards were mostly older men, unfit for frontline duty. The women were registered, issued work overalls and blankets. Each rushed to claim a sleeping bunk. Then they raced to the first sinks they had seen in years, turned up the faucets, stuck their thumbs in the taps, and proceeded to have a water fight.

Meanwhile, Franci and Kitty climbed out onto a window ledge and, speaking a mixture of French and German, discovered that they were in Hamburg, that the men were Italian prisoners of war, and that their quarters were warehouses off loading docks for river barges from the Elbe. The Italians, who received mail and had access to news, told the women that the Allies had reached Rome, had landed in Normandy, and were advancing through France. Franci told them that they were Jewish women from Czechoslovakia who had left a concentration camp called Auschwitz.

A string of men and women took their turns at the windows, some of them simply gazing at one another and repeating one another's names; others conducting intense conversations. It was in this way that my mother met Bruno, a prisoner from northern Italy. He explained to Francesca, as he called her, that the POWs received regular packages of food, cigarettes, and clothing. He had a plan, he said, and asked her to come back to the window later. After the women had settled down for the night, Franci returned to her window. Bruno, in his window twenty yards away, tied a small package to the end of a laundry line and swung it until my mother caught it. The package contained some chocolate, a comb, a toothbrush, a pair of socks, a pencil and writing paper — and a letter written in French. Bruno was a factory worker from Treviso, which I recognized from my research as the home of the Collalto family of Brtnice. He had been drafted into the Italian army but had defected to fight with the partisans in Yugoslavia, where he had been captured and sent to prison camp. He wrote that he had fallen in love at first sight and wanted to marry Francesca.

Franci shared the chocolate and the letter with Kitty. The experience of being perceived as a woman was a revelation to the prisoner who had begun to think of herself as A-4116, who was wearing stiff overalls and sharing a bunk with rats. Her depression lifted. When the Allies began bombing Hamburg, she welcomed the bombs. In Auschwitz Franci had searched the sky for Allied planes. Now, as she held Kitty's head in her lap and covered her cousin's ears, Franci reveled in the sound of explosions.

Every morning the women worked clearing debris. Franci and Kitty were in a group taken by boat to a damaged but still functioning oil refinery, where they were ordered to pile the rubble into large mounds. The work was brutal for women who had never held a brick or shovel in their hands before but it was out in the open and afforded contact with other kinds of prisoners. One French POW who had built himself a radio began to give them regular news reports. Kitty met another, who slipped her food, winked whenever he caught her eye, and improved her spirits after the bomb-fractured nights.

Being recognized as a pretty woman was as important, my mother later wrote, as their thick potato and turnip soup. Many of the women from her transport soon had a Flavio or Benedetto or Pierre. After watching Franci shiver one morning during lineup, Bruno had swung over one of his sweaters. Although she knew she risked ending such aid, Franci wrote back that he should know she was a married woman. Bruno replied that he would always love her as a sister and their rope correspondence continued.

Their male friends drove a wedge between the women who had arrived as one from Auschwitz. Only the younger ones were receiving letters and gifts and although they shared food, many women were left out of the loop. The disparity between haves and have-nots, the twelve-hour work shifts, and night after night of interrupted sleep broke down their solidarity. They split into small groups they called "communes" that looked out for one another. As summer ended and the weather turned cold, their sharing of food and clothing could make the difference between illness and health.

In October of 1944, the POWs reported that they were to receive civilian status and be integrated into the local labor force. The women were to be transported to another camp. These rumors set off another frenzy of gift giving. In July, the women from Auschwitz had arrived in Hamburg with nothing. When they lined up to leave, many were carrying bundles. Franci had a small pouch around her neck which held two hundred German marks that Bruno had given her as well as a pack of cigarettes in the pocket of her overalls. Petrovich pulled them out and demanded to know where they came from.

"I find them, *Hauptscharführer*," said Franci, who had regained some of her sarcasm and, when he asked where, said, "In the same place every day." Petrovich replaced her cigarettes, then loaded the girls onto trucks that took them to a small camp on the outskirts of Hamburg.

It was at this small, new camp that Franci was identified as an electrician. The commander was a carpenter turned SS officer whom the prisoners knew only as "Spiess," or "Sarge." Friedrich-Wilhelm Kliem, as he identified himself before a British war crimes unit in 1946, was then forty-seven years old. A man of complex personality, he threatened his prisoners with a revolver and a rubber hose but risked his position by protecting his pregnant Czech typist, Mimi, from deportation. Spiess was a good carpenter and as his camp was not built to his standards, he determined to remodel it. He needed the help of an electrician, sent for A-4116, and informed her that he needed his telephone line moved.

My mother later recalled that she had not the faintest idea of how to move a telephone. But she noticed an assortment of colored pencils on Spiess's desk and, using them, drew a diagram of the box of wires, disconnected it from the main cable, spliced the wires of a new cable to the old one, ran it along the wall to the new office, reconnected the wiring, and, in a cold sweat, waited for a dial tone. When Spiess returned, she handed him the receiver. He decided to make better use of his surprising prisoner.

He had been thinking about converting a dilapidated old shed into a staff kitchen but had not done so because electrical current had to be brought in from a high-voltage pole and there had been no one to do it. A-4116 would. Spiess made drawings. He waited for a dry day, then ordered her to work, providing a long ladder and a pair of his own leather gloves.

"*Pulling together all her wits she worked on that line the whole day,*" my mother wrote in *Roundtrip*, using the third person when she described herself as a prisoner. "*And by evening, behold, there was actually light, although the cable swung dangerously in the wind. After this escapade, a grudging sort of respect for A-4116 came over Spiess.*" He seemed to enjoy conversations with his prisoner and took to lighting one of his cigarettes, placing it at the edge of a table, and leaving the room. He appointed her camp maintenance woman, a change that had profound ramifications for her well-being.

Instead of shoveling rubble in the cold autumn air of northern Germany, Franci became part of the crew who unloaded camp supplies and performed a variety of indoor tasks. She replaced fuses, maintained circuits and overloaded wiring, and fixed the numerous small appliances that belonged to the SS women. She worked alone and mostly in warm, dry places where she could lie down on a rafter unobserved and daydream. She moved freely between camp and headquarters, sometimes passing a German civilian who wished her good day as though she were an ordinary citizen.

She knew that the Americans and British were advancing from the west and the Russians from the east but had no sense of where they were or how long it would take them to get to Hamburg. Meanwhile, the women in her group — no longer the recipients of POW largesse or attention — began a rapid decline. By November, when the ground was covered with frost every morning, a shipment of old coats arrived. But adequate shoes continued to be a problem. In leaving Auschwitz, no one had been able to hold on to her own pair of shoes, including Franci, who had lost the ones Gisa had just returned to her. No one had a pair that matched or that did not need to have the holes papered over. Many women walked in bundles of rags tied together with string. Franci was particularly worried about her cousin Kitty.

Although Kitty enjoyed the privileges of a room elder, she had developed a skin infection that escalated into boils. The boils spread into her armpits and she began to run a fever. Vitamins were absent from their diet; there was no medicine. The camp doctor was able to lance some of the boils but Kitty's condition worsened and the women in her room began to treat her like a leper, complaining that she continued to distribute their bread. To prove to her cousin that she was not a pariah, Franci took to sleeping under the same blanket with her at night and draining her boils with the sewing needles she had held on to since her incarceration. But Franci could make no progress against the infection until one day — recalling that yeast contained large amounts of vitamin B — she stole several blocks of it from the bakery to which the "inside" crew was sent for bread. Counting on the friendliness of the German civilian who regularly greeted her, she persuaded Kitty to write to her fiancé in Prague. Franci would offer the German ten of her two hundred marks to post the letter and bring back a reply.

The German agreed and, some three weeks later, a small package of bandages and ointments arrived with a letter that did far more for Kitty than the medications. She memorized it, quoting her fiancé's expressions of love and regret and his mother's prayers for her return until all her bunkmates knew them by heart. During the long, cold nights, to the sound of bombing in the distance, Kitty and Franci would huddle under their thin blanket and take imaginary walks through Prague with the rest of the women in their barracks, awarding points to those who could remember the name of an obscure street or store. They reconstructed the satirical revues of Prague's Liberated Theater. They shared worries about their husbands or boyfriends and how it would be when things returned to normal. Their most popular fantasy was lying in a deep, hot bath.

Franci Solar began to do what she had not allowed herself for two full years: she began to think and fantasize about Pepi. She had spotted an empty notebook one day on Spiess's desk, taken it, and — during the hours she spent ostensibly working — was writing all that had happened to her since that September day they had been separated in Terezín in the form of letters to her mother.

She wrote in Czech, the language she and Pepi had always spoken together when they were alone, the language of her transport, the language that had become most precious to her. Her notebook became not only a diary of her life as a slave laborer in Hamburg but a meditation on all she had seen and experienced since being deported from Prague. She recounted her life in Theresienstadt, her friendship with Margot and Gisa, Joe's continued smuggling, his arrest and confinement in the Small Fortress, and her fear that he had divulged the names of the other men in his network. She described her transport to Auschwitz and reunion with Kitty, how everything they had been taught as girls was cast into a different light by *koncentrák*.

Once again, the women had no concrete sense of the progress of the war. The weather in northern Germany was icy. Many fell ill. They kept up their morale by working on an "entertainment" to be performed for the entire camp on Christmas Eve that had grown out of their reminiscences of the Liberated Theater. Spiess had permitted them the use of the mess hall, allowed the use of some camp materials, and required only that the whole production be in German. A former opera singer prepared selections from German operettas to be accompanied by an orchestra of combs. A former journalist on the staff of the *Prager Tagblatt* wrote skits. A former Berlin nightclub performer recreated her routine. Franci served as lighting director. The costumes were being made from five hundred handkerchiefs that had arrived in camp instead of shoes. They prepared two versions of the production: one in German, one in much racier Czech.

Franci wrote to her mother that the performances were a hit with the prisoners as well as their guards but that the first days of 1945 were frigid and grim. The waterpipes froze, as did the latrines. As camp maintenance woman, it was her job to lower herself down to the drain and hack a hole into the frozen sewage. Her roommates refused to go near her and complained about her odor as much as they had complained about Kitty's boils. Then the first of their women died of pneumonia and Spiess designed a coffin. Franci found herself telling him that Jewish law required a simple box and realized that, somehow, sometime since she had left Prague, she had begun to think of herself as a Jew.

Spiess's secretary, Mimi, delivered a baby boy, she wrote Pepi. He was strangled and buried in the forest. A shipment of one hundred wooden shoes finally arrived. Another woman, who had become pregnant by one of the Italians, was starting to show. When her pregnancy came to Spiess's attention, he ordered that she be deported to the concentration camp of Bergen-Belsen and ordered Franci to take her post as block elder.

She was given a cold reception. The women had all been invested in the pregnancy; it was difficult for them to adjust to their loss and made impossible when, two days later, two SS women conducting a routine inspection confiscated a cache of food — potatoes, turnips, some jars of fruit — that they had found and hidden under a loose board. Franci was ordered to deliver the lot to headquarters but, unable to resist a jar of cherries, she had hidden it in her new block elder's cubicle.

When the women returned from work and Franci told them what had happened, they were furious, accusing her of divulging their hiding place to the SS to score points. Franci was not able to convince them otherwise and eventually retreated to her cubicle, where one of the women burst in to find her with her fingers in the jar of cherries. She began screaming and started an uproar. For days, the women refused to speak to Franci or carry out her orders. She was wheeling out the barracks garbage when she was spotted by Spiess. What kind of elder was she? Demoted back to her old block.

Her reception there was as frigid as the January weather. Even Kitty said, "How *could* you?" and then refused to listen to her explanation. Feeling guilty but more misunderstood, Franci withdrew into work and wrote to her mother, covering dozens of pages with tiny, careful script. It was not long before the SS women discovered the notebook and brought it to Spiess, who called Franci into his office.

What was written in the notebook?

When she replied that it was letters to her mother, Spiess handed it to Mimi, his secretary. He demanded that she translate, word for word.

Mimi began reading Franci's most intimate thoughts to Spiess in German, softening or skipping what she could.

After a few pages, Spiess stopped her.

Did A-4116 realize that she had produced an illegal document? Did she realize it was his duty to report her?

Franci nodded.

Spiess handed the notebook back to her. Then he motioned toward the wood stove that heated the room.

Franci opened it, dropped the notebook into the flames, and watched them devour the pages. Then Spiess ordered her back to barracks.

She did not tell anyone that she had been forced to burn her letters to her mother but Mimi did. Sympathy for Franci's loss canceled out censure for her behavior as block elder. Most important, Kitty returned to her.

At the end of February, Spiess was ordered to load his prisoners onto open trucks and drive with them to an industrial section of Hamburg called Tiefstack. En route, they saw the results of Allied bombing. Rows upon rows of houses were burnt out or reduced to rubble. The cousins themselves were sick: Kitty with recurrent fever, Franci with a broken toe. In March, they were both lying in sick bay, chatting, when the air raid siren went off. Then they were thrown headfirst onto the floor.

When rescue crews came to dig them out, they found twenty girls dead. They lifted a dust-covered Kitty out of the debris and moved beams so that Franci was able to crawl out by herself. In the chaos, a few members of their transport managed to escape and survived the war hiding in Hamburg but, although the cousins discussed the possibility of escape, neither of them felt strong enough to try.

The bombing intensified. In the morning, they worked in what seemed a sea of flame. At night, the relentless bombing for the first time pierced through Franci's layer of numbness and she was terrified by every flare and sound. On April 5, Spiess loaded his prisoners onto freight cars. The train moved, stopped, reversed direction, moved, stopped again for more than twenty-four hours. The women learned that they were at a camp whose commander refused to accept them and that the train conductor refused to return them to Hamburg. Finally the doors were opened and they were herded out into a landscape more ghoulish than any they had yet seen.

They were in the concentration camp of Bergen-Belsen where, in April of 1945, piles of corpses lay beside living people waiting to die. The ground was crawling with lice that spread typhus. There was no food. The sleeping bunks had been used as firewood. The two cousins lay down on the floor of a bare barracks with what remained of their Czech transport, trying to conserve their strength, waiting.

When, on April 15, the British army entered Bergen-Belsen, there were sixty thousand prisoners still alive. Fourteen thousand of them died during their first week of freedom; another fourteen thousand in the weeks that followed.

The two cousins restrained one another from joining the

prisoners scrambling for food and cigarettes that the British soldiers sent flying over the barbed wire. They were determined to
get away from the lice and managed to drag themselves and their
blankets up the steps of a now deserted watchtower, from which
they watched for a few hours, waving to their liberators, and in
which they then fell asleep.

That first week of liberation, they were quarantined, fed, de-
loused, issued new shoes and clothing. Because they spoke fluent
English as well as Czech, German, and French, Franci and Kitty
were recruited as interpreters. They had been assigned living
quarters in the British army camp and were being taken there
when Franci collapsed.

She was moved to a hospital, where she was diagnosed with
typhus. Running a high fever, Franci drifted in and out of con-
sciousness for three weeks. Except for the tattoo on her left forearm, she had no clue to where she came from or who she was.

17

As Franci Solar struggled against typhus in a British army hospital in Germany, the Soviet army was moving toward Prague from the east and the American army from the west. The Americans were within striking distance of the city when they received unequivocal orders to halt: Winston Churchill, Joseph Stalin, and Franklin Delano Roosevelt had agreed at Yalta that the Red army would liberate Prague. The Czechs, however, took matters into their own hands.

On May 5, they occupied public buildings in Prague, built barricades from cobblestones, and, heavily out-armed, fought against the last major Nazi outpost in Europe. By the time the Red army entered the city, two thousand Czechs had died, thousands more had been wounded, and Prague's beautiful old Town Hall badly damaged. The Czechs buried their dead as they celebrated liberation, unable to understand why the American army had stopped its advance and not come to their aid.

At war's end, most of the Republic's political, financial, edu-

cational, and cultural leaders were dead or in exile. Its agricultural and industrial resources were in ruins. A major transfer of
populations was in process: thousands of Germans were fleeing
or being forced out of the country and thousands of Czechoslovaks were returning home. Franci Solar heard descriptions of the
chaos from her bed in the British army camp in Celle, near
Belsen, where she listened to the BBC, read newspapers, and
talked with her visitors. One woman, who had been with her the
whole way from Terezín to Birkenau to Hamburg to Belsen, had
returned to Prague and come back to Celle with grim news. Her
own parents and husband were dead; Franci's parents were dead
and Joe Solar unaccounted for; Kitty's parents were dead and her
fiancé, whose love letter had thrilled the entire barracks in December, had married a Czech girl in February. Housing and every
other commodity was scarce in Prague and the public mood had
already shifted from exultation to cynicism. "They were not giving food and clothing away anymore," Heda Kovály would later
write of those first months,

> but selling it on the black market. . . . Partisans who
> throughout the war had lived in the woods, widows of the
> executed who for years had slept on the floor of some
> basement, and ailing survivors of the concentration camps
> all spent day after day waiting in lines at the Housing Au-
> thority while butchers and grocers and other wartime prof-
> iteers walked in by the back door and were seen first. . . .
> Hadn't the butchers and grocers supplied the bureaucrats at
> City Hall with meat and flour throughout the war? Weren't
> they entitled to a little recognition for their efforts?
>
> Meanwhile, in the waiting room, a clerk would yell at
> the women who stood there weeping: "What do you want
> me to do? So many of you came back — how do you think
> we can find housing for you all? You expect miracles?" And
> people would walk out, humiliated, their fists clenched in
> rage.

Every week, an old Prague sightseeing bus arrived in Celle
and repatriation officers of the Czechoslovak government tried

to persuade the Czech Jews to ride back with them. Kitty and Franci did not respond. *"In our eyes, they were idealists who perhaps, just perhaps, were not totally representative of the general population,"* my mother would later write. *"The mere fact that they were driving dilapidated buses for thousands of miles proved that they were the ones who had always been our friends. Alienated as we were and schooled in six years of German propaganda, many of us were unable to grasp the outstretched hand."*

They were also unready to face the enormity of their loss. Franci was twenty-five years old; Kitty, twenty-three. They were, for the moment, one another's entire family and Franci's weakened health gave them a valid excuse to stay with the British. Typhus had left her partially deaf, her body swollen, her hair falling out, and on a strict regimen of diet, rest, and exercise that addressed her psychological as well as physical needs. Every afternoon, her doctor ordered, Franci was to be driven by jeep through the countryside by a rotating crew of British soldiers so that she could see something other than barracks and regain contact with the natural world.

Those jeep rides became crucial to her recovery. The English men and women who cared for her were different from any group of people she had known before. Franci knew they were horrified by what they had seen when they liberated Belsen, but they did not speak of it. They were reserved, solicitous but not overbearing, kind but unintrusive. A motherly colonel from South Africa took Franci under her wing, suggesting she register the names of every member of her family with the International Red Cross, that she see the camp dentist, supervising her recovery, even encouraging her relationship with a British officer who sometimes drove with her into the countryside.

Although some of the Czech ex-prisoners had become engaged to the British soldiers who had liberated them, Franci viewed Captain Jason, as the cousins called him, as a strictly temporary companion. He was a taciturn young man who respected her silences, taught her how to drive a stick shift, and — mercifully — asked her no questions. During her convalescence, Franci mulled over her prewar life, developing a distaste for the girl she had been and the husband she had chosen. She wrote a long letter to an address she and Joe Solar had agreed on before they were deported, explaining why she wanted a divorce. She was not cut out for marriage. She had no need of a husband. For the last three years, with the exception of the weeks in Hamburg, she had viewed herself as a soldier rather than as a woman. Even her body had shut down: the menstrual period that she had been expecting the week she was taken to Prague's Trade Fair Hall in the fall of 1942 had not arrived until six weeks after liberation — in June of 1945. She liked Joe. He had always been her playmate, the eternal prankster. But she was no longer interested in play. She was sure she would never marry again.

Franci began working as a translator as soon as she was able and, in her free time, making clothes again. Carrying written orders from the South African colonel, accompanied by a British driver, Franci rang the doorbell of a house in a pleasant residential area in Germany that summer of 1945 to requisition a sewing machine. When the door opened, she looked into the fearful eyes of a young German woman and, for an instant, recognized herself six years before. The woman was relieved that all they wanted was a sewing machine and astonished when they gave her a receipt. For Franci, their interaction was one she would later remember as a stop on her journey back to normal life. Once again, she began to sew.

Kitty, burying her grief in an affair with a British major, was her principal client. Although Kitty's back would be scarred for the rest of her life, the boils that had covered it had healed. She wore her blond hair in a shiny pageboy that evoked Ginger Rogers. She had retained her prewar deftness with lipstick and mascara. By July of 1945, neither she nor Franci looked like Bergen-Belsen survivors anymore but like pretty, normal young women. They worked during the day and went to dances, movies, and lectures at night. The routines of British army life in Celle replaced the routines of the concentration camps in which they had been prisoners.

One evening, the movie *Song of Russia* was shown, preceded by a newsreel showing the liberation of Bergen-Belsen. Sitting beside Jason, Franci watched the images of walking skeletons and piles of corpses as if she were seeing them for the first time. When the screen showed two girls standing in a watchtower and waving to the camera, the British captain grabbed Franci's arm and exclaimed, "By God, that's you and Kitty!" But she shook her head. Except for an occasional bolt of recognition such as she had experienced at the door of the German woman with the sewing machine, she lived in the present.

The officers close to the cousins became aware of their reluctance to plan for the future. Gently, they began to suggest that they think about returning to Prague. Franci and Kitty did not put up an argument. Although their tattoos marked them as Jews, they still thought of themselves as Czechs. Prague was their home. Of course they would go back. But they delayed until finally one evening, the South African colonel and the two men closest to the cousins organized an intervention. They explained that members of the liberating army would soon be sent home and replaced by other soldiers. These soldiers would not have seen the liberation of the camps. They would be unable to distinguish between a former concentration camp prisoner and an ordinary civilian. Kitty and Franci understood it was time to go home.

The first week of August 1945, the cousins set off for Prague, loaded down with gifts from the British. Kitty rode the old sightseeing bus; Franci followed in a dilapidated truck that carried their thirteen pieces of luggage and a radio. The two vehicles, burning blocks of wood for fuel, made their way east through the ruins of the Third Reich, breaking down every fifty or sixty miles. In the American occupation zone, Franci found mechanics with names like Jim and Bob who had never seen such a contraption but who helped get it running again. They chewed gum, offered her Spam, asked naive questions about her tattoo. In the Russian occupation zone, the soldiers pointed to her lipsticked mouth and asked *"Ty kurva?"* or "Are you a whore?" provoking waves of merriment from the four Czechs accompanying her. Finally in Prague, the cousins were dropped off at their destination: a two-room flat that belonged to a former classmate of Kitty's, his mother, and grandmother.

That first morning in Prague, Franci was served a huge breakfast by people she was meeting for the first time. Then she and
Kitty hurried onto the second car of a tram to go downtown. Although there were empty seats, neither cousin realized she was
now allowed to sit down. They stood in the rear like well-trained
dogs. Then they walked to the Jewish Community Offices, beside
the Old-New Synagogue. Before the war, Franci had never set
foot inside the building. During the occupation, she had been one
of thousands of Czech Jews forced to register in its offices. Now
that the war was over, the *Kehillah,* or *Obec,* in Czech, was once
again the mandatory clearinghouse for all Czech Jews. A tiny
remnant. Of the 85,000 who had been deported from their homes
in the protectorate of Bohemia and Moravia, only 3,250 returned.

Few of those 3,250 people had documents. No passport, no
identity card, no bank book, no school diploma, no certificate of
birth. They were obliged to fill out a series of forms and apply to
a series of government offices where they could obtain others.
They were told that, since they had returned so late, housing was
unavailable and priority was given to families and married couples. The apartments in which they had once lived were now occupied by Czechs who had thrown out the Germans who had
thrown out the Jews. By the time Franci had examined the lists of
the dead and missing, the euphoria of the journey back to Prague
was gone, replaced by a familiar numbness.

That first day, Franci met with the friend whom the Solars had
asked to serve as their contact after the war. As she waited for
him in Wenceslas Square, not far from the former premises of Salon Weigert, Franci realized that the dress she prized as a British
gift was made of cheap cotton and that her bare legs and sandals
looked wrong in the city. When the friend came toward her
through the crowd, she saw only his meticulously cut suit and a
summer tan. As the spouse of an "Aryan," Max had been spared
the camps and spent only the last two months of the war in
prison. He seemed uneasy and, after they had sat down to coffee,
handed her the letter she had written to her husband, asking for
a divorce. Joe had not contacted him. It was all but certain that he
was dead.

Franci sat, silent, holding the letter in her hand. It had not occurred to her that Joe would not survive the war. How should one feel, having asked a dead man for divorce? Max grew uncomfortable in Franci's silence. He pushed some cash across the table, invited her to dinner at his home that evening, then stood up and left.

Next, Franci forced herself to walk to Salon Weigert and ring the doorbell. Marie was as ill at ease as Max. After inquiring about Pepi and Emil, Marie said that she possessed nothing that had belonged to the Rabineks. She had put the furniture and mirrors and sewing machines and mannequins in storage to avoid any charges of having enriched herself with Jewish property. She and her tailor husband had refurbished the salon, had taken out a new lease, had developed a new and different clientele. Marie wrote out for her the address of the warehouse and, mutely, Franci left.

That evening in Max's living room, she was served a dinner celebrating her return. She held her mother's silverware between her fingers and stared at the corner of a tablecloth embossed with the letter *R* that the Rabineks had left with the family before their deportation. Only slowly did she understand that these things had not been brought out in her honor. Surviving the war with a Jewish husband had been very difficult, Max's wife said by way of conversation. Fear. No income. Starvation rations. Coupons. The black market. The children had been thrown out of school. They had been forced to sell some Rabinek possessions and barter others for food. Franci nodded and tried to hide her dismay when Max's son entered the room wearing one of Joe Solar's suits. She said she understood. But she understood nothing and had stopped feeling anything at all.

Vava Schön would later describe calling a former theater colleague to let him know she was back and hearing back, over the wire, "You must have whored for the Germans — there's no other way you could have stayed alive!" Heda Kovály would write that

a survivor might need a lawyer to retrieve lost documents
and he would remember the name of one who had once

represented large Jewish companies. He would go to see him and sit in an empire chair in the corner of an elegant waiting room, enjoying all that good taste and luxury, watching pretty secretaries rushing about. Until one of the pretty girls forgot to close a door behind her and the lawyer's sonorous voice would boom through the crack, "You would have thought we'd be rid of them finally but, no, they're impossible to kill off — not even Hitler could manage it! Every day there's more of them crawling back, like rats. . . ."

Vava and Heda, less introspective women than Franci, were better able to shake such incidents off. Vava auditioned for a play fourteen days after her return, won the role, and was immediately pulled into rehearsals. Heda reunited with her childhood sweetheart and began building a postwar life. Franci reconnected neither with her work nor with any person. At night, lying next to Kitty on the living room couch of Kitty's old classmate's two-room apartment, the classmate, his mother, and the grandmother crammed into the bedroom, Franci said that a displaced persons camp would have been better than this. The classmate was an angel. So were his mother and grandmother. But the situation was untenable. How long could they live with strangers? Where else could they go? They had been thrown out of their world, that world had continued without them. They had lost their places in it.

Kitty tried to placate her cousin. She also heard idiotic comments: "What an idea to write your telephone number on your arm!" or "You girls are so smart, you'll be married before you know it!" She also was asked the unanswerable question: How did you survive? But they were home. Things would fall into place. In the camps, it had been Franci who forced Kitty up in the mornings. Now it was Kitty who forced Franci through the postwar bureaucracy, to the homes of former friends and customers and prisoners who already had flats of their own.

Franci went through the motions. *Koncentrák* had forever changed the nature of authority in her mind. Uniforms frightened her, rules enraged her, and she had no tolerance for interrogations, inspections, or proofs of any kind. A friend had offered her a job for his export firm that entailed extensive travel and she had even begun to muster some enthusiasm for the work. But she needed a passport and when she applied, she was asked to provide her national affiliation according to the Republic's census of 1930. She learned that Emil Rabinek had registered himself and his then ten-year-old daughter as German nationals. Her French diploma would solve the problem and serve as proof of Czech nationality but obtaining it entailed another round of lines and explanations. Instead, Franci gave up the job and did not look for another.

"I didn't expect any triumphal arch and brass band to welcome me home," my mother would say years later, "but I expected some kind of official or general pleasure in the population to see me back, some pleasure that we had made it, that we had somehow managed to survive. Instead the pleasure was only isolated. Our very close friends of course were delighted to see us. The more casual acquaintances had a sort of wait-and-see attitude. What did you do there that you survived and my best friend didn't? Finally, I got to the point where I only wanted to see the people I was in prison with. I didn't really trust anyone else. Or I wanted to see only new people."

One of the people from prison was Karel, the former Czech policeman who, with his brother, had helped Franci and many other Jews in Terezín. He invited Franci to dinner after he heard of Joe Solar's death. Following traditional Bohemian custom, Karel gave her a detailed account of his property and expressed his wish to court and eventually marry her. He knew it was too early for her to make a commitment but he wished to let her know at once. Franci was grateful for his good manners but taken aback by his proposal. What she would later remember most about her dinner with Karel was the diamond ring on his finger and the pearl in the lapel of his navy blue suit. She was sure both had belonged to Jews. No death certificate had yet been issued for Joe, she replied. She had decided never to remarry, she said, and felt depressed, inadequate, wrong.

Those feelings surfaced when she traveled to Rakovník, where she was invited to stay with a middle-aged woman for whom Pepi had, years before, designed a wedding dress and trousseau. The former client now owned an automobile agency with her husband. They were wealthy and childless. The woman plied her with food and gifts, prevailed upon her to stay a week instead of a day, and insisted that she accept three times the amount of money that Pepi had left in their safekeeping. At the end of the week, the couple asked that she consider staying with them and said that they loved her as a daughter. Franci thanked them but said she was twenty-five, far too old to be adopted. Again feeling at fault, she returned to Prague.

Kitty had managed to obtain new accommodations for them: a spacious apartment on Old Town Square belonging to a middle-aged Czech bachelor who had employed Kitty as a secretary before the war and who had fallen in love with her. He had made clandestine visits to Terezín to see her and had even served time in prison for his attachment. His family now offered them lodgings on the assumption that Kitty would eventually marry their son. The two cousins had their own room; the location was extraordinary, but Franci did not seem to notice the improvement in their situation.

Half-heartedly, she searched for her old friend Helena. When she called Jan Slavíček's home, a stranger said only that Helena had left the painter at the end of the war. She visited Honza Pollak, the man whose integrity she had so admired in Terezín and Birkenau. He was dying of tuberculosis in a state hospital where he lay coughing up blood. As she sat at his bedside, the injustice of surviving the camps only to die a slow death in Prague struck her so forcefully that she fell into the state that had followed her separation from her parents three years earlier.

For days, Franci sobbed and refused to leave the house. She had still not been able to verify the fate of her parents and her husband. On the lists posted in the Jewish Community Offices, Emil and Josefa Rabinek were listed as "transported to Riga" but she could not find anyone who could confirm that they were really dead. September became October, the weather turned cold, and Kitty insisted that she see a doctor. It was in his waiting room that she once again met up with Margot Körbel, her Theresien-stadt bunkmate.

Margot had been liberated at the concentration camp of Maut-hausen and nursed back to health by a Czech colonel who had himself been a prisoner for six years. She had returned to Prague with him and the colonel had used his connections to obtain the special permit that she, a former German citizen, needed to re-main in Czechoslovakia. She had found out that her husband, Arthur, had collapsed on one of the death marches at the end of the war. Now she was living with the colonel, who had, she told Franci, spent the last year of the war with Joe Solar. After Joe's arrest, he had been put into a cell block of Czech army officers in the Small Fortress. When their group was deported to Auschwitz, the fact that Joe was a Jew was overlooked. None of the Czechs betrayed him. As the Red army neared, the Czech prisoners were sent to Mauthausen. Joe had died there while Franci was ill with typhus.

It was in October that the International Red Cross, with whom Franci had registered the names of all her relatives, noti-fied her that Peter Sachsel, the son of Pepi's older brother Emil, was alive in New York. "I AM THE ONLY ONE LEFT FROM THE WHOLE FAMILY STOP," she cabled him on October 25, 1945. "PLEASE WRITE AT ONCE STOP YOUR COUSIN FRANCES."

The cable was followed by some fifty letters exchanged by the twenty-five-year-old cousins, who had not seen one another since they were fifteen. I did not know of their existence until I found them with my mother's business records in an unmarked manila folder in my own study. The set of letters is not complete but even one is enough to hear my mother's voice and to understand the abyss that had opened up between concentration camp sur-vivors and almost everyone else in the world. The first letter is Pe-ter's:

New York, November 18, 1945
Dear Franzi,

    This is the third letter I am writing to you, in English this time. I'll repeat what I said in the other ones. You can-not imagine how happy I was to hear from you. I thanked

God for preserving at least one of the people dear to me. I really didn't have any hope left at all. And I am going to help you as much as I shall be able to. First of all, I sent you two packages with coffee, tea, sugar, cigarettes and the like. Then I am going to try to get you over here. For this, I'll have to know everything about you — not only personal data, but everything that happened in the last years. I cannot promise anything because it's very hard at the present time, but anything that can be done will be done.

Once more, Franzi, you cannot imagine my emotion and happiness when I heard from you. My cousin Franzi must be quite a girl — to go through hell and come through not only alive but also in good spirits. My respect and admiration to you, Franzi. After this, there will not be any obstacles for you anymore. I was sorry to hear about your husband and parents. I do hope they did not suffer too long. My parents and brother most probably had the same fate. Could you, Franzi, try to get some more information?

Now, as far as I'm concerned, I'm just plain lucky. You know that I left for France in July 1938. I finished in July 1941. I received some kind of diploma calling me chemical engineer specialized in tannery, and as I was lucky and had two uncles in America, I could get out of France in November 1941, four years ago, almost to the day. I went to Cuba, where I stayed until March 1943, when I finally was admitted to this country. I first worked as a research chemist with a company making chemicals for leather; after a few months, I volunteered for the army but they actually said it would do more good if I'd stay in industry and they just didn't call me. I joined my uncle Walter, who has made a big success in the leather business, like in Europe, and I hope I'll stay with him for many years. I didn't make very much money in chemistry; there isn't any in it if you are not in your own business, and as this is a very necessary thing in this country — to make money — I joined Walter, where of course I had to begin at the bottom. I'm not married yet but it undoubtedly will happen in the near future — I guess.

Write, Franzi. Tell me what you need. . . . Stockings, wool, all kinds of food, whatever you can think of. Just write.

With my love, and my very best wishes, your Peter.

Prague [undated, in Czech]
Dear Peter,

I only just received your first letter dated November 18. It's hard to describe how I felt. To thank you for your help seems to me almost banal. You gave me much more, you gave me back a piece of my mother. . . .

You write that after all I've lived through, there can be no obstacles for me. How wrong you are! It seems to me that I'm surrounded only by obstacles and sometimes I think that there was no point in my surviving the war. You have to understand that I returned to Prague and found nothing there. Every step reminds me of my mother and the past. Worst of all, I can't find a place to live. This is a catastrophe because after all these years of constant moving I need a corner of my own as a dog needs a doghouse.

I still live with friends and it's horrible. There are also material worries. Not that I need money, but I'm concerned about the current legal situation regarding the return of business permits. . . . And, finally, I live in such an emotional vacuum. You know, I don't really grieve for my husband. That's something that can't be changed. And maybe God was right because my marriage was not a happy one and the whole time I was in camp I was afraid of meeting up with him again because I didn't want to return to him. Of course, I'm almost afraid to remarry. I'm probably the kind of person who feels better free.

You're right. It would probably be best if I left Prague. Maybe I could make a living there. I do have a few skills. I don't know if you are aware of the fact that I'm a trained dressmaker, cutter, and pattern-maker and that I managed

Mother's business alone those last years. I even put it back on its feet. Besides, I've mastered four languages so there should be something I could do there.

You know, Peter, I'm not feeling sorry for myself but I have to find some meaning in life again. And that's very hard for people who came out of that hell. What would you like to know from me? It would be a novel and were I to tell you everything, your hair would stand on end. . . .

You ask what I need. Look, everything available here is expensive and poor quality — if you can even find it. If you can, send me some stockings, fabric, and — most important — shoes. Maybe it would be possible to send leather for shoes and I'll have them made. Please don't send me money. I would prefer it if you bought me something. Please send me cigarettes. I smoke like a chimney and cigarettes here are bad and expensive. . . .

At the end of November, Kitty's benefactor began to press her to set a wedding date. Kitty felt unable to marry him merely because of gratitude and the two cousins were compelled to move out of the apartment on Old Town Square, each to a new address. Half a year after the end of the war, they were moving in different social circles. Kitty liked to party with a fast set of friends whom Franci considered materialistic and flashy. Franci moved in a more artistic circle and, much to Kitty's consternation, had taken to going home after a play or concert with whatever man had paid for the tickets. One regular was a Slovak partisan who told her stories of the wartime underground. Another was a married man, a former friend of Joe's who had married an "Aryan." His mother had died in Theresienstadt and now he was obsessed by the remark she had once made before the war that he should have married a Jewish girl like Franci. Most important was a Jewish physician who had returned to his Christian fiancée in Prague only to find that she had been the mistress of an SS officer for the previous three years. He could not make up his mind whether to return to her or have a relationship with Franci. When he accepted a job in the provinces to get away from the dilemma, Franci moved into his empty apartment.

"Your mother would go to bed with anyone then," Kitty told me nearly fifty years later as we walked arm-in-arm through Old Town Square, which had survived the Nazis and the Communists and was now undergoing a capitalist face-lift. "That was her way of dealing with depression after the war. She'd sleep with someone a few times and then decide she didn't want to see him again. I didn't go to bed with anyone. I was immeasurably sad. The man I loved had married a Czech girl who convinced him that I'd not be able to have children after the war. He met me for coffee and said that under any other circumstances he would divorce his wife but she was pregnant now and that made it impossible. Of course, she was lying about both herself and me. She was not pregnant. She was never able to have children. And I later got married and had a baby."

Prague, December 20, 1945 [in Czech]
Dear Peter,

You cannot imagine how eagerly I wait for any news of you. I'm so infinitely sad, to the point that I sometimes think it would have been better had I died in the camps. I cannot find any meaning in my return. I think that all of us who returned from that hell have had a certain mental collapse and sometimes that collapse is worse than all the suffering. You know, there, we still hoped that when the end came, each of us would find someone who would love us, and then the end came, and I'm standing here completely alone and I am a terrible burden to myself.

You have to understand that I'm not talking about any material concerns but that I have absolutely no one who cares even a little whether I'm dead or alive. There's nobody here who needs me and if I didn't exist, there's no one who would miss me.

The whole time, I believed that the two of us would meet again. I think we always had a very nice and warm relationship but you are so terribly far away and you have so many other things to think about. There is a girl you want to marry and it would be selfish of me to ask you to take care of me. I would so like to sit with you the way we did as children long ago in Bratislava and talk and weep about everything that's hurting us. I don't know if you can understand it but I feel we would understand one another very well.

You have to understand, Peter, when I asked you in my last letter for some things, those things are not as vitally important to me as finding a human being in the true sense of the word, who did not pass through the mud of the camps, and who still has some semblance of mental health. I know if you were here, you would be the one who would put back together what was broken in me. I'm like a runaway dog who has no master. After all, I'm only a woman. I didn't lose my nerve all through the war but I can't go on. I'm mentally totally "down."

Please don't get upset that I'm intruding on your life with this kind of talk but I have no one else in the world to whom I can say this. I'm smart enough to know that you cannot help me. If only I could come to you. But I'm afraid that it's too difficult, even knowing that I would not be so dependent on you financially since I can earn money and a relatively fair amount of it. But I wouldn't want to be with you because, perhaps, you would pity me. A person should never do anything out of pity because the time comes when it becomes uncomfortable. I would come to you without a thought and immediately if I thought that you needed me as a comrade and as a kind of surrogate for what you've lost.

Don't think that all I do is think about this emptiness in my life. I'm a great pragmatist but even the greatest pragmatist needs a home. I don't live like a nun. I very much like a physician whom I met in camp. However, he is in roughly the same mental state that I myself am in. Moreover, he had a fiancée whom he loved very much and who broke up with him when he returned. I can't ask him to fall in love again — I'm well aware of this — but still, it hurts me. . . .

But I think I've already bothered you enough with this

talk — I don't want to infect you with this depression. I'm very glad that you were spared it and I so much want you to be happy because I love you. After all, we're family and I would like at least one of us to be happy. Poor darling, I'm sorry you have to hear all this. I can also be all laughs but sometimes I just can't. Peter, please write soon and send me photographs. I'm so curious what you look like now that you're grown up. I wish you and your uncles all the best for the New Year and with many warm greetings,

Your Franci

Her physician friend had finally decided to forgive his fiancé. Franci moved out of his flat. She still had no work. She had no interest in living. My mother would, later on in America, examine the first six months of her return to Prague on a psychoanalyst's couch. She would spend weeks analyzing her return to life and, in *Roundtrip*, wrote about the last few days of 1945 in this way:

For the first time in years I was now living entirely alone. At times I enjoyed my solitude but it also invited the incessant re-thinking of the past. Somewhere along the way I had acquired the notion of a certain complicity in the murder of my parents that I found myself incapable of reasoning out. . . . Christmas drew near and my pride made me refuse several invitations, con-sidering them as bones thrown to a hungry dog. . . . On New Year's Eve, I spent a few hours in the place I felt most comforted when depressed: a hot bathtub. A little mouse emerged from a hole in the wall and slowly made her way toward me on the rim of the tub, peeking curiously at me. Lost and undecided about which way to go, she seemed a symbol of my own existence. We stared at each other for quite a while and then she decided to re-turn to her hole. Suddenly, I felt this as the last unbearable loss, and fled the apartment intending to go to a party after all. But instead I started to walk through the passageways of the Old City to the river, down to the lower embankment, which used to be a lovers' lane and where I had had my first kiss some nine years before.

I arrived at a recess in the river wall with a step to the water and a large iron ring for tying up boats. Suddenly I recalled that as a five-year-old I had seen a drowned man fished out of the water and tied to the boat ring. He must have been in the water for a long time, all green and slimy, reeking of dead fish and decay. That night I dreamt a dream confusing the drowned man with the legendary Waterman of Czech folklore who lures innocent girls into the depths of the river — a fate that my nursemaids had often threatened me with when I misbehaved as a little girl. Now the image was alive again but the man was not dead. He was calling my name and telling me how dark and soft the water was.

I stood there transfixed, staring at my beloved river with its slowly moving ice floes, remembering how I had skated on it and how much I had loved to go swimming in it just across from the spot where I stood. The water looked cold but peaceful with the reflection of the streetlights dancing on it like little stars.

I felt a hand on my shoulder and a white-haired policeman said: "Miss, this is not a good place for a midnight walk alone. Tell me where you live. I'll walk you home."

That night, in my mother's account, was the turning point of her return to Prague. She went home and slept. The next day was sunny and cold. She packed a suitcase, gathered up the skis and ski boots that friends had hidden away for her during the war, and took the train to the mountains. For the first time since her eighteenth birthday, just before Hitler's annexation of Austria, she was going skiing.

18

~

When Franci Solar returned to Prague from her ski vacation in January of 1946, there was a jauntiness in her voice that had been missing for years. "I'm employed," she informed Peter Sachsel at the end of the month.

> As a matter of fact, I'm the *directrice* of a big dress factory for export. True, the factory is in Domažlice, but its central office and workroom are in Prague so I'm here most of the time and go to the factory once a week. I have a salary good enough to live fairly well. I don't think I could earn more on my own, not to speak of the worries I'd have being an employer. I see my boss twice a week and do what I want. As you see, life can throw me around every which way and I always land on my two feet.
>
> Second, I have a firm promise of a studio apartment where I'll finally live by myself. What that means to me is probably difficult for you to imagine so just try to imagine

that for the past three years I've been sleeping in the same room with anywhere from twenty-five to two hundred other people and since I've come back, I've been living in a series of places belonging to friends where I don't have a corner to crawl into that's my own.

These two things have put me on my feet — and at five minutes to midnight. . . .

Eight months after liberation, as Franci Solar was struggling to re-create a normal life, Czechoslovakia was struggling to do so on a national level. Both the American and Red armies had withdrawn from the country, leaving the Czechoslovak army in control. But that army was deeply divided between those who had spent the war within the protectorate, those who had fought with the Red army, and those who had fought with the Allies. These divisions were becoming clear in all facets of Czechoslovakia's postwar life as people who had spent the last six years in the Soviet Union or in England or in the protectorate jockeyed for power in the reconstituted state.

"Nothing is more difficult than to overthrow a totalitarian regime once it has been installed in a country, to erase the traces of a 'protectorate' and to create all the conditions indispensable to the restoration of an independent state," Hubert Řípka would later write. "The catastrophe of Munich had crushed the nation. From free citizens, we had become slaves. The Czechoslovak State had disappeared from the map of Europe."

One of the casualties of Masaryk's humanist Republic was his notion of a "higher Switzerland" in which different ethnic groups would cooperate. In January of 1946, two million Sudeten Germans were officially expelled from the country. An orderly expulsion had been planned by the Allies at Yalta and Potsdam as an appropriate correction to Nazism but the so-called transfer of populations was not orderly and was sometimes brutal. Every day, hundreds of Germans, carrying their 50 kilograms of luggage, were deported from Czechoslovakia to Germany. Every day, Czechs and Slovaks from all over the country moved in to grab up their former homes and property.

The expulsion of the Sudeten Germans following the annihilation of the Czechoslovak Jews — both highly educated, skilled, and largely middle-class segments of the population — left Czechoslovakia with an economic vacuum that the government hurried to fill. Within months, some 60 percent of the nation's workers were employed in nationalized industries. The government that administered these industries comprised politicians trained in the Soviet Union, those trained in the West, and those who had remained in the protectorate. But it had been created on Russian soil and its Communists were backed by Joseph Stalin. The first set of postwar elections was scheduled for May and the Communists expected to win big.

Just as the general population broke down into three groups, the tiny remnant of Jews that had returned to Prague did not retain their cohesion but scattered in different directions. Some found return too painful and, wanting to get as far away as they could, emigrated to England, North America, and Australia. Some, like Margot Körbel and Vava Schön, had become Zionists and were determined to leave for Palestine. Some became Communists. Still others, like Kitty Vohryzek, were trying to ignore the interruption of the war and living the way they had before the occupation. At twenty-three, Kitty was a party girl. She did not talk about the war. She ran with a fast crowd bent on making up for lost time, rarely letting on that she had ever been a prisoner.

Franci observed all the choices her friends made but found none of their solutions comfortable. She could not throw off the past as Kitty seemed able to do. Nor could she consider emigration. "I don't really understand why you don't feel a longing to come home," she wrote to Peter,

but probably you didn't grow up with our Republic the way I did. Even though it's not exactly ideal right now, it's interesting and it has a certain charm to be here when people are starting to build on the ruins. Every day things are better and in a few years, we won't even know that there was a war. I'm certainly no chauvinist but despite my internationalism, I have a great weakness for our small country and it would feel like desertion for me to leave it. . . .

Margot argued that Franci should come with her to Palestine. Nazism was the natural consequence of centuries of European antisemitism, she argued. It would never disappear. But Franci had not been impressed with the Zionists of Theresienstadt. She did not want to live in a parochial Jewish state that, she believed, would feel like a larger concentration camp. Hitler had succeeded in identifying her Jewish roots but Franci still did not consider herself first and foremost a Jew. When Peter Sachsel confessed that he had changed his surname to Scott, she replied, "Please! Why do you apologize to me? Do you think that out of some kind of stupid religiosity I'm stuck to a name? I'm all for assimilation."

Franci felt closest to her artistic friends who called themselves Communists, although most were not Party members. The Communists had been among the most helpful and decent people she had known in the camps and they were the idealists as well as the pragmatists of postwar Prague. They included her studious cousin Helli, who had returned to Prague from England, as well as many crude, slogan-spouting people that she remembered from before the war. Although she was a child of the First Republic and — as a woman and a Jew — one of its beneficiaries, Franci agreed with the Communist view that Masaryk's government had, in the final analysis, been a failure.

"Our democracy had allowed the growth of the fascist and Nazi parties which had in the end destroyed it," her contemporary Heda Kovály would later summarize the argument.

Worst of all, it had failed to defend the country against Hitler. After Munich, where our treacherous allies had forsaken us, our democratic government had surrendered to the Germans without a struggle. Did we want to repeat the same mistakes and live out a new version of Munich? Who had sold us out to Hitler? Our allies, the western capitalists. Who had offered to help when every other country

had abandoned us? The Soviet Union. Who had liberated
Prague while the American army stood watching? The Soviet Union.

Communist ideology, with its condemnation of all forms of
racism and its insistence on social equality, held strong appeal for
concentration camp survivors like Heda and Franci, who had
never before given much thought to politics. Like so many
Czechs of her generation, Franci believed the Communist
promise of egalitarianism and began, with the enthusiasm of an
amateur, to frame her thoughts in Communist language.

"I was in Bratislava this week on business," Franci wrote in
March.

> There are still evening dances at the Carlton and the Slo-
> vaks are as *gallant* as they were before the war. It would be
> even better if they were able to decide their political status
> and stopped flirting with former fascists. You know, Slova-
> kia is a state unto itself. They do what they want there, and
> it isn't always the smartest thing. There, they bad-mouth
> the Czechs and here, they bad-mouth the Slovaks but in
> my opinion, it's all a waste of time because we need them
> and they need us. I know a Slovak Communist representa-
> tive and he's an intelligent and nice man and there are
> more of them. We Czechs are always inclined to regard
> them as half idiots and they understandably refuse to put
> up with it. . . .

At the beginning of May:

> Maybe you'll say that a woman shouldn't worry about pol-
> itics but . . . you can't just say politics is a dirty profession
> that you want nothing to do with when politics affects
> every part of your life, especially the economic and cul-
> tural parts. It's no longer possible here to turn your back
> on politics. I have to confess that when I came back from
> camp I was a terrible Anglophile but now a year after the

war I had to acknowledge that only in a socialist world is there a hope of preventing another war. As long as a few millionaires rule the world in their own interests instead of in the cause of human peace, there won't be any peace. I'd be interested in what ordinary Americans think about this. . . . If you had lived through what I did, you'd probably be a Communist too.

On May 25:

You can't imagine what's been going on here over the past few days. We had elections. For the first time since the war, people are able to express themselves out loud politically, and even get into fistfights over politics without anyone prohibiting it. . . . It turned out well. We — that is the Communists — won about 40 percent. Three parties split up the remaining 60 percent — about 35 percent for the right wing and 15 percent for the Social Democrats. Frequently some of my friends complain of my lack of Czech feeling. They say that I'm first of all a Communist and only then a Czech. Really, if I had to explain to you my worldview, I would put in the first place if not always, the Communist idea, certainly from the standpoint of the equality of all people and all nations. Mindless German nationalism brought us to the last war and neither Czech nor Jewish nationalism is all that far from it. . . . Don't think that our Communists here are just workers. Today I'd say that all the intelligentsia have oriented themselves toward the left and it's not unusual to find a factory owner who's a Communist or a high official.

Franci believed that Czechoslovak Communists would create a specifically "Czech" road to Communism in the humanist tradition of Jan Hus, Amos Comenius, and Thomas G. Masaryk. Many more seasoned Czech politicians thought so too, viewing Communism as the best way of rebuilding their devastated country. When the postwar government was put together in Russia, the Communists had taken control of key government ministries. They moved quickly to extend their control to the media, the police, the unions, and — perhaps most important — the local agencies that handled such things as the restitution of prewar property and the granting of business permits. The Communists could expedite matters for a returning Czech exile, a farmer in the country, or a dressmaker in the city — or they could make them very difficult. The May elections of 1946 showed the results of that power. They received the most votes and, in coalition with the Social Democrats, the Czechoslovak Communist Party controlled 51 percent of Parliament.

That spring of 1946, Franci was spending her days cutting patterns and supervising a workroom of seamstresses. In the evenings, she often went to concerts where she ran into former clients. Many expressed their dismay that she was working for a factory and urged her to reopen Salon Weigert. Franci answered maybe, someday. Right now, she was trying to reconstruct a life. She had visited the warehouse where Marie had placed their property in storage and seen her mother's Louis XV salon chairs moldering in a half-covered shed. Their sewing machines were filthy and in pieces with only the heavily oiled machine heads still usable. At the restitution agency, she was told that there was a backlog of applications and rumor had it that no one was in a hurry to return Jewish property. But friends and former clients kept after her, arguing that Pepi would not have liked to see her daughter working for anyone else. Finally, when one of Pepi's former customers offered her space and her political connections, Franci decided to apply for a business permit. Nothing happened.

"Dear Peter," she wrote at the beginning of her second postwar summer.

> I always think when I write that it's best to paint my existence in the rosiest possible way because there's nothing you can do to help me and it's not exactly amusing to read about other people's troubles. But I've decided to disregard this fundamental rule and speak to you. . . .
> I still don't have my own flat. You'd have to know the

conditions here to understand that it's not my fault. I live at a friend's — or better said — one of my customers whom I know pretty well, whose family I began to see a lot of after my return home. They are very nice to me but there's hardly any space here and I practically live out of my suitcases. And I can only stay here for the summer because their child and nurse are in the country and when they come back I won't have anywhere to sleep. You can't imagine how depressing this is. Since I came back, I've lived at the homes of six different people, put my possessions in storage, and felt like a dog without a home. And that train of thinking leads into another complex. I start to think how unnecessary it was for me to survive the war because if I hadn't returned, no one would have noticed. You understand there are lots of cheap arguments against this, but basically it's the truth.

The next chapter is my social life or rather my lack of it. As you know I have a very good friend in Kitty, who is in the same situation, and besides, she's dating someone and we rarely see one another outside of work. My story with men is also an issue. Because I am, as you put it, a "merry widow" everyone thinks that I'm wild and free and wants to have an exciting fling with me. Believe me, I've had enough. I have no interest in being a married man's lover or to date someone because I have nothing better to do. And to fall in love in this crazy postwar period is only to invite trouble.

I try to deal with all of this by burying my head in work. I work from 7:30 in the morning to 5 in the afternoon and then I go from 6 to 10 to a master dressmaking school. I've put in a request for a business permit and hope that in the fall I'll open my own firm. Since, as you know, I'm also a music fan, I go to almost all the good concerts. But in spite of all this, life seems so terribly meaningless and empty that I sometimes wish the devil would take it.

Shortly after she posted this letter, Franci was notified that her business permit had come through. She now had the papers and the premises in which to open a *salon*. Now she needed start-up money to equip the workroom, furnish the fitting room, and assemble a staff. She wrote Peter, who was now in the American army, to send money, fabric, and the latest *Vogue, Mademoiselle,* and *Harper's Bazaar.* Could he send them air mail? She planned to work at her current job until the end of July, then go to a spa in Slovakia to get some rest, and open the *salon* in the fall. "My nerves are completely shot," she wrote to Peter on June 22. "It's not hysteria this time — just overwork. . . ."

The letter that followed two weeks later was not posted from Slovakia and it contained a surprise.

Dear Peter,
I'm writing to let you know that I've gotten engaged. It all happened very quickly, actually all in one week, but the final result is that I'm getting married and that for the first time in my life I'm really happy. Because I imagine that you'll want details, I'll begin with my husband. His name is Kurt Epstein. . . . He's forty-two years old, a head taller than I am and very good looking (he's a well-known athlete, a swimmer, and related to the Petschek family). I've known him since I was twelve, when he was our trainer at the swim club and I hated him with all my heart because he was so obnoxious to us teenagers that I always thought of him as an awful, arrogant person.

And all of a sudden Mr. Epstein wasn't obnoxious at all. . . . Of course, this changes nothing in regard to my intention of setting up my own business even though Kurt makes enough money for us both — he works in the chemicals business. But I have the example of my parents, where my father was a millionaire when they got married and in the end we were glad that we had Mother's shop. Kurt isn't that young and a person never knows what can happen. He of course doesn't totally agree with me, mostly because we want to have children and he thinks, of course, that I won't know what to do first, but even so I'm going to open the business and then we'll see. I'll probably not get married until the winter, not until my documents are in order and we get a flat. It's easier to get one if you're married and things in general are better now. Don't you think that here in Europe we sometimes proceed at American speeds?

You've definitely not seen two people so much in love with each other as we are — so much so that I'm afraid it won't last. I'm too accustomed to bad luck to be able to grasp that happiness is something that I also have a right to. Well, that's all I wanted to tell you.

Lots of love,
Franci

Kurt Epstein, to Franci's circle of friends, was something of a throwback to another time, much like the peddler Judah Sachsel when he married the innkeeper's daughter Therese Furcht. His grammatically flawless Czech, his assumptions, and his courtly manner all identified him as the product of a world that was pre–First Republic. Kurt had been born in 1904, when Franz Joseph was still emperor, and raised in the provincial town of Roudnice-nad-Labem, where the Epsteins had settled sometime after the Spanish Expulsion of 1492. Kurt's grandfather had been the first Jew allowed to build a house outside the ghetto and the first to establish a factory in Roudnice. Kurt's father had inherited the factory and was one of the pillars of the Jewish community, serving as president of Roudnice's synagogue and the director of its choir. Kurt had grown up in a provincial Bohemian-Jewish household, with violin lessons, summer vacations on the Baltic, a mother who supervised a household staff but took pride in her baking, and Hebrew lessons three times a week with the revered rabbi Richard Feder.

But the Epsteins were unusual in two significant ways. They were Czech nationalists who made a point of speaking only Czech to their children. And they were loving, indulgent parents who encouraged their sons to follow their own interests. When Kurt, their second son, began to spend most of his free time rowing and swimming in the Elbe, they did not object. When he announced his wish to enter athletic competition, they encouraged him. Kurt did not join any of the Jewish sports clubs. In 1921, he and three friends formed the nondenominational Independent Swim Club of Roudnice. Then he joined the national Czechoslovak Swim Club. By 1928, he was playing water polo for Czechoslovakia in the Olympic Games.

Water polo was a popular sport in Czechoslovakia and he became a well-known athlete, touring Europe and North Africa with his team, and in 1936, choosing to represent Czechoslovakia at the Nazi Olympics rather than joining the international boycott observed by many other Jews. He was an idealist who believed that sports should be above politics. His reputation was that of a purist, an athlete focused on his swim training.

Since her return to Prague, Franci had not given much thought to swimming. The pool at Barrandov where she had trained as a teenager closed down every fall and reopened in late spring. She had not thought of the health benefits of swimming laps — a philosophy that had imbued her adolescence — until a fellow swimmer recognized her in the street and demanded not how she had survived the camps but why he hadn't seen her at the pool. What was she doing on weekends? Could she come out the next day? Franci purchased a bathing suit and took the tram out to Barrandov. She entered the familiar locker room warily, expecting reentry here to be as uncomfortable as elsewhere. But there was something different about this world where everyone wore the same caps and suits. Greeting old acquaintances at poolside, she thought that of all the sectors of prewar Prague, the swim club seemed to be the most intact. The talk was all laps and strokes and scores and water temperatures — everything she remembered from the age of twelve.

The big difference was Kurt Epstein. When she and Kitty had been teenagers, Mr. Epstein had been head coach of the women's division, an exacting trainer almost a generation older than they, who had no time for the girls who giggled, gossiped, and complained about him. Now Epstein was greeting her with the level gaze of a fellow ex-prisoner. He had been one of the one thousand Jewish men sent to Theresienstadt in December of 1941. Kurt was more familiar with Terezín than most of the other men.

It had been his military garrison, he told Franci. In September of 1938, he had reported there as a reserve lieutenant in the Czechoslovak army.

By the time Franci Solar arrived in Theresienstadt, Kurt Epstein was one of the eight quartermasters charged with overseeing the delivery, preparation, and distribution of food. Unlike Joe Solar, Kurt Epstein was widely regarded as a straight-arrow. Incorruptible, he was known as a quartermaster who tried to ensure that the food he signed for actually arrived in the mouths of the prisoners it was intended to feed. Now they discovered that his parents had been deported to Auschwitz in the same transport as Franci. Kurt had followed in October of 1944. He, too, had stood before Dr. Mengele and had been sent to a labor camp. He was the sole survivor of his family. His fiancée had been murdered in the war. I had once thought my parents' decision to marry within twenty-four hours precipitous. Now, writing their story, it seemed obvious.

"He's a wonderful person who holds rather old-fashioned views of women," Franci wrote in September,

> which is good because he behaves with a certain honor-ableness that younger men don't have. He also loves me — which does not blind him to my faults. It's in every way the opposite of my first marriage, where my husband idolized me and let me do all kinds of stupid things. In the end I only hated him for his weakness and lost my last bit of respect for him. It looks like Kurt won't make this mistake and will keep a certain authority. It helps that he's sixteen years older than me. You know, my girlfriends are the happiest about all this. I was always such an *"enfant terrible"* and everyone who knows me is glad that finally there's someone who won't let me dance around his head.
>
> As far as finances go, Kurt makes enough money but I want to have my own business. I don't feel good when all I have to think about is a household. Also one never knows what will happen and it would be madness to abandon my clientele. I would be terribly unhappy at home and Kurt

knows that I have too much energy for my life's achievement to be dusting.

Kitty, who rushed back into her cousin's life when she heard about Kurt, was delighted that her cousin had finally found a steady guy. She begged Franci not to sleep with him and not to let him get away. But many of Franci's friends thought she was making a mistake. They thought Kurt Epstein something of a dinosaur crossed with a Puritan. He was not only clean-living but square. He spoke an outdated Czech, laden with rural proverbs. He fell asleep when Franci took him to concerts or the opera and, despite all his prowess as a swimmer, had never once been on skis. Helena Slavíčková thought Kurt would be a good husband but did not believe Franci was truly in love with him. He had no languages. His sports reputation would not travel. It was obvious that he had no street smarts at all. If they emigrated, Helena thought, Franci would have to support the family.

Helena Slavíčková had reappeared in Franci's life sometime during that summer of 1946 and the two women quickly reestablished the friendship that had been cut off in 1938, when Helena had married. As was their habit, the two women were satisfied with fragments of each other's stories. During her long honeymoon abroad, Helena had seen the foreign places she so craved to see and was able to continue her work as a secret courier. But she soon realized the implications of Slavíček's drinking. So long as they were living in Italy, it had been a convenience that afforded her great freedom. But once back in occupied Prague, Slavíček had become abusive, throwing sculpture and furniture when he was drunk, bringing in prostitutes, and becoming so violent that she often had to barricade herself inside their bedroom. Once, when Helena defied the curfew and ran out of the house in the middle of the night, Slavíček had called the Gestapo to find her. He had been able to continue selling paintings right through the war while Helena trained as a nurse for the Resistance and hid dozens of people in their basement.

She had looked for Franci then and remembered ringing the bell at Salon Weigert. She had pretended to be a client but Marie had not been forthcoming about the Rabineks' whereabouts and she had been careful. It was dangerous to ask too many questions. All through the war, she had kept a cyanide pill hidden under a crown in her mouth. When it was finally over, Helena had worked with medics repatriating concentration camp survivors, but, although she searched the lists for Franci's name, was unable to find her. She had become a Communist, of course, despite her distaste for the Russians she had encountered. The war had killed her enthusiasm for every nationality. She had seen all of them — the Czechs, the Italians, the French, the British, and the Americans — at their worst. By 1946, all Helena wanted was a peaceful home and a normal life. She was twenty-eight, and living in her parents' summer home outside of Prague. She was working at the Swedish embassy and in love with a man whose name she would not divulge, pregnant with his child, and full of plans about life as a single mother.

On my visits to the rustic house in Černošice, where Helena lived into the 1990s, Helena would recall that the Franci she met in 1946 was not very different from the one she remembered from 1938: "She was thinner, her hair was shorter, but her attitude toward life didn't seem to have changed. She was full of zest for living and mostly we chatted about things that were unimportant. As soon as I saw that something caused her pain, I stopped talking. She needed to get back to her life here. She didn't want to talk about the war. None of them did. I told her funny stories I thought would amuse her. How I stole an SS uniform and smuggled a Frenchman out from under the noses of the Nazis. How the Resistance planted me as a cleaning lady at the Hermann Goering Works with papers that said I had only four years of elementary school. How I pushed a mop and how it never occurred to them that I might understand or read German!"

Helena learned that Franci had also married young, that she had been separated from Pepi in Terezín, that she had survived the camps as an electrician. She understood that Franci, who had never before regarded herself as a Jew, had undergone a profound change of identity. For the first time, she used the word *pogrom* and was concerned about the recurrence of antisemitism in Europe. That concern, Helena recalled, raised the prospect of emigration. But it did not prevent her from trying in every way to reestablish a life in Prague. Franci desperately wanted a home, a family, a child — exactly as Helena herself did. She was pursuing those goals, living at a dizzying pace, making up for the six years that had been stolen from her life.

"*Cher monsieur Pierre*," Franci wrote on new stationery that located her *salon* at 20 Old Town Square, "*J'ai l'honneur de vous annoncer that I opened my* maison de couture *on September 15 and business is pretty good.*" She chose to name her salon with her first husband's name, calling it Salon Franci Solarová just as Pepi had named her place of business Salon Weigert. In November, she wrote that she had seven seamstresses in her employ, was planning a trip to Paris to see the spring collections, that some of Pepi's clients had come back and she had attracted many new ones. "It's beginning to be thought modern in Prague," she gloated, "to get your clothes made at Solarová's."

She and Kurt Epstein were married on December 21 and in May, after months of worrying that three years of missed periods in *koncentrák* had left her infertile, Franci wrote Peter that she was pregnant. Her letters were now filled with discussions of powdered milk, baby clothes, and diapers and free of any reference to political life. Her hurried lunches with Helena Slavíčková, too, focused around Helena's baby daughter and how her friend managed breastfeeding while commuting to a full-time job. The Epsteins had managed to secure new living quarters that would house the *salon* and between preparing to move, running a business, and tending her marriage and pregnancy, Franci was very busy. Then, one day in June, she woke up to find the insides of her thighs sticky with blood.

Franci became hysterical. She had lost her father. She had lost her mother. She had lost her husband and relatives and friends and six years of her life. Now she was sure she was going to lose her baby. Her obstetrician, the much-respected Karel Steinbach, who had been a friend to most of the prominent figures of the First Republic, tried to comfort her by explaining that her body knew best. She had been starved and overworked. She had suffered a severe bout of typhus. It was only two years since she had returned to normal life and, perhaps, her body was not yet ready to have a child. Kurt, too, tried to persuade her to remain calm. If this pregnancy did not work out, they would try again. But Franci would not be consoled until Dr. Steinbach gave her pills from America, put her to bed, and warned that emotional upset would only aggravate the problem. Kitty used her black market contacts to bring her calves' brains, then considered beneficial to pregnant women. Margot Körbel sat by her bedside and the devout among her seamstresses prayed.

In July, Dr. Steinbach pronounced the pregnancy secure and Franci returned to the work that had accumulated in her salon. Everything but baby and work became background. The Epsteins barely noted the political crisis that summer, when the Americans proposed an economic plan to aid postwar Europe and the Czechoslovak cabinet voted unanimously to join it. Then Stalin condemned the Marshall Plan as inimical to the Soviet Union and insisted that the cabinet reverse itself and reject it. Astute observers saw in its capitulation to Stalin a second Munich, but the Epsteins were not among them.

One year earlier, when Winston Churchill had declared that an Iron Curtain was descending across the European continent, few Czechs paid attention. Czechoslovakia was a bridge between Eastern and Western Europe, a democracy which had room for many parties. Czech Communists were, after all, not Russians or Poles but a different breed.

Neither one of the Epsteins worried much about politics during that summer of 1947. Kurt Epstein had much on his mind. Apart from working as a partner in a chemicals company, he was an active member of the Czechoslovak Olympic Committee, frequently served as a water polo referee, and had returned to his strict swimming regimen. He read the sports section; he did not spend much time pondering the "Cold War," the continual denunciation of "wartime collaborators," and the perpetual scandals involving the Czech police. Franci noted with annoyance that there were fewer and fewer American and British films showing in the cinemas. She did not suspect that the Ministry of Information had agreed to import 70 percent of all foreign films from Russia.

Unlike the rest of the countries that had been liberated by the Red army, Czechoslovakia had a coalition government made up of Communists and non-Communists, who engaged in passionate debate. It appeared that all segments of the population — students, farmers, factory workers, civil servants — were leading a free political life.

Although some of their friends had decided to emigrate, the Epsteins planned to remain in Prague. That summer, they moved to their new apartment at the foot of Wenceslas Square, where Margot Körbel joined them.

"We're moved!" Franci wrote to Peter.

Our windows — five of them — look out onto Wenceslas Square and all our friends have already let us know that they're coming to see all the parades. . . . I'm only going to work fourteen more days and then go to Moravia to a big fishpond where I'll watch the clouds go by, collect mushrooms if there are any, knit coats for your new niece or nephew, and go for walks. I'll also bathe — but not too much anymore. . . . Your two packages of wool arrived in good shape and I'd just like a few more things: baby soap and soap flakes. We don't have any here and my guess is that they're not expensive over there.

In October:

I feel fine but even so, I'd like to be two months older already. I'm terribly curious about what I'm bringing into the world. . . . I have a lot of work but still very little material. All our good textiles are produced for export and nothing's left for us here at home.

In November:

I feel good but sometimes I have quite enough of this pregnancy because the rascal kicks so much that I can't sleep at night. My doctor is unfortunately in New York and I don't know if he'll be back in time. I'm very used to Dr. Stein-

bach and he's such a pleasant person. . . . Kurt is the absolute model of a husband. He goes to sleep with me at
nine o'clock every night or sits with me and listens to the
radio since he doesn't want to go to the movies alone.
Business is good but there's a terrible scarcity of material.
I'm afraid we'll soon be worse off than we were during the
war. The situation isn't exactly the best as far as food and
staples go either but we aren't in bad shape. *Tu sais, on se
débrouille.* We're young and nothing on earth can throw us
off so easily. Please write earlier than half a year from now.

Love,
Franci

During the fall of 1947, polls found that Communist influence
had peaked and predicted that, in the next elections, the Party
would take a beating. Diverse groups were expressing dissatisfac-
tion with the Communists. There were a series of police and government scandals and even assassination attempts on the lives of
three democratic ministers but no mention of them appears in
the correspondence between the Epsteins and their cousin.

"Today, at two in the morning, our little girl, whose name is
Helenka, was born," Kurt Epstein wrote on November 27.

Franci is a wonderful person. Yesterday evening she
worked until nine o'clock. At ten, she left for the hospital
and in four hours the child was born. Without drugs, without screams. . . . We are very happy. . . . I would never
have thought that after all we lived through in the last few
years, we would ever be so happy.

"Dear Uncle," Franci wrote on January 9, 1948.

I've become a totally besotted mother. . . . Helen will have
a nurse but she isn't here yet so for the moment I'm doing
everything myself. For the time being, the baby doesn't
need much and no one can breastfeed her for me anyway.
Of course it takes time and I have a lot of work right now.
I need the day to have at least thirty-six hours. But I defi-

nitely like this role of mother and have already decided (with the father, of course) that we'll have more. Kurt is completely infatuated with his daughter and she stops crying immediately when he sings to her!!! I'm more prone to start [crying]. She's crying right now so I have to go see whether she's wet — that supposedly won't happen in twenty years. I told her that she has to be good because I was writing to Uncle Peter and she took it to heart. It's a pity you can't see her. . . . I still like to go to the theater or go dancing but the fact is that when I go I worry whether my little girl isn't crying at home. It's a good thing I'm breastfeeding since the scarcity of milk is catastrophic. . . ."

That last letter was written during the last full month that Czechoslovakia was functioning as a democratic state. The lack of milk Franci mentions was only a symptom of the drought, exacerbated by Soviet policies, that had put Czech agriculture in crisis. Other sectors of the economy were in crisis as well. But the most dramatic newspaper headlines were political. By January of 1948, clashes between Communists and non-Communists were a daily feature of political life. The coalition government, aware that elections were only four months away and that the Communists stood to lose, was unable to agree on anything.

In February, the non-Communist ministers submitted their resignations to President Eduard Beneš, expecting that he would follow constitutional procedure and call for elections. But the president was old and ill. The Communists, following strategies that had been tested throughout Eastern Europe, organized massive demonstrations. A Soviet envoy arrived in Prague to emphasize Stalin's support.

On February 25, the eve of Franci Epstein's twenty-eighth birthday, President Beneš bowed to Communist pressure. Instead of dissolving the government, he accepted the resignations of the democratic ministers and confirmed the appointment of a new Communist government. The last European battleground of the Cold War had been decided. Czechoslovakia had been taken over by a Communist *putsch*.

There is no letter documenting my parents' decision to leave

Prague. All that remains is the family story of how Kurt surveyed the armed militia marching in the streets and said that these were Nazis in different uniforms and that he would not make the same mistake twice. They had a child to think about; they were getting out, even if they had to leave in their bathing suits. Franci replied that she was not going anywhere. She had just celebrated her twenty-eighth birthday. She had a three-month-old baby. It was then, for the first and only time in their marriage, that my father slapped her.

Franci Epstein stalked out of her new apartment into the February cold and marched around Wenceslas Square to think things over. Then she came back home. Any lingering doubts she had about emigration were dispelled on March 10, when the body of Jan Masaryk, widely considered the conscience of the country, was found in the courtyard below his office windows.

Thousands of Czechs fled immediately. Thousands more lined up at foreign embassies. Kurt Epstein was one of the first in line at the American embassy. He had registered for a visa there in 1945, when he had returned from the camps. His only surviving relatives were in England and in the United States. One of them was Franzi Petschek, a member of the Petschek family that had hired a special train to evacuate its extended family members and bank employees before the war. My father was told that his number — 99 — was now at the top of the list and that it would also accommodate his wife and daughter. Franci did not want to be a poor relative, especially not of the Petscheks, whose bank Emil Rabinek had always blamed for his bankruptcy in 1932. She would have preferred Peter Scott to be their American sponsor, but her cousin had neither the legal nor financial resources of the Petscheks.

They flew out of Prague on July 21, 1948, carrying 50 kilograms of luggage each and me in a canvas bag. Just as she had in the hot summer of 1942, Franci layered her body with all the clothing she could tolerate. She left most of her wedding gifts in Prague but, along with diapers and baby things, packed the old family photographs and Pepi's three porcelain figurines that had been saved by friends during the occupation.

Whenever I asked her what it had felt like to arrive in New York, Franci invariably replied that the trip had taken twenty-six hours, that the temperature was over 100 degrees, that she was sweating under all those clothes, and that, of the ten dollars Franci and Kurt had each been allowed to take out of the country, the New York Port Authority had taken eight. The Petscheks met them at the airport, loaned them money, and settled them in the Hotel Colonial, across the street from the planetarium on Manhattan's Upper West Side. She never mentioned any emotion.

As Helena had predicted, Kurt Epstein was lost in New York. It was Franci who oriented them to the new country. She located friends and her obstetrician, Dr. Karel Steinbach, who was now at the hub of the Czech emigré community. Within two weeks, Dr. Steinbach found her a client. Czech soprano Jarmila Novotná was singing at the Metropolitan Opera and needed a dress.

It was illegal to work in the Hotel Colonial. Franci found a basement apartment off Riverside Drive, a few blocks away, borrowed money to buy a sewing machine, and moved the family. Within a month, she was once again sewing.

Epilogue

In the late 1950s, after my mother had reestablished her *salon* in New York, she met a Czech woman who had been deported east from Theresienstadt on the same transport as Emil and Pepi Rabinek. Their transport, she said, had terminated in the Latvian city of Riga. The Jews from Theresienstadt were marched into a forest. Then they were shot into a common trench. It was, however, harvest time and, at the last minute, she herself — then barely twenty — had been selected out for a harvest brigade. *"At last I had an answer to the question that had tormented me all these years,"* Frances wrote. *"Almost grateful that the end had been mercifully short, I could finally accept the reality of my parents' death and lay them to rest in my mind."*

In 1963, my mother was reading the *New York Times* and in a book review of *Herod's Children*, an Austrian novel set during the Second World War, she recognized the characters described as members of her father's family. She wrote to its Viennese author, Ilse Aichinger, and found an entire branch of Rabinek descendants. They were scattered throughout Europe and the United States — in London, Belfast, Woodstock, and Berkeley — and they were stunned and delighted to hear that my mother, who they thought had been murdered by the Nazis, was alive and making dresses in New York.

Most members of Emil Rabinek's immediate family had been baptized. None had retained a tie to Judaism. Some had become Catholics, some considered themselves agnostics; those who could came to New York to visit. My mother was thrilled to present a living family to her children, even if they lived so far away that we rarely got to see them. They were energetic, intense, critical, and multilingual — like my mother. One part of the family had changed its name in the United States. Once Hirsch, they were now Hearst.

Emil Rabinek's niece Lily Hearst was born in May of 1897 and, in honor of her upcoming one-hundredth birthday, her son John had planned a gala celebration in the city she had loved and fled. In the fall of 1996, I flew to Vienna to celebrate Lily's upcoming centenary and to visit Therese's grave.

Vienna still makes me uneasy with what my writer cousin Ilse calls its mixture of "brutality and charm" and I probably would not have gone were it not for my cousin John, who had become increasingly intrigued by my research. He and his wife, Jean, promised to accompany me to the cemetery and help me find Therese's grave.

Arriving in Vienna, watching Lily's excitement as she and her children revisited their prewar apartment, attended the opera, and were served by waiters in a luxurious hotel where they would have been refused entry half a century earlier made me act out in many ways. I refused to speak German. I wore T-shirts and jogging shoes in the red velvet breakfast room. I whistled "Don't Cry for Me, Argentina" in the ornate, slow-moving elevator. I was relieved to be sharing my room with one of John's colleagues, a scientist born and raised in China, and pleased when another colleague and his Japanese-American daughter asked to join our expedition to the cemetery. I was fighting for distance. The farther removed anyone was from Europe the better.

Five of us set out for Vienna's Central Cemetery by trolley. The place is vast and on that September day was gray, sweet-smelling, empty, and peaceful. We walked past the imposing tombstones of prominent Austrian Jews: the grave of playwright Arthur Schnitzler, who immortalized the "sweet young thing"; the grave of Leopold Kompert, whose stories of rural Bohemian Jewry were my first introduction to Therese; the graves of the Zwieback brothers, who established the department store where Pepi served as apprentice. The Viennese rabbi Moritz Güdemann was buried here along with members of families whose names are familiar in America, names like Baumgarten, Wertheimer, Spitzer, Rosenthal, Weiss, Loewy, Boehm, Taussig. If I had grown up in Prague, if I had had a simple family history, I thought, I would have come here to tend my great-grandmother's grave. I would have come here when I quarreled with my husband or was frustrated with my children or just needed a quiet place and time to think things through.

As our small party of Americans walked through the empty rows, looking for plot 19, 19, 84, the number that I had received in a letter five years earlier, we saw a young gardener. He stopped his work to lead us to the plot. There were an estimated eighty thousand Jews buried in the Jewish section, he said, and some sixty thousand identifiable graves. Since 1938, when the Jews could no longer tend them, the cemetery had become a jungle, with large trees and thick brush overgrowing the stones and monuments. In 1991, a group of Viennese decided to clean it up. They mobilized the police, the army, and volunteers from all parts of the community, carting out about two thousand tons of wood. Then they identified all the gravestones they could, and put them all on a computer. He led us to a granite tombstone about four feet high.

"*Hier ruht Frau Therese Sachsel geborene Furcht,*" read the tombstone in German.

Here rests Therese Sachsel, born Furcht, joined together with her beloved son who died at the age of 17. We re-member our unforgettable mother and thankfully remember our unforgettable brother who left us too early. Now rest softly in heaven's peace until we meet again in front of God. . . ."

There was ivy growing up the side of the tombstone and the sweet smell of juniper all around. My cousins stayed and took photographs. Then they left me there alone. There is a long Jewish tradition of placing a stone on a tombstone but, given the length of time no one had visited, a stone seemed too cold a thing to leave. I wanted Therese to have something alive. The next day, I returned with a pot of heather and a trowel. It began to rain. People were saying that it would be a wet fall. I did not know when I would be back but it seemed possible that the purple heather I planted would prove hardy and take root.

Acknowledgments

My first debt of gratitude is to the three Jiřís of the Czech Republic: Jiří Fiedler, Jiří Rychetský, and Jiří Tichý. Thanks also to Leo Pavlát, director of the Jewish Museum; Jiřina Šedinová of the Jewish Studies faculty at Charles University and Jiřina Šiklová, director of Charles University's Center for Gender Studies; art historian Arno Pařík (who searched the photo archives of the Jewish Museum and found the photographs taken during the Nazi occupation); Eva Uchalová of Prague's Museum of Decorative Arts (who found photographs of clothes my grandmother designed in the 1920s, advertisements for Salon Weigert, and even an article about it in the course of her own research on Prague's fashion industry); Helena Klímová and the researchers and museum workers in Prague, Kolín, Brno, Jihlava, and Brtnice who helped me find documents. Kitty Egererová (1922–1994), Helena Rissová, and Heda Margolius Kovály all served as surrogate mothers to me in Prague as well as interviewees, readers, and critics. For extended hospitality, my thanks to Michael Egerer and his family and Eva Lorencová and her family.

I researched this book as a visiting scholar, then affiliate, of the Minda de Gunzburg Center for European Studies at Harvard University. I thank Stanley Hoffmann, Charles Meier, and Abby Collins for their support and Anna Popiel and Loren Goldner for going out of their way to make me feel at home. I am indebted to Isadore Twersky for admitting me to his classes in premodern Jewish history and to Karen von Kunes and Alfred Thomas for admitting me to their Czech classes. Zuzana Nagy, Harvard's Slavic librarian and friend, located numerous books, corrected my Czech, critiqued drafts, and provided endless diacritical markings.

There are many scholars to whom I am indebted. Foremost is Wilma Iggers, whose books *Women of Prague* and *The Jews of Bohemia* are indispensable resources and from which many of my historical quotations are drawn. I thank her for permission to reprint those quotations, for her criticism and interest. Eduard Goldstücker put his encyclopedic knowledge of the history of the Jews in the Czech lands at my disposal in the early stages of my research. Harry Zohn, Vienna-born professor emeritus of Brandeis University, assiduously tried to make me understand Vienna just a fraction of the way he does, read, translated, and played devil's advocate. Ruth Deutsch, Prague-born professor emeritus of Wellesley College, translated from the German and never faltered in her support for the book. I also thank Jerold Auerbach, Gary Cohen, Atina Grossmann, Deborah Hertz, Ted Kaptchuk, Hillel Kieval, Hillel Levine, Shulamith Magnus, Ladislav Matějka, Beth Noveck, Susan Pedersen, Gila Ramras-Rauch, Barbara K. Reinfeld, Edward Shorter, Diane Spielmann, Michael Stanislawski, Moshe Waldoks, and Tom Winner.

I enjoyed the help of many members of the Czech emigration to America: the late soprano (and daughter of a Prague tailor) Jarmila Novotná; the late physician Karel Steinbach, Fred Hahn, Milan Herben, Miroslav Kerner, Hana Stránská, and Joan Winn. Lewis Weiner, former editor of the *Review of the Society for the*

History of Czechoslovak Jews, had the entire manuscript read to him by his housekeeper so that he could discuss it with me. I also thank the Israeli contingent: Nava Shan, Ruth Bondy, Hana Greenfield, Yael Na'aman, Nava Semel, Lily Schoen, and Erwin and Etha Frenkel.

Many friends read parts of this manuscript. I am particularly indebted to the late Ernst Pawel, author of the peerless biographies of Kafka, Herzl, and Heine, and to his wife, Ruth Pawel, who attended the Prague *lycée* at the same time as my mother. Thanks also to Brad Bellows, Dany Dayan, Vera Eisenberger, Helen Fremont, Eva Fogelman, Rosalie Gerut, Muriel Gillick, Peter Jacobsohn, Rochelle Rubenstein Kaplan, Greta Schreier Löbl, Ellen MacDonald, Andrei Markovits, Susan Miron, Yael Muller, Beth Noveck, Tereza Pánková, Rachelle Rosenblum, Peter Scott, Ellen Winner, and especially Ruth Gutmann.

Early versions of my research appeared in *Cross Currents: A Yearbook of Central European Culture,* number 11; the *Review of the Society of Czechoslovak Jews,* volume 4; and *New York Magazine,* November 27, 1989.

I have, throughout, enjoyed the steadying and unflappable support of my editor, Jennifer Josephy, and my agent, Peter Ginsberg. Apart from their intelligence and professionalism, both were enthusiastic from the start about an arcane and esoteric subject. Thanks also to my copyeditor, Betty Power.

Artist Susan Erony not only designed the cover for this book but, over the years, read and discussed with me every chapter from its first draft to the final product.

My husband, Patrick Mehr, and my sons, Daniel and Sam, lived with this book and the travels it entailed for many years. I thank them for giving me — ultimately if not always graciously — the space and time to research, write, and think. I could not have written it without their love and the blissful normalcy of our domestic routines.

This book is dedicated to Margo Jefferson. For more than twenty-five years, Margo and I have shared our mothers, our family and cultural histories, and our writing. There is no one whose judgment I trust more. Margo has one failing that is particularly meaningful to me: she has never been able to correctly pronounce the name Auschwitz. For this and everything else, I thank her.

Helen Epstein
Cambridge, Massachusetts

Selected Bibliography

My primary sources were 12 pages of family history written by Frances Epstein in the 1970s; her unpublished memoir, *Roundtrip;* a 144-page oral history I took in 1974 for the William E. Wiener Oral History Library in New York; and two other audiotaped interviews. My main archival sources were the Czech State Central Archive in Prague and the local archives of Kolín, Jihlava, and Brtnice.

Most pertinent to my mother's story were the memoirs of other Czech Jewish women of her generation: Heda Margolius Kovály's *Under a Cruel Star,* Vlasta Schönová's *Chtela jsem být Herečkou (L'hiot Sachkanit* in Hebrew), Helen Lewis's *A Time to Speak;* Jana Renée Friesová's *Fortress of My Youth;* Maria Bauer's *Beyond the Chestnut Trees;* Vera Gissing's *Pearls of Childhood,* and Hana Greenfield's *Fragments of Memory.* Gerda Hoffer's multicentury family history, *The Utitz Legacy,* provided excellent background as did the privately published histories of the Weiner, Barth, Bamberger, and Roubitschek families.

I was immeasurably helped by the work of Carolyn Heilbrun, Maxine Hong Kingston, Toni Morrison, Adrienne Rich, Elaine Showalter, Joan Wallach Scott, and Alice Walker. I would like here to express my thanks to them and to Jane Kramer, who, since my student days, has shown me the power and possibilities of good journalism.

Arendt, Hannah. *Rahel Varnhagen: The Life of a Jewish Woman.* New York, 1974.

Ashkenazi, Yaakov. *Tz'enah Ur'enah.* Jerusalem, 1983.

Barea, Ilsa. *Vienna.* New York, 1966.

Bauer, Johann. *Kafka and Prague.* New York, 1971.

Bauer, Maria. *Beyond the Chestnut Trees.* Woodstock, 1983.

Baum, Vicki. *It Was All Quite Different.* New York, 1964.

Beckermann, Ruth. *Die Mazzesinsel.* Vienna, 1988.

Beller, Steven. *Vienna and the Jews 1867–1938.* Cambridge, Mass., 1990.

Berger, Natalia, ed. *Where Cultures Meet: The Story of the Jews of Czechoslovakia.* Tel Aviv, 1990.

Berkley, George E. *Vienna and the Jews.* Cambridge, 1990.

Blaukopf, Kurt. *Mahler: A Documentary Study.* Oxford, 1976.

———. *Gustav Mahler.* New York, 1985.

Boucher, François. *20,000 Years of Fashion.* New York, 1987.

Brisch, Hans, and Völgyes, Ivan. *Czechoslovakia: The Heritage of Ages Past, Essays in Memory of Josef Korbel.* New York, 1979.

Brittain, Vera. *Testament of Youth: An Autobiographical Study of the Years 1900–1925.* London, 1933.

Brod, Max. *Pražský kruh.* Prague, 1993.

———. *Franz Kafka: A Biography.* New York, 1947.

Buber-Neumann, Margarete. *Mistress to Kafka.* London, 1966.

Burk, John N. *Clara Schumann: A Romantic Biography.* New York, 1940.

Burke, John. *Czechoslovakia.* London, 1976.

Buxbaum, Gerda. *Mode Aus Wien.* Residenz Verlag, 1986.

Chagall, Bella. *Burning Lights.* New York, 1947.

Chazan, Robert. *Church, State and Jew in the Middle Ages.* New York, 1980.

Churchill, Winston S. *The Gathering Storm.* Boston, 1946.

Cohen, Gary B. *The Politics of Ethnic Survival: Germans in Prague, 1861–1914.* Princeton, 1981.

Collegium Carolinum. *Die Juden in den böhmischen Ländern.* Munich, 1983.

Corti, Egon. *Elizabeth Empress of Austria*. London, 1936.

Craig, Gordon A. *The Germans*. New York, 1982.

David, Katherine. "Czech Feminists and Nationalism in the Late Habsburg Monarchy," in *Journal of Women's History*, vol 3., no. 2, 1991.

Deák, István. "Jewish Soldiers in Austro-Hungarian Society," in *Leo Baeck Institute Yearbook*. London, 1990.

De La Grange, Henry-Louis. *Mahler*. New York, 1973.

De La Haye, Amy, and Tobin, Shelley. *Chanel: The Couturière at Work*. Woodstock, 1996.

Demetz, Hana. *The House on Prague Street*. New York, 1979.

———. *The Journey from Prague Street*. New York, 1990.

Deslandres, Yvonne, and Muller, Florence. *Histoire de la Mode au XXe Siècle*. Paris, 1986.

Dignowity, Anthony Michael. *Bohemia under Austrian Despotism*. New York, 1860.

Donath, Oskar. *Böhmische Dorfjuden*. Brunn, 1926.

Eisner, Pavel. *Franz Kafka and Prague*. New York, 1950.

Erdely, Eugene V. *Germany's First European Protectorate*. London, 1942.

Exton, Inez. *Children of Nowhere*. Riverside, 1991.

Fiedler, Jiří. *Hrady, zamky a tvrze jižní Moravy*.

———. *Jewish Sights of Bohemia and Moravia*. Prague, 1991.

Fout, John C., ed. *German Women in the Nineteenth Century*. New York, 1984.

Fraenkel, Josef. *The Jews of Austria: Essays on Their Life, History and Destruction*. London, 1967.

Fraisse, Geneviève, and Perrot, Michelle. *A History of Women: Emerging Feminism from Revolution to World War*. Cambridge, 1993.

Franck, Irene. *Clothiers*. Facts on File. New York, 1987.

Frevert, Ute. *Women in German History*. Oxford, 1989.

Friedländer, Saul. *When Memory Comes*. New York, 1979.

Friedman, Otto. *The Breakup of Czech Democracy*. London, 1950.

Friedman, Saul S., ed. *The Terezín Diary of Gonda Redlich*. Lexington, Kentucky, 1992.

Friesová, Jana Renée. *Fortress of My Youth*. Tasmania, 1995.

Fučík, Julius. *Notes from the Gallows*. Salt Lake City, 1990.

Gay, Peter. *Freud: A Life for Our Time*. New York, 1988.

Glückel. *The Memoirs of Glückel of Hameln*. New York, 1977.

Gold, Hugo. *Židé a židovské obce v Čechách v minulosti a přítomnosti*. Brno, 1934.

———. *Die Juden und Judengemeinden Mährens in Vergangenheit und Gegenheit*. Brno, 1929.

Goldstücker, Eduard. "Jews between Czechs and Germans around 1848," in *Leo Baeck Institute Yearbook*. London, 1972.

Graupe, Heinz Moshe. *The Rise of Modern Judaism: An Intellectual History of German Jewry, 1650–1942*. New York, 1978.

Greenfield, Hana. *Fragments of Memory*. Jerusalem, 1992.

Grunfeld, Frederic. *Prophets without Honor*. New York, 1979.

Grunwald, Max. *The Jews of Vienna*. Philadelphia, 1936.

Gutman, Yisrael, and Berenbaum, Michael. *Anatomy of the Auschwitz Death Camp*. Bloomington, Ind., 1994.

Hájek, Hanuš. *T. G. Masaryk Revisited*. Boulder, Col., 1983.

Henry, Sondra, and Taitz, Emily. *Written Out of History: A Hidden Legacy of Jewish Women*. New York, 1978.

Herben, Jan. *Do třetího a čtvrtého pokolení*. Prague, 1956.

Hertz, Deborah. *Jewish High Society in Old Regime Berlin*. New Haven, 1988.

Heschel, Susannah. *On Being a Jewish Feminist*. New York, 1983.

Hockaday, Mary. *Kafka, Love and Courage: The Life of Milena Jesenská*. London, 1995.

Hoffer, Gerda. *The Utitz Legacy: A Personalized History of Central European Jews*. Jerusalem, 1988.

Hubmann, Franz. *The Jewish Family Album: The Life of a People in Photographs*. Boston, 1975.

Hyman, Paula. *Gender and Assimilation in Modern Jewish History*. Seattle, Wash., 1995.

Iggers, Wilma. *The Jews of Bohemia and Moravia: A Historical Reader*. Detroit, 1992.

———. *Women of Prague*. Providence, 1995.

———. "Leopold Kompert, Romancier of the Bohemian Ghetto," in *Modern Austrian Literature*, vol. 1, March/April, 1973.

Janák, Jan, ed. *Dějiny Brtnice*. Brno, 1988.

Jesenská, Milena. *Člověk dělá šaty*. Prague, 1927.

Joeres, Ruth-Ellen, and Maynes, Mary Jo. *German Women in the Eighteenth and Nineteenth Centuries*. Bloomington, Ind., 1986.

Johnson, Paul. *A History of the Jews*. Harper and Row, 1987.

Johnston, William M. *The Austrian Mind: An Intellectual and Social History, 1848–1938*. Berkeley, 1972.

Jones, Ernest. *The Life and Works of Sigmund Freud*. New York, 1961.

Jungk, Peter Stephan. *Franz Werfel*. New York, 1990.

Kafka, Franz. *Diaries, 1910–1913; 1914–1923*. New York, 1965.

———. *Letters to Friends, Family and Editors*. New York, 1977.

Kahler, Erich. *The Jews Among the Nations*. New York, 1967.

Kaplan, Marion A. *The Jewish Feminist Movement in Germany.* Westport, Conn., 1979.

———. *The Marriage Bargain: Women and Dowries in European History.* Binghamton, N.Y., 1985.

Katz, Jacob. *Out of the Ghetto: The Social Background of Jewish Emancipation, 1770–1870.* New York, 1978.

———. *Tradition and Crisis: Jewish Society at the End of the Middle Ages.* New York, 1971.

———. *Emancipation and Assimilation.* Brookfield, Vt., 1972.

———. *From Prejudice to Destruction: Antisemitism, 1700–1933.* Cambridge, Mass., 1980.

Kennan, George. *From Prague after Munich.* Princeton, 1968.

Kennett, Frances. *The Collector's Book of Fashion.* New York, 1983.

Kieval, Hillel. *The Making of Czech Jewry.* Oxford, 1988.

Kisch, Egon Erwin. *Sensation Fair.* New York, 1941.

Kisch, Guido. *In Search of Freedom.* London, 1949.

Klein, Dennis B. *Jewish Origins of the Psychoanalytic Movement.* New York, 1981.

Kohn, Hans. *Living in a World Revolution.* New York, 1964.

Kolář, Erik. *Vila Humboldt.* Prague, 1994.

Koltun, Elizabeth. *The Jewish Woman.* New York, 1976.

Kompert, Leopold. *Scenes from the Ghetto: the Ghetto Violet; Christian and Leah.* London, 1892.

Korbel, Josef. *The Communist Subversion of Czechoslovakia.* Princeton, 1959.

———. *Twentieth Century Czechoslovakia.* New York, 1977.

Kraus, Ota B. *The Painted Wall.* Tel Aviv, 1994.

Křesadlo, Karel, and Hyhlík, Vladimir. *Jihlava.* Prague, 1986.

Kulka, Erich. *Jews in Svoboda's Army in the Soviet Union.* London, 1987.

Laqueur, Walter. *Young Germany: A History of the German Youth Movement.* New Brunswick, 1984.

Lea, Charlene A. *Emancipation, Assimilation and Stereotype: The Image of the Jew in German and Austrian Drama.* Bonn, 1978.

Lea, Henry A. *Gustav Mahler: Man on the Margin.* Bonn, 1985.

Lebrecht, Norman. *Mahler Remembered.* Norton, 1987.

Lederer, Zdeněk. *Ghetto Theresienstadt.* London, 1953.

Lentin, Ronit. *Night Train to Mother.* Dublin, 1989.

Levine, Hillel. *The Economic Origins of Anti-Semitism.* New Haven, 1991.

Lewald, Fanny. *The Education of Fanny Lewald: An Autobiography.* New York, 1992.

Lewis, Helen. *A Time to Speak.* Belfast, 1992.

Lieberman, E. James. *Acts of Will: The Life and Work of Otto Rank*. New York, 1985.

Lion, Jindřich and Lukáš, Jan. *The Prague Ghetto*. London, n.d.

Low, Alfred D. *Jews in the Eyes of the Germans from the Enlightenment to Imperial Germany*. Philadelphia, 1979.

Lukács, John. *Budapest, 1900*. New York, 1988.

Lynam, Ruth. *Paris Fashion: The Great Designers and Their Creations*. London, 1972.

MacDonald, Callum, and Kaplan, Jan. *Prague in the Shadow of the Swastika: A History of the German Occupation, 1939–1945*. London, 1995.

Mahler, Raphael. *A History of Modern Jewry, 1780–1815*. London, 1971.

Maimon, Solomon. *The Autobiography of Solomon Maimon*. London, 1955.

Mamatey, Victor S., and Luža, Radomír. *A History of the Czechoslovak Republic, 1918–1948*. Princeton, 1973.

Masaryk, Jan. *Speaking to My Country*. London, 1944.

Mastný, Vojtěch. *The Czechs Under Nazi Rule*. New York, 1971.

Mautner, Hella Roubíček. *Hella*. Washington, D.C., 1996.

May, Arthur. *The Hapsburg Monarchy*. Cambridge, Mass., 1951.

Mayreder, Rosa. *A Survey of the Woman Problem*. New York, 1913.

McCagg, William O. *A History of Habsburg Jews, 1670–1918*. Bloomington, Ind., 1990.

Mendelsohn, Ezra. *The Jews of East Central Europe between the World Wars*. Bloomington, Ind., 1983.

Metternich, Pauline. *My Years in Paris*. London, 1922.

Meyer, Michael A. *The Origins of the Modern Jew*. Detroit, 1967.

Morrell, Sydney. *I Saw the Crucifixion*. London, 1939.

Morton, Frederic. *A Nervous Splendor*. Boston, 1979.

Museum of Decorative Arts in Prague. *Fashion in Bohemia: From the Waltz to the Tango*. Prague, 1994.

———. *Czech Fashion, 1918–1939*. Prague, 1996.

Neuda, Fanny. *Stunden der Andacht*, 1855. New York, 1910.

Olsen, Kirsten. *Chronology of Women's History*. Westport, Conn., 1994.

Opalski, Magdalena. *The Jewish Tavern-Keeper and His Tavern in Nineteenth Century Polish Literature*. Jerusalem, 1986.

Oxaal, Ivaar, et al. *Jews, Antisemitism and Culture in Vienna*. London, 1987.

Památník. *Terezín*. Prague, 1988.

Pawel, Ernst. *The Nightmare of Reason*. New York, 1984.

———. *The Labyrinth of Exile: A Life of Theodor Herzl*. New York, 1989.

Payne, Karen. *Between Ourselves: Letters Between Mothers and Daughters.* Boston, 1983.

Penn, Vreeland. *Inventive Paris Clothes, 1909–1939.* New York, 1977.

Perrot, Philippe. *Fashioning the Bourgeoisie: A History of Clothing in the Nineteenth Century.* Princeton, 1994.

Pollack, Herman. *Jewish Folkways in the Germanic Lands.* Cambridge, Mass., 1971.

Popp, Adelheid. *The Autobiography of a Working Woman.* Chicago, 1913.

Prinz, Joachim. *The Dilemma of the Modern Jew.* New York, 1962.

Pynsent, Robert B., ed. *T. G. Masaryk.* London, 1989.

Rakous, Vojtěch. *Vojkovičtí a přespolní.* Prague, 1986.

Reinharz, Jehuda, and Schatzberg, Walter. *The Jewish Response to German Culture.* Hanover, 1985.

Richarz, Monika. *Jewish Life in Germany: Memoirs from Three Centuries.* Bloomington, Ind., 1991.

Riff, Michael. "Czech Anti-Semitism and Jewish Response Before 1914," in *Wiener Library Bulletin,* vol. 29, 1939–1940.

Ripka, Hubert. *Czechoslovakia Enslaved.* London, 1950.

Robert, Marthe. *As Lonely as Franz Kafka.* New York, 1982.

Robertson, Priscilla. *An Experience of Women: Pattern and Change in Nineteenth Century Europe.* Philadelphia, 1982.

Rogers, Catherine. *The Troublesome Helpmate: A History of Misogyny in Literature.* Seattle, Wash., 1966.

Rosenbloom, Noah H. *The Religious Philosophy of Samson R. Hirsch.* Philadelphia, 1976.

Rosman, M. J. *The Lords' Jews: Magnate-Jewish Relations in the Polish-Lithuanian Commonwealth.* Cambridge, Mass., 1990.

Roth, Ernst. *A Tale of Three Cities.* New York, 1971.

Roth, Joseph. *The Radetzky March* (Berlin, 1932). Woodstock, 1983.

Saunders, Edith. *The Age of Worth.* Bloomington, Ind., 1955.

Sagarra, Eda. *Tradition and Revolution: German Literature and Society.* New York, 1971.

Schapiro, Raya, and Weiberg, Helga. *Letters from Prague, 1939–1941.* Chicago, 1991.

Scheinpflugová, Olga. *Byla jsem na světě.* Prague, 1988.

Schnitzler, Arthur. *Little Novels.* New York, 1929.

———. *Plays and Stories* (Vienna, 1900–18). New York, 1982.

———. *My Youth in Vienna.* New York, 1970.

———. *The Way to the Open.* Evanston, Ill., 1991.

Shepherd, Naomi. *A Price Below Rubies: Jewish Women as Rebels & Radicals.* Cambridge, Mass., 1992.

Shirer, William L. *Berlin Diary: The Journal of a Foreign Correspondent, 1934–1941.* New York, 1942.

Society for the History of Czech Jews. *The Jews of Czechoslovakia,* vols. 1–3. Philadelphia, 1971.

Spiel, Hilde. *Vienna's Golden Autumn.* New York, 1987.

———. *Fanny von Arnstein.* New York, 1991.

Spitzer, Leo. *Lives in Between: Assimilation and Marginality in Austria, Brazil and West Africa, 1780–1945.* Cambridge, Mass., 1989.

Steinbach, Karel. *Svědek téměř stotetý.* Cologne, 1993.

Steinem, Gloria. "Ruth's Song," in *Outrageous Acts and Everyday Rebellions.* New York, 1983.

Stekel, Wilhelm. *The Autobiography of Wilhelm Stekel.* New York, 1950.

———. *Conditions of Nervous Anxiety and Their Treatment.* London, 1923.

Stern, J. P. *The World of Franz Kafka.* New York, 1980.

Stock, Phyllis. *Better Than Rubies: A History of Women's Education.* New York, 1978.

Straka, František. "Vybledlé obrázky z Kolína před 50 lety," in *Věstník Klubu čs. turistů.* Kolín, 1935.

Stránský, Jan. *East Wind over Prague.* New York, 1951.

Szeps, Berta. *My Life and History.* New York, 1939.

Szulc, Tad. *Czechoslovakia Since World War Two.* New York, 1971.

Thomson, S. Harrison. *Czechoslovakia in European History.* Princeton, 1943.

Troller, Norbert. *Theresienstadt: Hitler's Gift to the Jews.* Chapel Hill, N.C., 1991.

Twain, Mark. *Concerning the Jews* (1898). New York, 1934.

Varga, Susa. *Heddy and Me.* Australia, 1994.

Vital, David. *The Survival of Small States.* Oxford, 1971.

Volavková, Hana. *Příběh Žiluvského musea v Praze.* Prague, 1966.

Von Bock, Gisela Reineking. *200 Jahre Mode.* Cologne, 1991.

Von Suttner, Bertha. *Memoirs.* Boston, 1910.

Vrba, Rudolf. *I Cannot Forgive.* New York, 1964.

Wardi, Dina. *Memorial Candles: Children of the Holocaust.* London, 1992.

Wechsberg, Joseph. *Prague: The Mystical City.* New York, 1971.

———. *The Vienna I Knew.* New York, 1979.

Weil, Jiří. *Life with a Star.* New York, 1990.

Weil, Simone. *The Need for Roots.* New York, 1952.

Weiner, Lewis, *The Weiners* (pamphlet). New York, 1996.

Weisskopf, Kurt. *The Agony of Czechoslovakia '38/'68.* London, 1968.

Weissler, Chava. *Traditional Yiddish Literature: A Source for the Study of Women's Religious Lives.* Cambridge, Mass., 1988.

Westphal, Uwe. *Berliner Konfektion und Mode.* Berlin, 1986.
Wistrich, Robert S. *The Jews of Vienna in the Age of Franz Joseph.* Oxford, 1989.
———. *Austrians and Jews in the Twentieth Century.* New York, 1992.
Yerushalmi, Yosef Hayim. *Zakhor.* Seattle, 1982.
Zweig, Stefan. *The World of Yesterday.* New York, 1943.

The *Encyclopedia Judaica* was indispensable in my research. The journals *Cross Currents, Judaica Bohemiae,* the *Leo Baeck Institute Yearbook,* the *Review of the Society for the History of Czech Jews, Yad Vashem Studies, Kalendář Česko-Židovský,* and *Židovská Ročenka* all provided useful background reading.

PENGUIN PUTNAM

online

Your Internet gateway to a virtual environment
with hundreds of entertaining and enlightening
books from Penguin Putnam Inc.

*While you're there get the latest buzz on the best
authors and books around—*

Tom Clancy, Patricia Cornwell, W.E.B.Griffin,
Nora Roberts, William Gibson, Robin Cook,
Brian Jacques, Catherine Coulter, Stephen King,
Jacquelyn Mitchard, and many more!

Penguin Putnam Online is located at
http://www.penguinputnam.com

PENGUIN PUTNAM NEWS

Every month you'll get an inside look at our
upcoming books and new features on our site.
This is an ongoing effort on our part to provide
you with the most interesting and up-to-date
information about our books and authors.

Subscribe to Penguin Putnam News at
http://www.penguinputnam.com/ClubPPI